Sound Move

This innovative study opens up a new area in sociological and urban studies: the aural experience of the social, mediated through mobile technologies of communication.

Whilst we live in a world dominated by visual epistemologies of urban experience, Michael Bull argues that it is not surprising that the Apple iPod is the first consumer cultural icon of the twenty-first century. *Sound Moves*, in using the example of the iPod, investigates the way in which we use sound to construct key areas of our daily lives. The author argues that the Apple iPod acts as an urban Sherpa for many of its users and in doing so joins the mobile army of technologies that many of us habitually use to accompany our daily lives.

Through our use of such mobile and largely sound based devices, *Sound Moves* demonstrates how and why the spaces of the city are being transformed right in front of our ears.

This text is essential for undergraduate and postgraduate students and researchers in the fields of Sociology of Culture, Urban Studies and Media and Communication Studies.

Michael Bull is Reader in Media and Film Studies at the University of Sussex.

University of
Chester
Warrington Campus

University of Chester Library
Tel: 01925 534284

International Library of Sociology
Founded by Karl Mannheim
Editor: John Urry
University of Lancaster

Recent publications in this series include:

Risk and Technological Culture
Towards a sociology of virulence
Joost Van Loon

Reconnecting Culture, Technology and Nature
Mike Michael

Advertising Myths
The strange half lives of images and commodities
Anne M. Cronin

Adorno on Popular Culture
Robert R. Witkin

Consuming the Caribbean
From arkwarks to zombies
Mimi Sheller

Between Sex and Power
Family in the world, 1900–2000
Goran Therborn

States of Knowledge
The co-production of social science and social order
Sheila Jasanoff

After Method
Mess in social science research
John Law

Brands
Logos of the global economy
Celia Lury

The Culture of Exception
Sociology facing the camp
Bülent Diken and Carsten Bagge Laustsen

Visual Worlds
John Hall, Blake Stimson and Lisa Tamiris Becker

Time, Innovation and Mobilities
Travel in technological cultures
Peter Frank Peters

Complexity and Social Movements
Multitudes acting at the edge of chaos
Ian Welsh and Graeme Chesters

Qualitative Complexity
Ecology, cognitive processes and the re-emergence of structures in post-humanist social theory
Chris Jenks and John Smith

Sound Moves

iPod culture and urban experience

Michael Bull

Routledge
Taylor & Francis Group

LONDON AND NEW YORK

First published 2007
by Routledge
2 Park Square, Milton Park, Abingdon, Oxon OX14 4RN

Simultaneously published in the USA and Canada
by Routledge
270 Madison Ave, New York, NY 10016

*Routledge is an imprint of the Taylor & Francis Group,
an informa business*

© 2007 Michael Bull

Typeset in Sabon by
Newgen Imaging Systems (P) Ltd, Chennai, India
Printed and bound in Great Britain by
MPG Books Ltd, Bodmin, Cornwall

British Library Cataloguing in Publication Data
A catalogue record for this book is available
from the British Library

Library of Congress Cataloging in Publication Data
A catalog record for this book has been requested

ISBN10: 0–415–25751–4 (hbk)
ISBN10: 0–415–25752–2 (pbk)

ISBN13: 978–0–415–25751–0 (hbk)
ISBN13: 978–0–415–25752–7 (pbk)

For Pierrette (1947–2007)

Contents

Acknowledgements

Time away from my desk to begin this project was generously funded by the AHRC which enabled me to sift through the primary research data which I collected in 2004.

Initial thoughts on the nature of iPod culture have been presented at lectures given at Transmediale in Berlin and at the universities of Maastricht, Budapest, Nottingham, Vadstena, Berlin, Bremen and Amsterdam. My thanks to the critical questions that I frequently received.

Much of my time whilst writing this book has been taken up in lengthy media interviews on the nature and meaning of the iPod phenomenon. These interviews permitted me to clarify my thoughts on the topic, and so I would like to thank the often inquisitive and intellectually curious journalists from *The New York Times*, *BBC Online News*, *The Economist*, *Newsweek*, *Il Manifesto*, *L'Express*, *L'Iberation*, *The Sydney Morning Herald*, *The San Francisco Times*, *The Los Angeles Times*, *Chicago Herald Tribune*, *The Edmonton Journal*, *Svenska Dagbladet* and *The Financial Times, Germany* amongst others, who interviewed me.

Thanks also to the staff at Routledge who have been most supportive of my 'late' manuscript which has been subject of the contingencies of the author's life over the last two years.

I would also like to thank Barry Selwyn and Stanley Unsworth for their support and friendship over the years and last but not least to Rosalinde for providing sanity and endless support at home and to Theo for bringing the sounds of laughter into my everyday life.

1 Sound moves, iPod culture and urban experience
An introduction

> My iPod goes everywhere with me. It's like my digital Sherpa for information and entertainment.
>
> (iPod user)

> I store my 'valuables' on the iPod. I completed three screenplays, which I data warehouse on my iPod. If the house burns down, I am not worried, because the iPod has the family jewels.
>
> (iPod user)

> When I leave the house I check my pockets for four things: my wallet, my keys, my mobile phone, and my iPod. I never go out without all four on my person.
>
> (iPod user)

> Spatial structures are the dreams of society. Whenever the hieroglyph of any such spatial structure is decoded, the foundation of the social reality is revealed.
>
> (Kracauer 1995: 30)

> The media do not simply occupy time and space, they also structure it and give it meaning.
>
> (Livingstone 2002: 81)

The Apple iPod is the first cultural icon of the twenty-first century, representing a sublime marriage between mobility, aesthetics and functionality, of sound and touch – enabling users to possess their auditory world in the palm of their hand. It has sold over 100 million units worldwide since its introduction in 2001, and has spawned its own commercial eco-system with more than 4,000 accessories made specifically to accompany its use at home, in the automobile or on the person. The iPod is the cultural equivalent of the Citroën DS, written about so elegantly by Roland Barthes in 1957:

> I think that cars today are almost the exact equivalent of the great Gothic cathedrals: I mean the supreme creation of an era, conceived with passion by unknown artists, and consumed in image if not in

usage by a whole population which appropriates them as a purely magical object.

(Barthes 2002: 341)

From Gothic cathedral to Citroën DS to the Apple iPod represents a Western narrative of increasing mobility and privatisation. The Gothic cathedral: immobile, massive and austere, an entirely public edifice magnifying the glory of God whilst reducing the size of the individual to a mere speck on the horizon. Gothic cathedrals were the largest man-made structures in Europe at the time, just as the pealing of the cathedral bells was the loudest man-made noise that the population regularly heard.

Barthes, in his analysis of the Citroën DS, had already reduced the scale of the cultural icon from the size of a Gothic cathedral to that of a five-seater automobile – and, of course, one could inhabit and privately occupy the Citroën in a way that you could not inhabit the cathedral – the DS was something not merely to be looked at or desired, it was something to be owned and travelled in – an icon of social and physical mobility. Barthes discussed the enveloping nature and tactile sense of the automobile – the leather seats, the suspension, as well as the sleek external lines that make the Citroën appear to slide through the air, like a slip of paper, effortlessly.

Barthes's interpretation of the Citroën DS is of a domesticated icon. This icon, however, is largely a visual and tactile-orientated one, just as Barthes's brief description of Gothic cathedrals is visually based. Yet a parallel cultural history can be developed from Barthes's sharp insights into Western aesthetics – an acoustic history of increasingly mobile privatised sound.

For Gothic cathedrals were not merely to be looked at or to be entered for silent prayer – they were also cathedrals of sound in which sacred vocal music reverberated through the spaces of the church. The populace invariably went into these spaces not merely to pray but to enter envelopes of sound resounding through their bodies, amplified by the great arches of the cathedral.

By the 1950s, even as Barthes was shrinking the scale of our cultural icons to five-seater auto size, so our acoustic envelopes began to shift. First, hi-fi began to train its post-war listeners to demand deeply private, acoustically intensified, almost entirely non-resonant 'fidelity' sound. With the invention of the miniaturised transistor and the hand-held, battery-powered radio it made possible in the 1950s, a new culture of personal mobile sound emerged, re-imagined in the 1980s with the Sony 'Walkman' (equipped with privatising earphones) and ghetto boom-boxes (outfitted with loud-speaker-quality sub-woofers). Now, at the beginning of the twenty-first century, the culture has shifted again. No longer prey to the whims of corporate radio, our sonic envelopes, our cathedrals of sound, exist in the personal play list of the iPod. In the head and mind of the iPod user the spaces of culture have been redrawn into a largely private and mobile auditory worship. Technology, precisely in its miniaturisation – the whole digital world in your hand – acquires a magical quality. As one enthusiastic yet typical New York user commented:

> The design is just flawless. It feels good, to hold it in your hand, to rub your thumb over the navigation wheel and to touch the smooth white surface. It looks nice, I'm proud of owning such a device. It represents and holds an important part of my life, so I don't want an 'ugly' package around it. I have never cherished anything I bought as much as this little device. When I was a child, I used to watch a kids' show called 'The Music Machine' and I always dreamed of having something like that. A device that plays any song there is. The iPod comes pretty close to the fulfilment of this childhood fantasy.[1]

The iPod – more even than the Barthesian automobile with its multi-channel car radio – offers the user the unfettered auditory freedom of movement from home to street to automobile to office. Time is woven into a seamless web of controlled sound and space, as another urban user comments:

> I now listen to music any time I can. Walking to and from work, at work, on vacation, on a train or airplane, even at home when I don't want to disturb my partner. I have any song I want to listen to at my fingertips at any particular moment. That amazes me. It truly is my own personal jukebox, and puts the soundtrack to my life in my pocket and at my fingertips.

Revealing the commercial music infrastructure that supports her listening habits, this 'jukebox' owner believes in the individuality of her life's 'soundtrack'. It is a hyper-post-Fordist culture in which subjects construct what they imagine to be their own individualised schedules of daily life – their own daily soundtrack of media messages, their own soundscape as they move through shopping centres, their own work-out sound track as they modulate the movement of their bodies in the gym. With its enveloping acoustics iPod users move through space in their auditory bubble, on the street, in their automobiles, on public transport. In tune with their body, their world becomes one with their 'soundtracked' movements; moving to the rhythm of their music rather than to the rhythm of the street. In tune with their thoughts – their chosen music enables them to focus on their feelings, desires and auditory memories.

The iPod puts them in tune with their desire to eke out some aesthetic, cognitive and social control as they weave through the day. Enclosed within a zone of immunity and security, enveloped in what they imagine to be their own reality as they move through the city, each holding an Apple iPod – twenty-first-century icon and acoustic metaphor.

Mobile sound universalised

For the first time in history the majority of citizens in Western culture possess the technology to create their own private mobile auditory world wherever they go.[2] iPod culture represents a world in which we all possess mobile phones, iPods or automobiles – it is a culture which universalises the privatisation of public space, and it is a largely auditory privatisation. The Apple iPod stands as both example and metaphor for a culture in which many of us increasingly close our ears to the multi-faceted world through which we daily move.[3] The erasure, or reconfiguration, of the spaces that we move through is primarily an auditory reconfiguration. It is the price that is paid for the often intense private auditory pleasure of listening or talking. iPods are a sonic technology, whilst mobile phones remain primarily sound-based artefacts.

The Apple iPod is symbolic of a culture in which we increasingly use communication technologies to control and manage our experience of the urban environment. iPod users, in the present analysis, are followed as they move through daily life, listening to their iPods, using their mobile phones and driving their automobiles. These three mobile technologies have transformed the meaning of what it is like to live in an urban culture. iPod culture represents a fully mediated culture in which increasingly large parts of our experience are constructed through the use of these mobile communication technologies. It is a culture of auditory mobility in which the privatising impulse of Western culture has come to a state of maturity. The present work uses the example of the Apple iPod to shed light on the nature of contemporary urban experience. Media Studies and Urban Studies become intertwined in the present analysis. Media use is increasingly amorphous and mobile, whilst urban space is largely mediatised. It is no longer possible to adequately understand the nature of urban culture without also understanding the nature and meaning of the daily use of mobile communication technologies.

The dialectic of mediated isolation

Sound moves focuses primarily upon the isolated, yet mediated, urban subject. This is not to deny, or indeed to suggest, that collective forms of behaviour, whether it be in the home, the street or elsewhere, are not important, merely that the trend towards 'mediated urban isolation' is of growing significance. Marc Augé has called for the need to develop 'an ethnography of solitude' (Augé 1995) in order to understand the nature of urban experience. He argued for this 'need' against a backdrop of what he perceived to be the experiencing of and development of 'non-spaces' of urban culture, by which he meant new shopping centres, airports, motorways and the like – spaces with no historical narrative attached to them. These urban spaces supposedly alienated the human subject as they passed through them. In the present analysis, in contrast to Augé, I argue that all urban spaces are potentially 'non-spaces'. In iPod culture we have overpowering resources to construct urban spaces to our liking as we move through them, enclosed in our pleasurable and privatised sound bubbles. Today, such an ethnography of solitude must be one of a technologically mediated solitude – we are increasingly alone together.

Focusing upon the solitary individual is justified empirically by the daily mobility patterns within urban culture. Solitariness and the daily movement of people through the city are two dominant hallmarks of contemporary urban experience. This solitariness is not necessarily enforced. Sole occupancy is often the preferred mode of travel in automobiles throughout Europe and America (Brodsky 2002; Putnam 2000). The desire for solitude in the automobile is mirrored in the desire for solitude in the street and the home as many retreat into the most private spaces of their already privatised home, accompanied by the sound of the television, radio or their music system (Livingstone 2002). Privatising the street is itself conditioned by the privatising of the home (Bauman 2003). The intimate nature of an industrialised sound world in the form of radio sounds (Tacchi 2004; Hendy 2000), recorded music and television increasingly represent large parts of a privatised everyday lifeworld of urban citizens. iPods are by their very nature primarily a privatising technology, whilst mobile phone users intermittently fill the urban spaces of the city with their 'own' reassuring noises (Puro 2002), in effect privatising it.

In parallel to this privatising tendency within urban experience there exists a compulsiveness towards proximity and contact in daily life (Katz and Aukhus 2002). Bauman has noted, in relation to mobile phone use, for example, that for many 'silence equals exclusion' (Bauman 2003). In iPod culture we might adapt the Descartian maxim 'I think, therefore I am' to 'I talk or listen, therefore I exist'. It is no accident that for Descartes identity was something constructed in silence whereas contemporary consumers invariably feel a sense of discomfort when confronted with silence (Bull 2000). The greater the craving for solitariness the greater the fear of being socially isolated. This contradictory desire for privacy and fear of social isolation is resolved through the use of mobile sound media.

The sounds of mediated we-ness

iPod users live in a world of mediated we-ness. The phrase derives from the work of Adorno, who argued that the consumption of mechanically reproduced music was increasingly used as an effective substitute for a sense of connectivity that modern cultures lacked. We-ness refers to the substitution of technologically mediated forms of experience for direct experience. Music, for Adorno, enabled the subject to transcend the repressive nature of the social world precisely by integrating him or herself more fully into the everyday, through the consumption of music. Music provides both the dreams and the chains for the urban subject. Mediated aural proximity constitutes states of 'we-ness' whereby 'direct' experience is either substituted or transformed by a mediated, technological form of aural experience. Music represents to the urban subject a utopian longing for what they desire but cannot achieve. Music substitutes that which is desired for itself, producing 'an illusion of immediacy in a totally mediated world, of proximity between strangers, the warmth of those who come to feel a chill of unmitigated struggle of all against all' (Horkheimer and Adorno 1973: 46). From the television set at the heart of family life to the iPod through which 'the world, threateningly devoid of warmth, comes to him like something familiar, as if specially made just for him' (Adorno, in Leppert 2002: 52)

The warmth of media messages is contrasted with the chill of the immediate and the inability of the structured forms of the social to satisfy the desire for proximity and warmth. Adorno perceived the urban subject as increasingly dependent upon forms of mediated company within which to live; 'we might conceive a series leading from the man who cannot work without the blare of the radio to the one who kills time and paralyses loneliness by filling his ears with the illusion of "being with" no matter what' (Adorno 1991: 78). Putnam, more recently, has commented upon the 'false sense' of companionship and intimacy created through the use of television (Putnam 2000: 242), as has Claude Lefort, who refers to these phenomena as a 'constant illusion of a between-us, an *entre-nous* in which the media provoke an hallucination of nearness which abolishes a sense of distance, strangeness, imperceptibility of otherness' (Lefort, quoted in Merck 1998: 109). Forms of 'accompanied solitude' thus become increasingly habitual in iPod culture. Yet compulsive mediated proximity does not necessarily endorse the 'one-dimensional' thesis of media colonisation, which collapses subjectivity into the objective structures of culture. A dialectical analysis of iPod culture points to a disjunction between the objective and the subjective moment of culture in which iPod users attempt to transcend the social precisely by immersing themselves in it.

Sound ideologies and iPod culture

The auditory self of iPod culture in which sound becomes 'a way of perceiving the world' increasingly inhabits acoustic space (Attali 1985: 4). We both increasingly move to sound and are simultaneously moved by sound. Tia deNora has pointed to the frequency with which the metaphor to be 'transported' has been associated with music. She argues, 'music can be conceived as a kind of aesthetic technology, an instrument of social ordering' (DeNora 2000: 7). The nature of this social ordering is both cultural and historical – what is true for music is also true for sound – the pealing of church bells in the nineteenth century was as much an instrument of social ordering as the sounds of a Monteverdi Mass in Venice in the seventeenth. Music itself performs an ideological role in the mediated household of the contemporary consumer. Adorno caustically remarked that the 'greater the drabness of existence, the sweeter the melody' (Adorno and Eisler 1994: 22), whilst Lefebvre concurred, stating that music 'brings compensations for the miseries of everydayness, for its deficiencies and failures' (Lefebvre 2004: 66). The consumption of technologically mediated sound, in the twentieth century, represents a significant mode of 'being-in-the-world'. The self claims a mobile and auditory territory for itself through a specific form of 'sensory gating', permitting it to screen out unwanted sounds, producing its own 'soundscape'. Media technologies are simultaneously private and structural: meaning cannot be isolated from the structural conditions within which it arises. The negative moment of media isolation has been commented upon by Debord, who interprets the media as an arm of capitalist culture intent upon weakening the collective bonds between urban citizens:

> The economic system founded on isolation is a circular *production of isolation*. The technology is based on isolation, and the technical process isolates in turn. From the automobile to television, all the goods selected by the spectacular system are also its weapons for a constant reinforcement of the conditions of isolation of 'lonely crowds'.
>
> (Debord 1977: 26)

Isolation in Debord's analysis ties people into the social system precisely by isolating them, making them weaker – more dependent. iPod culture appears to have furthered the culture of mediated isolation whereby connectivity is increasingly engaged with absent others.

Isolation in the past was often equated with silence – the freeing up of the individual to be alone with their thoughts – the Enlightenment precondition for autonomy. The use of sound-based technologies has changed the search for silence into a search for noise. Sound technologies from the Lambretta to the iPod have enabled users to 'create a transparent but impenetrable wall of sound, transporting [them] out into the world while isolating [them] from it' (Levi 2004: 30). iPod culture reorders the social spaces of the city, giving greater prominence to media-generated forms of privacy whilst distancing users from the 'proximity' of others. iPod users live within a mediated and perpetual sound matrix, each user inhabiting a different auditory world.

The rhythms of iPod culture

The iPod appears to privilege private life, enhancing the conception of the consumer as an isolated subject. In doing so users appear able, and often desire, to liberate themselves from the perceived oppressive rhythms of daily life: the daily commute to and from work, the oppressive and inevitable working week, working month and working year. As working life is scripted, so are the managed rhythms of leisure time, increasingly packaged by the milli-second (Lefebvre 2004). The technologies that come to our aid in the management of the daily rhythms of life simultaneously steal time away from the subject as the whole of life appears subject to the demands of the mobile phone, the internet, the fax machine – daily life appears to some iPod users as a luxurious workhouse:

> Well, I think I've come to the conclusion that overall I feel pretty out of control in my life. Stores play music to get me to buy more. Work tells me what to do and when. Traffic decides how quickly I get from here to there. Even being in public places forces me to endure other people and their habits (the guy slurping his soup, the brat crying for a piece of candy). I didn't realise how much I yearn for control and probably peace and quiet. Strange, since I'm blasting music in my ears. I think I'm really tired of living on someone else's schedule. The iPod has given me some control back.
>
> (Janet)

iPod culture is one in which users become sensitive to living their life to 'someone else's design' (Sennett 2006), as the above user so eloquently describes. As Janet struggles to free herself from the oppressive rhythms of daily life she does so through the mediation of her iPod – itself a rationalised and rationalising media technology[4] – yet it differs significantly from other communication devices in so much as it always obeys her will – unlike the mobile phone, which is a technology of the discontinuous, the contingent. The use of an iPod is both an inclusive act – the listener communes with the products of the culture industry – and an act of auditory separation.

Sound itself is normative, mediating and reflecting the cultural predispositions of the listener who 'gates' experience. The manner of this auditory screening is dependent not merely upon the values of the subject but also upon the technologies themselves. Not only do we get the technologies that we deserve, we also get the ones we desire.

iPod culture represents a distinctive and new 'temporal sensibility' on the part of the subject who attempts to break away from and overcome the structured rhythms of contemporary urban life. Digital technology has enabled consumers to redefine the nature and meaning of many of their daily schedules. iPod culture is one in which users seek to control the rhythms of daily life; in doing so, islands of communicative warmth engulf the chilly spaces of urban culture.

The dialectic of urban chill and warmth

Isolation in the midst of connectivity – this is the urban tale to unravel and conceptualise, demanding a theoretical articulation of the twin phenomena of urban isolation and connectivity. iPod culture embodies a dialectical relationship between the desire for an ever-present intimate or personal connectivity and the impoverishment of the social and geographical environment within which it occurs. This dynamic is expressed theoretically in the present work through the concepts of 'warm' and 'chilly' – 'warm' representing the proximate, the inclusive; 'chilly' the distant and exclusive. The more we warm up our private spaces of communication the chillier the urban environment becomes, thus furthering the desire and need to communicate with absent others or to commune privately with the products of the culture industry. Media technologies simultaneously isolate and connect. This is the dilemma at the heart of our understanding of how we increasingly inhabit the public spaces of urban culture.

Mobile media provide privatised citizens with the means to create islands of communicative warmth in oceans of urban chill – chilly urban space is heated up. Mediated isolation itself becomes a form of control over the spaces of urban culture in which the 'minimal' self 'withdraws into a world small enough that it can exert almost total control over it'.

iPod culture represents an expression of personal creativity coupled with a denial of the physicality of the city. The city becomes individualised in iPod culture – a unique and pleasurable experience, as one New Yorker commented: 'This [New York] is a great city where you might not want to be infiltrated by anyone else's distracting or disruptive energy.' iPod culture is best understood as a mono-rhythmic approach to urban experience, as against the traditional understanding of urban life as polyrhythmic – a world of certainty as against a world of contingency. iPod use makes the city what it is for users – rather than the city as inhabited by embodied 'others'. iPod culture is a culture in which individual experience is cultivated, fostered and attended to through the micro-management and filtering of experience. The iPod user who states, 'When I plug in and turn on, my iPod does a "ctrl + alt + delete" on my surroundings and allows me to "be" somewhere else,' points to the empowering potential of use. Whilst the ears become able to redial their auditory map, they can do so only through media technologies themselves. The independence of the ears is dependent, just as the motive to separate out from others is often fuelled by a desire for connectivity to others or indeed oneself. Connectivity in its multifaceted nature is increasingly achieved through mediation – through the use of communication technologies creating a sense of 'warmth' for the individual as they move through the 'chilly' spaces of urban culture.

Normative cities

City spaces are normative spaces. The history of cities is a history of how we come to inhabit and share social space. Integral to the sharing of social space is the recognition of others, changes in the ground rules governing modes of recognition thus reverberate within culture. iPod use precisely represents such a transformation. iPod culture is a culture of the dematerialisation of the other – a culture increasingly focusing upon the intimate yet absent other at the other end of a mobile phone – or the seduction of the user's own sound narrative embodied in the iPod. If 'the establishment of relations of mutual recognition [are] a precondition for self realisation' (Honneth 1995: xi) then how do we understand a transformed social arena in which these traditional forms of recognition are increasingly embodied in distance relationships – not in the immediate social space which one inhabits?

Media theorists have recognised the ethical dimension attached not just to forms of media production but also to the mundane consumption patterns of media technologies by consumers themselves. (Morley 2000; Silverstone 2006). The use of media artefacts is inherently relational – they are in some sense interpersonal – whether in terms of direct physical inter-action (Bull 2000) or in terms of a more general ethical sensibility towards absent others (Morley 2000). Whilst theorists of mobile phone use concur that the etiquette of interpersonal relations is undergoing a period of change through the use of mobile phones (Castells 2007; Katz 2006) it is by no means certain that these transformations encourage forms of social recognition, change them or diminish them. iPod users, equally, never voluntarily interact with others whilst using their iPods in public. Both iPod and mobile phone use represent an already denuded concept of public urban space embodied in the ubiquitous presence of the automobile (Kay 1997; Stallabras 1996).

Binding social forces in iPod culture have migrated to a narrow network of interpersonal connections, supplemented by an increasingly media-generated sociality (Castells *et al.* 2007; Sennett 1990) This transformation of the social does not necessarily represent the impoverishment of subjec-tivity – rather the opposite. Mediated communication with absent others or the culture industry itself vies with face-to-face encounters in an already impoverished public world (Bauman 2003; Sennett 1990). The nature of our social world is changing right in front of our ears!

iPod culture represents both a continuum and a shift in Western urban experience. The continuum represents new developments in the search for public privacy and a discounting of the 'public' realm, whilst the transfor-mation lies in urban citizens' increasing ability and desire to make the 'public' spaces of the city conform to their desires. As we increasingly inhabit 'media-saturated' spaces of intimacy, so we increasingly desire to make the public spaces passed through mimic our desires, thus, ironically, furthering the absence of meaning attributed to those spaces. This is the dialectic of iPod culture.

The iPod is used as a platform in the present work upon which to develop an auditory sociology of urban movement. It operates as a prism through which to understand the nature of the public world in which we live. This world is dominated by an auditory reconfiguration of urban experience that impacts upon, constitutes and embodies users' sense of the social. This is a study of how the solitary urban citizen becomes rooted in mobile urban space, of how they acquire their 'being in the world' through the creation of privatised sound atmospheres. It is a study of the processes of auditory gating and filtering that embodies the urban world that most of us inhabit. Primarily this book is an exploration of how we come to share social space with others in urban culture.[5]

2   Sound epistemologies
Strategies and technologies

> A history of representational space and the social imagination can no longer afford to neglect materials pertaining to auditory perception.
>
> (Corbin 1995: xii)

Historically the ears have been interpreted as both passive and democratic; passive in so much as the ears are open to all sounds – we cannot close our ears to the world, and it is this very openness that constitutes their democratic nature. iPod culture is, however, neither passive nor democratic but rather discriminating and distinctive. The passivity of the ears is merely an historical effect, now technologically superseded. Technology has come to the aid of the ears through the invention of headphones (or, even more intimately, earphones) empowering the auditory self, which becomes a discriminating self. We can now choose what we want to hear, screening out the world to create a private auditory universe through the use of mobile technologies like the iPod. In doing so we transform our relationship to the social world we live in, to others around us and to ourselves – our cognitive processes through which we channel all experience. iPod culture is a fully mediated world in which users increasingly universalise the benefits of mediated 'warmth', of communication in a world grown cold. To be separated out from others is simultaneously a mark of distinction (Bourdieu 1986) and a mark of alienation. City spaces become enacted spaces, which are enjoyed and modified (de Certeau 1988; Lefebvre 1991: 34); and also structural spaces which contextualise all behaviour. An auditory epistemology of the privatising of urban experience encompasses both urban and media studies. It is a tale of the coming together of the 'chilly' urban street and the 'warm' sounds of privatising media technologies.

Mediating the city: A dialectic of warmth and chill

The consumption of technologically mediated sound, in the twentieth century, represents a significant mode of 'being-in-the-world'. The self claims a mobile and auditory territory for itself through a specific form of 'sensory gating', permitting it to screen out unwanted sounds, producing its own seductive 'soundscape'.

In iPod culture we are simultaneously connected and disconnected from the urban world that we inhabit. Connected through the use of our mobile technologies whilst simultaneously disconnected from the physical world through which we move. Connectivity is associated with the 'warmth' of the communicative process, disconnection and isolation with 'chill'. In the present work the concepts of 'warmth' and 'chill' are dialectically linked, describing our relationship with urban space through the mediation of sound-based mobile communication technologies – the iPod, the mobile phone and the automobile. 'Warmth' is associated with the desire for 'connectivity', whilst 'chill' is associated with our relationship to the urban spaces that we pass through; the warmer one gets, the chillier the other becomes. The use of a mobile phone in the street, for example, transforms the space of reception from chilly to warm. In the act of phoning the space beyond the user becomes chillier as they colonise urban space with speech to an absent other. As Harper noted, 'mobile phones are changing co-proximate behaviours in ways that are making the world perhaps a lonelier place than before … mobile phones are changing interactions between people who are near to one another' (Harper 2002: 212).

One side of the dialectic, the 'chilly' urban street, is inscribed into mainstream urban studies. This chill is variously located in the geography of the city itself (Sennett 1977, 1990, 1994; Augé 1995; Bauman 2000, 2003); in the sensory overload of the city (Simmel 1997); in the technologies of the city, which repel and isolate (McLuhan 1997; Kay 1997; Putnam 2000); and in the very values of Western urban culture – a Protestantism of the senses that manifests itself in the desire to withdraw (Sennett 1990). Urban chill is understood to be the multiple products of these variables in the present analysis. Rather than isolating out each variable, they are understood as overlapping and cumulative in their effect upon us.

Sociological thought has located the 'chill' of urban relations in the rise of modern urban culture itself. Tonnies's division of society into relations of *Gemeinschaft* and *Gesellschaft*, the one warm and intimate, denoting pre-industrial modes of community, the other cold and distancing, indicative of relations in urban culture in which the utilitarian values of 'use' and 'instrumentalism' reign supreme in the everyday life of cities. These categories of *Gemeinschaft* and *Gesellschaft* are not primarily psychological categories but, rather, social and structural ones into which the subject falls. For Tonnies a society typified by relations of *Gesellschaft* in effect had restructured itself without community. Urban culture consisted of individuals who lived, for better or worse, through the chill of urban relations.

Simmel, following in the tradition of Tonnies, was perhaps the first 'chilly' sociologist who attempted to explain the significance and desire of urban citizens to maintain a sense of privacy, to create a mobile bubble, whilst on the move in a world dominated by values of impersonality. Simmel's concerns were with sensory overload, crowds, strangers and the noisy maelstrom of the city from which citizens were thought to retreat. Simmel charted the changing nature of bourgeois civility within the increasingly technologised urban geography of the early twentieth century, addressing the relational nature and problems associated with people continually on the move in the city (Simmel 1997). For Simmel, we should get off the streets as quickly as possible!

Simmel famously begins *The Metropolis and Mental Life* with the statement 'The deepest problems of modern life derive from the claim of the individual to preserve the autonomy and individuality of his existence in the face of overwhelming social forces, of historic heritage, of external culture, and of the techniques of life' (Simmel 1997: 178). Simmel associated urbanism with an overbearing oppressiveness and a new sense of freedom. The individual became defensive in the face of a sensory onslaught of close proximity – a surfeit of noise and people, coupled with a lack of perceived personal space. The sensory oppressiveness of the city paradoxically produced the ground upon which the individual could flourish, unhindered by the claustrophobia of similarity, which encumbered earlier generations of town dwellers. Isolation bred individuality.

Retreat has subsequently become a dominant urban metaphor used to describe strategies whereby citizens attempt to maintain a sense of 'self' through the progressive creation of distancing mechanisms from the urban 'other', who may, or may not, be just like them. The chill of urban relations is thought to reside in the fabric of the city itself – a consequence of a neutralising value system. Richard Sennett describes urban space as 'a bland environment [which] assures people that nothing disturbing or demanding is happening "out there". You build neutrality in order to legitimise withdrawal' (Sennett 1990: 65). The chilly spaces of the city become uninhabitable without the warmth of communication for many an urban citizen. Urban space is perceived a threat in this narrative, isolating, hostile and bland.

Building urban chill

Urban chill is said to reside in the streets we walk through, the buildings we pass by, the modern shopping centres we are inevitably drawn to, the anonymous spaces of airports, train stations, parking lots and the endless motorways that many of us progressively live in as we shuttle backwards and forwards in our cars. Augé, in his analysis of urban space, used the term 'non-space' to describe an urban culture of semiologically denuded spaces: of shopping centres, airports, motorways and the like. He thought of these spaces as if they had been dropped on to the urban landscape at random. They were invariably architecturally bland – who can tell one shopping centre from another, for example? Urban spaces from this perspective increasingly functioned as the endless transit zones of urban culture – emblems of the increasing mobile nature of urban culture:

> If a place can be defined as relational, historical and concerned with identity, then a space which cannot be defined as relational, or historical, or concerned with identity will be a non-place. The hypothesis advanced here is that super-modernity produces non-places, meaning spaces which are not themselves anthropological places ... where transit points and temporary abodes are proliferating ... where the habitués of supermarkets, slot machines and credit cards communicate wordlessly, through gestures, with an abstract, unmediated commerce; a world thus surrendered to solitary individuality, to the fleeting, the temporary and ephemeral.
>
> (Augé 1995: 77–8)

In iPod culture, however, any urban space can become a non-space. The defining feature of our relation to urban space is not necessarily how culturally situated they may be. Augé is also incorrect in assuming that his narrowly defined 'non-spaces' of urban culture can have no meaning for urban subjects. Historical narrative is not the sole condition for endowing places with meaning. Shopping malls can become places of meeting; places endowed with particular personal narratives; places of pleasure or crime. Whilst Augé recognises that 'the word "non-place" designates two complementary but distinct realities: spaces formed in relation to certain ends (transport, transit, commerce), and the relations that individuals have with these spaces' (Augé 1995: 94) he nevertheless over-determines the structural meaning of representational space, thus minimising the subjective response of subjects to the spaces they transit through. In iPod culture any urban space may become a 'non-space', it is not dependent upon the 'anthropological nature of the space itself' but increasingly upon the subjective response to that space or, indeed, the prior negation of that space through the cognitive predilections of the subject. In iPod culture many do not notice the nature of the space passed through, whilst hermetically sealed in their sound world. And whilst Augé rightly believes that many urban spaces appear to exist in the continual present, 'the radio plays continuously in service stations and supermarkets. Everything proceeds as if space had been trapped by time, as if there were no history other than the last forty-eight hours of news' (Augé 1995: 104). Augé's analysis of the experience of urban space is too static. Even at the time he constructed the term 'non-space', consumers could appropriate both space and time through the use of mobile technologies like their personal stereos and car sound systems. The dynamic of the appropriation of the public spaces of the city is furthered through the users of iPods, who can choose the manner in which they attend to, and inhabit shopping malls or any other urban space. Urban and social theory has been deficient in understanding the transformative power that urban citizens have over the nature and meaning of urban environments passed through. This transformative power is achieved through the mediation of the automobile, iPod and mobile phone.

The chill of automobility

The automobile became a dominant means of escaping the street as the twentieth century wore on (Kay 1997; Putnam 2000; Sachs 1992), producing city spaces in which urban citizens congregated without meeting. Lefebvre argued that the automobile was primarily responsible for 'the disintegration of city life', a sentiment echoed in much subsequent urban analysis. Cities and suburbs have increasingly been given over to the automobile, with 25 per cent of London and almost half the land mass of Los Angeles the preserve of the automobile (Urry 2006). The automobile has permitted the global development of the urban sprawl in which most of us now live, in towns and endless suburbs served increasingly by out-of-town shopping malls (Stallabras 1996). In many US suburbs there are no pavements to walk on, whilst around 50 per cent of US iPod respondents use their iPod primarily in their cars, as they so infrequently walk anywhere.

Media theorists such as McLuhan also argued that the public spaces of the city should be avoided. McLuhan directly related the automobile to the creation of the chilly urban landscape: 'As the city filled with mobile strangers, even next-door neighbours became strangers. This is the story of the motor car … . The car has quite refashioned all the spaces that unite and separate men' (McLuhan 1997: 224). According to McLuhan the urban chill would reach such proportions that we would increasingly decide to stay at home with our new communication technologies rather than venture out into the semiotically empty spaces of the street in which the pedestrian feels 'friendless and disembodied'. McLuhan's vision of urban space was one in which the automobile had eroded the terms and conditions of urban civility. His solution to this was to advocate retreat into our domestic interiors through the use of media technologies – a further retreat into the privatisation of urban culture. It is not my intention here to provide a litany of anti-car and anti-suburban thought, merely to point to the privatising role that the car has played in urban culture. Automobiles are not merely a way of moving from one place to another, they also objectify personal and social values. These values are complex and often contradictory, from the love of the automobile itself, with all that this embodies, such as the values of individualism and mobility paraded out endlessly in automobile advertisements to the values embedded in car use representing forms of anti-urbanism in which car use enables a separation from the 'other'. Henderson found that automobility was often embraced as a tool of 'spatial secession' rather than as a pleasure in itself: 'mobility is not just movement but also an extension of ideologies and normative values about how the city should be configured and by whom' (Henderson 2006: 295). Automobility privatises the streets passed through, thus empowering the driver. Secessionist automobility refers to the use of a car 'as a means of physically separating oneself from spatial configurations like higher urban density, public space, or from the city altogether' (Henderson 2006: 294). Secessionist values play a central role in the chilly world of iPod culture: from the street to the automobile – users enact a range of isolationist strategies.

The chilly values of iPod culture

The disenchantment of city spaces is variously located in the values intrinsic to capitalism – rationalism itself (Weber 2002) and the resulting disenchantment of the subject thrown back on their own resources who 'was previously incorporated into the dance of forms filled by the world, is now left solitarily confronting the chaos as the sole agent of the mind, confronting the immeasurable realm of reality ... thrown out into the cold infinity of empty space and time' (Kracauer 1995: 120). This is the tale of the melancholic urban subject, victim of the spiritual secularisation of the age, living an increasingly privatised and mobile existence. This secularised and privatised space itself breeds suspicion, potential fear and further withdrawal – becoming a cycle of progressive urban chill. 'If physical proximity – sharing a space – cannot be completely avoided, it can perhaps be stripped of the challenge of "togetherness" it contains, with its standing invitation to meaningful encounter, dialogue and interaction' (Bauman 2003: 105).

'Chill' becomes dislocated from city spaces to become the dominant metaphor of urban habitation itself – thus the quiet suburban street together with the crowded urban street both become spaces of isolation. Theorists of the suburbanisation of culture are virtually universal in their description of suburban spaces as 'the last word in privatisation' (Putnam 2000: 210). The important point here is that the move to suburbanisation is structural both in terms of the spatial configuration of urban culture and in the value system embodied in the world view of urban subjects themselves. Mumford was correct in his assessment of suburbia as 'a collective effort to lead a private life'. Chill extends to all urban space in a marriage between the neutrality of urban geography and of cognitive orientation. Bauman for example makes it a moral imperative of the urban citizen to escape the street:

> For every resident of the modern world, social space is spattered over a vast sea of meaninglessness in the form of numerous larger and smaller blots of knowledge: oases of meaning and relevance amidst a featureless desert. Much of daily experience is spent travelling through semiotically empty spaces – moving physically from one island to another.
> (Bauman 1993: 158)

Technologies such as iPods, mobile phones and automobiles act as tools enabling the urban citizen to move through the chilly spaces of urban culture wrapped in a cocoon of communicative warmth whilst further contributing to the chill which surrounds them.

Sound values: the archaeology of iPod culture

Sound both moves and removes us. Sterne has located the origins of the privatising auditory impulse to the cultural training and expectations located in the early communication technologies of the West – the telephone, phonograph and radio. These technologies problematised our understanding of the relationship between interior and exterior sound worlds (Sterne 2003). Sterne demonstrated that 'audile technique was rooted in a practice of individuation: listeners could own their own acoustic spaces through owning the material component of a technique of producing that auditory space – the "medium" that now stands for a whole set of framed practices. The space of the auditory field became a form of private property, a space for the individual to inhabit alone' (Sterne 2003: 160). Sterne's is a compelling tale of auditory evolution in which the privatisation of sound is located in the ears of the bourgeoisie – an impulse and desire progressively democratised throughout the twentieth century with the mass take-up of radios, telephones and automobiles. The use of technologies like the iPod, from this viewpoint, becomes the latest phase of a historical trajectory. Yet auditory privatisation pre-dates the communication technologies that have done so much to define the nature of, and our relation to modernity. The power of sound and our attempt to master experience through it can be found at the earliest stages of Western history, in Homer's *Odyssey* – brought to life as part of a Western narrative in Horkheimer and Adorno's *Dialectic of Enlightenment*. In a well known passage from the *Dialectic of Enlightenment* Horkheimer and Adorno analyse a section from Homer's *Odyssey* in which Odysseus pits his wits against the Sirens whose song represents the seductive yet fatal allure of song and knowledge. The Sirens' song evokes 'the irresistible promise of pleasure [yet] they demand the future as the price of that knowledge' (Horkheimer and Adorno 1973: 33). All who hear the Sirens' song perish. Odysseus aims to outwit the Sirens by having himself tied to the mast of his ship, thereby enabling him to listen to the enticements of the Sirens' song without being destroyed upon the rocks to which the Sirens beckon the unwitting desirer. For Odysseus's strategy to succeed he introduces a very simple artefact – wax. He orders the oarsmen of his ship to block their ears with it, thus rendering them deaf. The oarsmen are unable to hear either the Sirens' song or Odysseus's increasingly desperate orders to steer the ship on to the rocks. Horkheimer and Adorno correctly point to Odysseus's desire for pleasure as being sublimated into aesthetic experience; he can hear but do nothing about it. They, however, gloss over the specific auditory nature of the experience. It is precisely the aural configuration of the experience which is important in the context of the present work, specifically the confrontation of Odysseus with the Sirens in terms of the seductive quality of sound and its relation to the space that Odysseus and the Sirens inhabit.

The auditory nature of their meeting means that for Odysseus to experience the Sirens' song he merely needs to hear it. The Sirens' song literally enters Odysseus. As Odysseus listens, tied safely to the mast of his ship, the Sirens' song transforms the distance between his ship and the rocks from which they sing. Their song colonises him and yet he uses the experience in order to fulfil his own desire for pleasure and knowledge. In doing so Odysseus becomes a rational and successful shopper of experience. Aesthetic reflection is a price worth paying for gaining the seductive experience of song. Odysseus's ability to experience the Sirens' song is purchased at the expense of the sailor's lack of that experience. Odysseus's aestheticisation of the world is premised upon the absence of the auditory for the oarsmen. Power, control and the enticement of song are at the heart of this tale.

The sound of the Sirens' song originates beyond Odysseus: it is the Sirens who construct Odysseus's soundscape. Yet Odysseus intervenes into the nature of this soundscape by having the oarsmen's ears blocked with wax. The soundscape now encompasses only Odysseus and the Sirens; it exists only between him and them. Socially speaking, Odysseus is in his very own sound world.[1] This passage from Homer is significant in part as it is the first description of the privatisation of experience through sound, experienced now as commonplace in iPod culture.

Odysseus is a traveller who makes himself through his journey. He outwits the Sirens and in doing so furthers his self-development. Sound thus plays a central role in the self development and narrative of Odysseus (Todorov 1993). Unlike the seductions of sound in contemporary consumer culture, Odysseus has only to experience the Sirens' song once; he doesn't need to 'replay' the experience for it to remain embedded in his narrative. The Sirens form an aesthetic presence in his biography, representing, in part, the draw of the 'exotic' and the forbidden as embodied by sound and encountered in his travels and mastered through his intellect. Possession, desire and movement are also the theme of Ovid's tale of Pan and the syrinx. Pan sees the beautiful water nymph and chases her to the river, where:

> Since the waters were barring her way, she called on the nymphs of the stream to transform her. So, just at the moment when Pan believed that his syrinx was caught, instead of the nymph's body he found himself clutching some marsh reeds. But while he was sighing in disappointment the movement of air in the rustling reeds awakened a thin, low, plaintive sound. Enthralled by the strange new music and sweetness of tone, Pan exclaimed, 'This sylvan pipe will enable us always to talk together!'
>
> (Ovid, *Metamorphoses*, 705–10)

Pan carries with him the metamorphosed syrinx wherever he goes. He possesses her, but only through the making of music. Bloch observes that his music is 'a call to that which is missing ... this pipe playing is the presence of the vanished ... the vanished nymph has remained behind as sound' (Bloch 1986: 1059–60). Mobility and possession, class exploitation and gendered violence are inscribed into the Western narrative of sound and music from the outset.

Mediated auditory magic

The stories of Odysseus and Pan occur before the dawn of mechanical reproduction, before the commodification and routinisation of sound/ music. With the rise of mechanical reproduction the 'exotic' appears to come home in the space where the magical and technology meet. As Thomas Edison recites 'Mary had a little lamb' into the first phonogram in 1877, playing it back to himself he exclaims in delight and fascination at hearing his own voice played back to him, as if by magic. Inventors and users alike of the new communication technologies of the voice often pursued the 'magical'-cum-scientific transformation of experience at the beginning of the twentieth century. Schmidt has pointed to the creation of the 'psychophone', created and used by spiritualists in the early 1920s to hear 'supernatural voices': the psychophone, little more than a telephone, becomes a technology 'of the disembodied voice ... turned from exposing the illusions of supernatural voices to providing acoustic proof of them' (Schmidt 2000: 241). Many early accounts of aural reception point to the 'magical' quality of the experience of hearing the recorded voice before the experience became routinised through the steady incorporation of reproduced sound into domestic and public spaces. Technologies of sound and their use disclose something about both the user and the culture from which they come. Taussig describes the early use of the phonograph among explorers, who often took a gramophone with them into the 'colonial' spaces they were to study and exploit. Their aim, he argues, was to display the scientific magic of the West to the rest, to record the 'exotic' and to play records to them. In his analysis the gramophone already has an element of routinisation attached to its consumption.[2] The sometimes obsessive nature of this activity is captured in:

> Werner Herzog's delirious effort in his film *Fitzcarraldo*, set in the early twentieth-century Upper Amazonian rubber boom and constructed around the fetish of the phonograph, so tenaciously, so awkwardly, clutched by Fitzcarraldo, the visionary, its great earhorn emerging from under the armpit of his dirty white shirt, Caruso flooding the forests and rivers, the Indians amazed as Old Europe rains its ecstatic art form upon them. Bellowing opera from the ship's prow, it is the great ear-trumpet of the phonograph.
>
> (Taussig 1993: 203)

Taussig's description differs considerably from the use and reception of sound found in Horkheimer and Adorno's account of Odysseus and the Sirens. On display in Taussig's account is the magic of Western technology and sound.[3] Fitzcarraldo takes his own Western sound world with him, and it is his sound world that re-creates the Amazon jungle for him, making it what it is. The jungle becomes aestheticised as a function of Fitzcarraldo's imagination mediated through the sounds of Caruso's voice. The presence of 'Caruso' in the jungle is maintained only through continuous sound, through the repeat. For Fitzcarraldo the aesthetic impulse is both 'literal' and dependent upon the sound of Caruso's voice, unlike Odysseus, whose experience of the Sirens travels with him, internalised and sublimated. In contrast to this, Fitzcarraldo needs the voice of Caruso to maintain his image of the jungle and his place in it. Contrast Fitzcarraldo's use of sound with the sound world of the indigenous population of the rain forest to discover the seductive similarity and dissimilarity of non-Western appropriations of sound:

> [Turnbull] elaborates on how Mbuti imagination and practice construct the forest as both benevolent and powerful, capable of giving strength and affection to its 'children'. For this to happen Mbuti must attract the attention of the forest, must soothe it with the strength of sound that is fully articulated in the achievement of song. 'The sound "awakens" the forest ... thus attracting the forest's attention to the immediate needs of its children. It is also of the essential nature of all songs that they should be "pleasing to the forest".'
>
> (Feld 2000: 255)

Feld points to the symmetrical nature of the sound world of the inhabitants of the rain forest, whereas Odysseus and Fitzcarraldo are both 'colonisers' of space and experience. Just as sound colonises them, so they use sound to recreate the spaces they inhabit in their image. Their experiences take place in the grand and 'heroic' vistas of a world 'tamed' through their aestheticisation of it.

There exists a powerful motivation to use sound to reorganise users' relation to space and place in Western culture. In the above examples, sound colonises the listener but is used to actively recreate and reconfigure the spaces of experience. Through the power of sound the world becomes intimate, known and possessed.

Technology has empowered the ears – it has turned the ears from the most democratic of the senses (Simmel 1997) to the most exclusive. This empowerment is embodied in earphones, which supplant the uncontrollable and chaotic noise of the street with the chosen sounds of the individual consumer. The price of technologically mediated empowerment is privatisation.

The filtering of sound in iPod culture

iPod culture is a filtering culture. Users filter out the polyrhythmic sounds of the city in order to regulate their daily lives. Filtering is a heightening strategy of cognitive control and a defensive strategy. The iPod acts as a 'framing' device, enabling a distinctive mode of auditory embodiment – governing the way in which iPod users engage and orientate themselves to the world and to themselves. The iPod user is an 'orchestrating' self who tones 'down stimuli from one sensory field [whilst] amplifying information coming through another channel' (Geurts 2002: 234). Turkle has recently referred to this form of continual connectivity as a form of 'tethering' of the subject to media technologies (Turkle 2006). The 'tethering' of the subject to sound technologies like the iPod casts light upon the meaning and significance of others with whom urban space is shared, and to the urban landscape/soundscape itself. The auditory filtering of experience represents the cultural template of iPod culture. Sensory filtering is central to the urban topography of daily life: 'Sensory orientations, therefore, represent a critical dimension of how "culture and psyche make each other up" and play a critical role in a person's sensibilities around inter-subjective dynamics and the boundaries between self and others' (Geurts 2002: 236).

Auditory filtering becomes 'second nature' in iPod culture as increasingly large portions of daily experience become mediated through the use of communication technologies. Communication technologies always embody a range of filtering practices, with the mobile phone filtering out body, touch and often vision; internet chat rooms filtering out all but the disembodied word, whilst the automobile filters out the bodily presence of others, noise, fumes and touch. All media, after all, combine a mix of sensory enhancement with sensory deprivation – each configuring culture with its own mix of sensory filtering aimed at controlling experience (Morley 2000; Robins and Webster 1999). Shove has demonstrated the more general desire of consumers to manipulate climate at will through the use of central heating and air conditioning – keeping the cold out whilst keeping the inside warm: 'whether at home, in the car or at work people inhabit a protected bubble of artificial climate' (Shove 2003: 27). iPod culture is the culmination of a century of media use in which sensory filtering has become second nature to most. Walter Benjamin recognised in the 1930s the significance of technologies in 'subject[ing] the human sensorium to a complex kind of training' (Benjamin 1973: 171). From the automobile to the iPod, urban culture embodies the multiple creations of individualised sound atmospheres, reorganising the sensory field of users. In iPod culture, representational space is constructed within the head space of the user through a mediated and privatised soundscape. In its simulated 'individuality' users repossess the representational spaces within which they move. The street is made up of multiple and overlapping representational spaces through the use of iPods and automobiles. Atomisation is taken to a new level in iPod culture.

The role of the media in the processes of both atomisation and connectivity, however, remains under-theorised. Atomisation or isolation occurs in automobiles with the splitting off of occupants from the outside world; in the home, as they increasingly become individualised nodules of consumption; or in the street, through the use of iPods or mobile phones (Bauman 2003; Livingstone 2002).

In a world in which the culture industry is continually trying to attract our attention (Lanham 2006) we turn to those industries to try to manage our experience – to carve out a mediated space for ourselves. We use the very same technologies that permeate our everyday lives to escape into our privatised auditory bubbles of autonomy. Connectivity has created a new sensibility, a 'tethered' self. The transformation of subjectivity through the use of new communication technologies takes on a dystopian aura as the pervasive use of new technologies potentially decreases the capacity of subjects to disconnect from their intoxicating use, tipping subjects into forms of social 'toxicity' (Rheingold and Kluitenberg 2006: 29). The negative moment of mediated technological connectivity has a long cultural history stretching from Heidegger to Marcuse. Marcuse – often ahead of his time – commented ominously as early as the 1960s that 'solitude, the very condition which sustained the individual against and beyond society, has become technically impossible' (Marcuse 1964: 68).

Yet the development of technologies of separation (meaning separation from the immediate environment) also indicates a restructuring of the social that isn't merely one of 'separation' but, rather, a reconfiguring of the social, whether it be through iPods (the construction of states of we-ness, the creation of auditory mnemonics, etc.) or by speaking through a mobile phone (*Gemeinschaft* at a distance) that potentially extends beyond a one-dimensional collapse of subjectivity in which the urban subject automatically identifies with all facets of a commodified culture. The auditory self rebels at the very same time as it is seduced – this is the dialectic of iPod culture, articulated in the following chapters.

3 Sounding out cosmopolitanism
iPod culture and recognition

Like all big cities it was made up of irregularity, change, forward spurts, failure to keep step, collision of objects and interests, punctuated by unfathomable silences; made up of pathways and untrodden ways, of one great rhythmic beat as well as the chronic discord and mutual displacement of all its contending rhythms.

(Musil 1995: 4)

All sounds have the same rhythm. All sounds have in them something of the churning of the ship's engine. The bootblack solicits business by drumming on the back of his brush on the lid of his shoebox. The streetcar and all the carts and wagons toot like automobiles. Everyone makes noise. Everyone beats the rhythm of the city. Everyone translates the music of the wave into his own language. The cry of the newspaper vendor is as imperious as a church's bells. And the church bells aren't too proud to mingle with the profane sound below. The continuous mixing of races and peoples is palpable, visible, physical, and immediate.

(Roth 2004: 131)

One nowhere feels as lonely and lost as in the metropolitan crowd.

(Simmel 1997: 181)

Different from, and indifferent to, is the hallmark of city life. This represents a process of disengagement whilst being immersed in difference. Difference becomes a mere parade of variety.

(Sennett 1990: 129)

The urban sound world confronts the subject as unordered, chaotic and polyrhythmic. Responses to this urban plenitude of noise have divided theorists and urban commentators alike. Both Robert Musil and Joseph Roth embraced the cosmopolitan soundscape of the European city of the early twentieth century. The Vienna of Musil's youth was endowed with its own specificity – he could recognise it with his eyes closed.[1] The picture painted by Joseph Roth of the rhythmic nature of the city is one of sound and mobility – the subject is caught up in this 'chronic discord' of clashing rhythms, existing in a state of constant fluidity. For Musil the subject is located as a biographical subject acting within the specific material and cultural constraints of the city: 'By this noise alone, whose special quality cannot be captured in words, a man returning after years of absence would be able to tell with his eyes shut that he was back in the Imperial Capital and Royal City of Vienna' (Musil 1995: 3).

Both Musil and Roth point to the non-synchronous nature of the urban sound world in its anarchic, uncontrollable dissonance. Whilst Musil's description of Vienna is endowed with personal nostalgia, Roth's description of Marseilles evokes the multilingual and multicultural sounds of a city in which 'everyone beats the rhythm of the city, everyone translates the music of the wave into his own language'. Roth's is a subject assimilated into the generality of the cultural sounds of the city, pointing the way in which subjects incorporate auditory multiplicity into themselves. Both these writers describe what Henri Lefebvre referred to as the polyrthyms of the city, 'he who walks down the street ... is immersed in the multiplicity of noises, murmurs, rhythms' (Lefebvre 2004: 28). From this perspective the urban citizen is primarily a 'listening' subject, open, more or less, to the cultural diversity of the city. For Musil the sounds of the city were specific to personal memory, a remembering possessing something like the 'grain of the voice' through which he recollects the identity of the city (Barthes 1985). Roth, an itinerant urban wanderer, perceives the soundscape of Marseilles very much as an informed flaneur as he travels through the cities of the south of France. Both descriptions are of an active immersion in the sounds of the city, deciphering it in order to make sense of its multiplicity and confusion. The loud polyrhythmic nature of city sounds is seductive in both accounts, its chaotic and unrhythmic nature brought to order by the attentive ear, enabling the subject 'to separate out, to distinguish the sources, to bring them back together by perceiving interactions' (Lefebvre 2004: 27).

The kaleidoscopic sensory environment of the city has a long literary pedigree even if there is no consensus as to how we should view or understand the subject's role within this sensory urban plenitude. This image of sensory richness derives from the observations of city centres, of Paris (Benjamin 1973; de Certeau 1988), of Berlin (Simmel 1997), New York (Sennett 1990) or, as we have noted, Vienna (Musil 1995), and not the far-reaching and quieter suburbs where so many people in the West now live (Clapson 2003; Putnam 2000; Silverstone 1997). None the less, it is the epistemology of the city centre that has captured the imagination of urban and cultural theorists in their accounts of how the urban citizen experiences, copes and manages city life.

The positive evaluation of an open sensory sensibility to urban experience equates the vast array of sensory delights confronting the citizen with providing the tools for self-realisation. Self-realisation, from this viewpoint, is gained by the understanding of 'difference', of 'otherness', offered by the multicultural city. Cities become cosmopolitan enclaves, spaces of opportunity and enlightenment in which 'life' itself means 'urban life'. Even in its apparent sensory and physical chaos the city provides nourishment for the subject's sense of displacement, seductively experienced as something to be desired (de Certeau 1988; Lefebvre 2004). The multi-sensory embracing of the city is commonly evoked through the concept of flanerie within urban and cultural theory and is emblematic of the city as a walking space and more latterly a driving space (Baudrillard 1989):

> Ever so often I am walking through streets, my eyes wide open, and I see lots of ludicrous, even abominable things, and eventually something beautiful. I walk through the long, crooked, narrow streets redolent with the smells of a thousand disgusting fumes … I twist myself through heaps of humans, screaming, running, panting, pushing each other … I look at someone, he looks back and we both have forgotten about each other before we turn the corner.
>
> (Kleist, quoted in Gleber 1999: 25)

Kleist captures the ambivalence attached to city walking as early as 1800 in his description of weaving a path through the crowded streets of central Paris. His is a description of one whose senses are open to the multisensory pleasure, repulsion and contingency of city life which both assaults and stimulates his senses.[2] Kleist seeks his place within the anonymous crowd, attempting to place himself within the polyrhythms of city life; he is the archetypal flaneur of nineteenth-century literature and twentieth-century urban and cultural studies (Freidberg 1993; Gleber 1999; Jenks 1995). Flanerie is a predominantly visual response to the city and its sensory stimulations whereas iPod culture, in contrast, represents an audio-visual experience of the city, which demands alternative theoretical explanations of our relations to urban space.

iPod culture represents an antithesis to this visualised understanding of cosmopolitan space. If cosmopolitanism remains as an experiential category in urban life, it has migrated from the street to the diverse and often multicultural nature of the user's playlists.

We each inhabit our own realities: the auditory solipsism of urban culture

iPod culture is usefully represented by an alternative and equally dominant motif in urban studies, one in which the city as a place of sensory overload threatens to engulf the citizen in a maelstrom of urban movement and contingency. In contrast to the above celebration of openness to the sensory and cultural richness of the city, this dystopian image of urban life responds to the very plenitude of urban experience with strategies of retreat and neutralisation. Some years ago Richard Sennett described New York before the arrival of iPods or mobile phones, but with automobiles aplenty, as a place of indifference where people passed each other but did not interact. Cities had, for him, become places in which the urban subject fell silent; 'there grew up a notion that strangers had no right to speak to each other, that each man possessed as a public right an invisible shield, a right to be left alone' (Sennett 1990). This image of urban experience derives in part from the urban writings of Georg Simmel, who begins *The Metropolis and Mental Life* with the statement that 'the deepest problems of modern life derive from the claim of the individual to preserve the autonomy and individuality of his existence in the face of overwhelming social forces, of historical heritage, of external culture, and of the technique of life' (Simmel 1997: 172).

Simmel had recognised that urban environments provided unprecedented conditions for the growth of personal freedom owing to their very anonymity; the city left the subject alone to be themselves – isolation became associated with individualism. Yet paradoxically, when confronted with so many other people, all equally subjects in their own right, the very individuality desired by the modern urban subject is threatened, diminished by its own relativity. For Simmel the city is managed by the urban citizen through the development of 'an organ protecting him against the threatening currents and discrepancies of his external environment which would uproot him' (Simmel 1997: 176). This 'tool' was the creation of a blasé attitude towards the polyrhythmic and sensual nature of the city. The blasé attitude negates difference through distancing itself from that which surrounds it; 'things themselves are experienced as insubstantial. They appear to the blasé person in an evenly grey tone, no one object deserves preference over any other ... The self-preservation of certain personalities is bought at the price of devaluing the whole objective world' (Simmel 1997: 179).

Simmel became the first thinker to propose that a rich and full interiority was premised upon the negating of the urban environment that confronted the individual. Thus the dystopian image of urban life is premised upon, and rejects, the physical presence or 'being' of cosmopolitanism. Rather, urban life becomes a dialectical process of freedom and insecurity in which the urban citizen progressively retreats into their own cognitive or physical shell whilst simultaneously neutralising the public spaces of the city. Urban retreat becomes the dominant metaphor in the dystopian image of urban life whereby the urban citizen attempts to maintain a sense of 'self' through the progressive creation of distancing mechanisms from the 'other'. Technologies of communication, from the automobile to the iPod, play their role in this neutralisation of urban space; these communication technologies empower the citizen in the very creation of the city as an alienated space. The automobile, train or bus, whilst facilitating the more or less successful movement of people through the city, vies with the pedestrian for space in the city. These pedestrians, in turn, increasingly use mobile technologies like the iPod in order to manage the contested spaces of the city.[3] The constitution of city life, from this perspective, becomes an arena of multiple sensory shocks in which subjects are obliged to adjust to the physical, technological and psychological demands of the city. Crowds have to be negotiated, as do traffic and the host of technologies that accompany automobility. Urban sensibilities become defensive and increasingly skilled in the management of urban space as the subject negotiates the movement of others, automobiles and the urban technologies that support the flow of movement through the city. As a result of this 'need for constant vigilant consciousness' the 'spontaneous capacities for experience [are] necessarily diminished' (Wolin 1994: xxxvi). Benjamin, in accordance with Simmel, but more attuned to the city as a technological environment, understood the city as reducing the subject's capacity for thought owing to the need for constant response to the contingency and plenitude of urban life. For Benjamin, urban 'technology [had] subjected the human sensorium to a complex kind of training' (Benjamin 1973: 171). This training enables the subject to retreat from urban space through neutralising it. Technologies of separation such as the iPod, the mobile phone and the automobile have progressively empowered the urban citizen precisely by removing them from the 'physicality' of urban relations:

> For every resident of the modern world, social space is splattered over a vast sea of meaninglessness in the form of numerous larger and smaller blots of knowledge: oases of meaning and relevance amidst a featureless desert. Much of daily experience is spent travelling through semiotically empty spaces – moving physically from one island to another.
>
> (Bauman 1993:158)

Urban experience undergoes a systematic 'ghettoisation' of which iPod use is the most recent and pervasive manifestation, furthering the technological intervention of subjects intent on urban retreat, transforming the polyrhythmic nature of urban space into the interiorised monorhythmic sounds of users. The overcoming of the polyrhythmic nature of the urban sound world is a dominant strategy of iPod users, who close their ears to the multi-faceted sound world of the city. In doing so they are responding to the perceived oppressive and enveloping nature of the cosmopolitan urban crowd, to the neutralising architecture of city spaces (Augé 1995; Sennett 1990, 1994) and to the contingent nature of urban experience itself. The preoccupation with the pleasures of solitary listening and the resulting cognitive control achieved through the management of their sound world is preferable to the contingency of the world existing beyond their auditory bubble. The foreclosing of the diversity of urban life is apparent when contrasting iPod users' descriptions of moving through the city with those of Musil and Roth:

> I enjoy having a soundtrack for New York streets. Having my own rhythm. I commute two hours a day. When I'm on the subway people

listening to music on headphones often surround me. We each inhabit our own realities.

(Karen)

It's as though I can part the seas like Moses. It gives me and what's around me a literal rhythm, I feel literally in my own world, as an observer. It helps to regulate my space so I can feel how I want to feel, without external causes changing that.

(Susanna)

iPod culture represents a world in which each person is locked into their own interiority, moving to their own rhythm and motivated by their personalised auditory soundtrack to urban life:

I keep some slow music that gives me a calm, peaceful feeling when I'm in busy or chaotic settings, like on the subway. Nora Jones is a great example. Then, I also like really upbeat, dance-style music. This is good not only for the gym, but also when I'm just walking around the city – puts me in an upbeat mood. Like, Britney Spears (who I normally don't listen to) has some good new dance songs, like 'Toxic'. They have great rhythm, very upbeat.

(Samantha)

Sometimes it seems to look a lot more hectic and almost like I'm in my own slow world, going only at the speed of the music I'm listening to. The lack of day-to-day sound effects totally changes living in a city, so listening to the iPod sometimes makes me feel like I'm missing something when I'm walking along.

(Mark)

Increasing numbers of urban dwellers are sounding out the sensory environment of the city, plugged into their earphones, listening to their own auditory soundtrack. Unlike the polyrhythmic descriptions of cities in urban literature, the city of the iPod user is made up of parallel and privatised soundscapes in which each iPod user looks around the subway compartment at others equally enclosed in their private soundscape, each 'inhabiting their own reality'. iPod users if they do stare at others – and they frequently do not – do so through their own hermetically sealed soundscape, their experience endowed with a privatised auditory rhythm. iPod users are representative of Bauman's urban citizens who 'whatever company they may wish to enjoy (or are willing to tolerate) they carry with them, like snails carry their homes' (Bauman 2003: 98). In iPod culture, movement through the city, unlike Lefebvre's understanding of city life, is no longer 'made up of chance encounters' (Lefebvre 2004: 30). Indeed, iPod users never willingly interact with others whilst listening.[4]

The solipsism of the cosmopolitan city

Urban space, especially in city centres, requires constant negotiation; through the use of iPods users negotiate their movements on their own terms through the mediation of their iPods. The following user typifies the strategies of iPod users as they move through urban space. Joey is twenty-eight years old. She lives and works as a photo researcher in New York, travelling across New York daily to work, as well as running work errands throughout the day. Like many iPod users, music orientates Joey at the out-set of her day, as she plans her music consumption through the creation of specific playlists – in the following instance, a high-energy morning mix, which stimulates 'mind and body':

> When I leave my apartment in the morning I grab my iPod and shove it in my pocket. By the time I get to the subway platform I am listen-ing to my morning mix. This mix is '80s music ranging from Eurhythmics to Blondie and the Smiths. It's an upbeat and a subtle mix that wakes me up and gets me motivated for my day. I always plan what I will listen to and it reflects what I want to hear or feel at that time.

Joey's experience of New York streets is described as a complex noise structure, which is unpleasant and to be avoided. Her description of sensory overload is uncannily reminiscent of Simmel's description of Berlin at the beginning of the twentieth century: 'sirens are going off, car horns honking, and people on their cellphones – so much urban chaos'. Joey's primary concern is with the auditory incursion of the street; she focuses upon the kaleidoscopic sounds of technologies of human movement and communication – cars and mobile phones – themselves technologies of separation. She brings the auditory city under control, drowning out extraneous noises through the loud and insistent sounds of her iPod play lists. The oppressive and confined spaces of the subway are also successfully managed:

> The subway is noisy with scratchy announcements and squeaking wheels. The noises make me irritated and nauseous, but if I have my headphones on it blocks the noises and makes me less irritable and impatient. If I wait on the subway platform for a half hour I do not mind if I have my iPod to listen to.

Sound is both a proximity and a distancing sense: with the ears open, sounds flood into the subject body – sound is intrusive, physically and cognitively; sensitivity to the noise of others has increased as urban citizens make more noise themselves. The everyday noises of the city are of concern to Joey, making her irritated and impatient. Sensorily, her body becomes a raw auditory nerve. The repelling nature of urban life is managed and transformed through her use of the iPod. Mundane and potentially 'boring' activities such as waiting for a train are transformed into pleasurable activities as Joey claws back time, repossesses it through its auditory management.

Sensitivity to auditory distraction is heightened for many iPod users. Joey is only able to read on the subway with the accompanying sounds of her iPod, not because, as some users, she needs a continual sound accompaniment to cognition, but rather the sound of others is in itself distracting. To read she needs her own managed soundscape which substitutes for silence:

> The only way I can read in public places is to read with my head-phones on. I think its because the music is familiar and I don't get distracted by it. It is background noise that is predictable, secure, and in my control.

iPod users banish the contingency of the auditory landscape, clearing a space for them which is predictable and secure. Out in the street Joey 'edits' her sensory experience as a strategy of control enabling her to successfully manage her experience physically and cognitively. She 'edits' not merely the unwanted soundscape of the city streets but also the 'looks' of others as she moves through the streets of New York. Auditory filtering is a central urban strategy of iPod users. Historically communication technologies have permitted users to engage in a diverse range of sensory filtering – the mobile phone filters out body, vision (sometimes) and touch, and internet chat rooms filter out all but the disembodied word, but in the city, where face-to-face co-presences arguably remain the norm, filtering strategies are developed by iPod users:

> I see them [people] as an obstacle. I have to deal with crowded streets and subways all the time, and the iPod helps me cope with this … I listen to my iPod while running errands around the city. You have men making comments at you like 'Yo, Baby' and then you have people trying to hand you religious flyers, or tourists trying to get directions, and all I want to do is grocery-shop and go to the bank. If I have my headphones on I am invisible and I do not have to get intimidated by jerky men or disrupted by lost tourists.

The experience of the city is a singular vision in which others are perceived as obstacles in opposition to the desire of the user for free mobility. Joey's narrative of the city street is an anti-urban narrative, of a place to navigate and overcome. iPod use creates a sense of social invisibility among users; the distinctive white wires dangling down from the user's ears signify to others that the user is 'otherwise engaged', that she is unavailable to receive the gaze or the speech of the other. The iPod is akin to an audio-visual pair of sunglasses – protecting and empowering the user, who no longer has to return the gaze of the other or hear their unwanted requests.

The city, in iPod culture, becomes a contested site, made up of 'others' desiring to intrude upon the conversational and visual preserve of the user: whether it be men making advances, tourists asking for directions or people distributing flyers, the use of the iPod empowers the user to brush them aside. iPod culture concerns the privatisation of public space; public space is possessed through the process of auditory privatisation and exclusion. The relationship between the iPod user and other urban citizens is one in which others are perceived as obstacles contradicting the desire and purpose of the user. Joey moves through the city 'as if' she were the only one – invisible to the gaze of others, 'parting the seas like Moses', firmly in the centre of her monorhythmic world, a world in which others fall away – in silence:

> I weave through a sea of people. I am usually in a big hurry and the music helps me do this weaving. I feel like I can slide in and out of people's pathways and not even brush up against them, like the continuous beat of a song.

iPod culture repositions the sensory experience of the city to that of an auditory or audio-visual experience in which touch and friction melt away as users glide through the street in a sensory world lacking opposition and voided of meaning. If space is 'a performed place' as Urry contends (2000) then the urban space inhabited by iPod users is a profoundly privatised space in which the multi-faceted otherness of the city is progressively denied and managed.

The pleasures of solipsism

iPod users glide through the urban street silently, and silence is imposed upon others as they passivise the looks and remarks of others. The silencing of the 'other' is a strategy of control, representing a refusal to communicate with others in public. The privatised sonic landscape of the user permits them to control the terms and condition of whatever interaction might take place, producing a web of asymmetrical urban relations in which users are, invariably, in control:

> A person with headphones on gives off an appearance of not wanting to be disturbed. There are times, mostly at work or walking to and from work, when I just want to be left alone. Wearing the iPod insulates me from other people in my surroundings.
>
> (Amy)

Users are aware of the symbolic meaning of the white wires of the iPod dangling from their ears: a combination of distinction and power. Empowerment is a product of withdrawal and withdrawal creates an empowering sense of anonymity:

> Anonymity. It [iPod use] lets me move through space and time at my pace.
>
> (Joanna)

> I use my iPod in public as a 'privacy bubble' against other people. It allows me to stay in my own head.
>
> (John)

iPod use permits users to redraw or redefine 'personal space'. Goffman considered personal spaces to be 'the space surrounding an individual anywhere within which an entering causes the individual to feel encroached upon' (Goffman 1969: 54). Goffman's own definition represented an unrecognised historical moment of bourgeois urban sensibility – the entitlement to personal space. iPod culture enhances this sensibility towards the ownership of space through the gating off, not only of the auditory, but also of the physical. The encroachment of others loses its physicality with iPod users as they fail to notice or respond to the physical touch of others; personal space becomes conceptual – in the saturated sound world of the user's cognition. The interpersonal nature of urban space is seen as a form of theft, an either/or which threatens to take away the autonomy of, and space for, thought.

Sound intolerance

> Listening to music makes me feel better about my environment. I don't particularly like living in the city, but it's a necessary evil right now. Using an iPod keeps me from feeling oppressed by being constantly surrounded by other human beings, and it makes me feel emotional or in-tune or empowered, or whatever else I need to feel at the time.
>
> (Stacy)

Sensitivity to the oppressive nature of urban sounds is class and culturally based (Smith 2004). Cultures with strong notions of 'private space' understood as a form of entitlement are more prone to dislike or discriminate against the noise of others. Historically the production of 'noise' was frequently perceived as uncivilised within a bourgeois Western and, specifically, northern European ethic in which silence was considered truly 'golden'. Creating an auditory space for oneself or one's family was increasingly a prerogative and strategy of elites who felt that noise was no respecter of urban private space. As a consequence, cities like London in the nineteenth century became the scene of intense auditory battles to control space, often in tune with the wishes of the middle classes, whose aim was to construct an interior environment in the home that banished the chaos and ugliness of the street beyond. The seeking of quietude was a class-bound value and ideology – ideological in so much as the desire was to forget the squalor which frequently existed beyond the domestic front door (Picker 2003). The middle classes were especially vocal in their defence of what they considered their right to privacy, as the following *Times* newspaper quote indicates:

> There is no protection, we say, for the ear is the most helpless faculty we have. It is at once the weakest and the most wonderful, the most ethereal and most persecuted of the senses … A sense that deliberately constituted we subject day and night to torture which is very nearly the equivalent to cutting off a malefactor's eyelids and then crucifying him with his face to the sun.
>
> (*Times* leader, 1856, quoted in Picker 2003: 66)

Charles Dickens, chronicler of the nineteenth-century industrial city, promoted government legislation to rid London of street musicians, whilst the nineteenth-century German philosopher Schopenhauer complained bitterly about the cracking of horse whips by carriage drivers disturbing his peace. The sensitivity towards urban noise has been transformed and extended in the twenty-first century. iPod users have successfully reclaimed not merely the private domains of the city but also public space. They have transformed the public spaces of the city into private enclaves of saturated sound. iPod users create a conceptual silence through the creation of a controlled, pleasurable and privatised sound world. The technology of the iPod has empowered ears precisely by privatising them.

> When I'm around others in a public place I use music to block them out. To begin with, people aren't as likely to approach someone wearing headphones. Secondly, small talk and chatter gets on my nerves, and I don't want to be drawn into other people's lives or conversations either vicariously or directly. Also the tonality and accent of certain people's voices is terribly grating to me.
>
> (Wes)

During the working week, which is when I use it most, I try to listen to it on my journey to and from work. I like to have it with me so I can

block out any annoying sounds or conversations that other people have
on public transport.

(Jane)

In NYC it's easier to avoid guilt-inducing encounters with the homeless,
or street beggars, because if they see that you can't hear them, they are
less likely to approach you (or persist in asking) for money.

(Ivan)

iPod users display a heightened sensitivity towards the mundane
existence of others in public space. The noise of 'otherness' is banished
and with it the 'quirkiness' of the other. For Wes, a twenty-four-year-old
programmer from the United States, this extends to the 'tonality and
accent' of other people's voices; for Ivan it permits him to silence the
homeless and needy; for Jane, a twenty-six-year-old librarian from
London, it is merely the general sounds of others as she commutes to
central London which are banished. iPod use enables them to operationalise their dystopian responses to urban life successfully. The more
users wish to remain in a private auditory space of control the more
sensitive they become to the contingent nature of the everyday world,
which they wish to push away. The cosmopolitan nature of city life is
negated through these 'gating' strategies. Tracy, a thirty-two-year-old
script writer living in Phoenix, Arizona, typifies these widespread urban
strategies of exclusion.

Tracy was an early adopter of MP3 technology, having had a player for
four years. Control is an overriding consideration in Tracy's description
of how she uses mobile technologies. The iPod is described as 'a tool'
enabling her to control whatever environment she occupies. Tracy is a
heavy user of the iPod, using it continually at work and elsewhere, 'Since
I'm a writer, I'm left mostly alone. If I had the option, I wouldn't take my
headphones off all day. Listening to music at work makes it slightly bearable. I've quit jobs that wouldn't let me listen to music.' Tracy uses music
to accompany her during most activities of the day. The need and desire
for musical accompaniment to a wide range of activities are taken for
granted in her description of use. Music is chosen to match her mood and
activity. Whilst doing yard work, for example, she describes needing
music with a 'faster beat. A Mozart sonata isn't going to motivate me.'
Continuity of listening is a way of organising the rhythms of the day –
continuity implies separateness for iPod users such as Tracy. Tracy
describes how she manages forms of interaction whilst continuing to listen to music on her iPod, 'If I go shopping from store to store I won't take
it off. I typically unplug one earphone when paying for my items so that
I can interact with the cashier.' This strategy ensures her continuity of
listening whilst simultaneously enabling a minimal level of recognition to
the subject employee. Forced interruption is described in the following

terms: 'Sometimes I feel violated if I have to turn it off for an unplanned reason.' The breaking of her auditory bubble represents recognition of the fragility of her auditory empowerment. Interruption becomes tantamount to the touching of an exposed nerve – the flow of subjective sound takes users away from the physicality of the world which is described as recessed by some, or not 'really being there'. An involuntary and sudden return to the world, as others experience it, is invariably experienced as unpleasant.

Maintenance of control implies a denial of difference within iPod use. Tracy's description of iPod use is of a subject in retreat, a subject who habitually 'gates' off her experience from others and the spaces she moves through:

> In America people are often loud and rude, and it's sometimes hard to concentrate effectively. In Phoenix we have a lot of Mexican immigrants. They don't learn English and they have no control over their children. I believe in mutual respect when in public places. It was becoming increasingly difficult for me to shop without encountering a bombardment of Spanish or screaming kids. The iPod lets me filter them all out. I'm much calmer now when I shop. The iPod lets me overlook the lack of courtesy. Using the iPod helps control my concentration. Since I'm familiar with the music, I can let it float to the back of my consciousness.
>
> (Tracy)

Tracy achieves a state of equilibrium precisely by withdrawing into herself, Sennett described this form of behaviour as representing 'an early sign of the duality of modern culture: flight from others for the sake of self-mastery' (Sennett 1990: 44). iPod use can usefully be understood as a filtering mechanism permitting users like Tracy to remain focused on themselves by negating the 'distasteful' and contingent nature of urban space.

The social politics of the street is one of proximity whereby the public spaces of the street are gendered, racialised and class-bound (Massey 2005). Among its diverse uses the iPod is used to erase the differential nature of these spaces.

The utopianism of iPod users becomes manifest in withdrawal from the world in which they move. Thus the world is experienced as bereft of meaning as the consumer derives pleasure and comfort from the mobile pleasures of commodity culture. Charles Taylor has noted the way in which an instrumental stance to subjective feelings increasingly separates subjects from one another. In the instrumental focusing-in upon atomistic goals a sense of shared experience declines (Taylor 1989). iPod use appears to represent for many users a 'device paradigm' whereby they withdraw from engagement with the world around them into the circumscribed world of auditory pleasure provided by the iPod, an urban world in which the 'other' is ignored, negated and denied.

Sound makes the city

In the cosmopolitan image of city life the city is partially a function of the life on the street. Through interacting with and being open to experience the citizen contributes to the fabric of city life. Whilst some iPod users report enjoying city life, their's is a mediated experience of the pleasures of the city. The city is viewed through the products of the culture industry in the form of music, talking books and of course the iPod itself:

> I refer to my iPod as my pacemaker, it helps me find that place. I almost exclusively travel to NYC when not in London. I have a dedicated playlist called 'NY state of mind'. This includes a lot of New York rap music and NY/east coast jazz. Something with NY in the lyrics, but also the sophistication, edge and energy of the place.
>
> (Sami)

The meaning of city spaces itself derives from the playlists of users. Cosmopolitanism becomes a fictional reality existing in the often eclectic mix of music contained in the iPod, in the user's music collection itself. For many iPod users the pleasure of the city comes from not interacting with others who 'disrupt' and 'distract' their energy but rather from listening to music, which may remind them of what it is to live in a city. A mediated cosmopolitanism is encased in the user's iPod.

The city as a cosmopolitan space is inscribed empirically, epistemologically and morally within Western cultural discourse. Cosmopolitan spaces are thought to construct cosmopolitan citizens. The centrality of cosmopolitanism to the health and well-being of urban culture is described by Silverstone in the following terms: 'In the ideal world such a figure is mobile, flexible, open to difference and differences. And such a figure is no longer seen as marginal but rather as central to the civic project' (Silverstone 2006: 12). Equally, Kwame Anthony Appiah has asked how urban citizens can maintain an ethical stance in a cosmopolitan culture in which they are confronted by a world of strangers (Appiah 2006). Mobile media such as the iPod which transform the nature of urban space appear to play a central role in the construction of the 'social, civic and moral space' of the city (Silverstone 2006: 5).

In doing so iPod culture appears to challenge a central tent of cosmopolitanism – the recognition of difference. Cosmopolitanism appears to reside in the contents of the iPod itself, in the culturally varied playlists of users or in downloaded news programmes informing users of what is occurring in the world beyond. This rich, interiorised cosmopolitanism stands in stark contrast to the strategies that iPod users employ to navigate urban space.

4 The audio-visual iPod
Aesthetics and the city

Whether at home or in some modern means of transportation, society's actions remain everywhere the same. Changes in the landscape, however, distract attention from the hypocrisy of societal events, whose monotony is forgotten in the adventure of the voyage ... Travel is one of the best means for a society to maintain a permanent state of absentmindedness, which prevents that society from coming to terms with itself. It assists fantasy along mistaken paths; it occludes one's perspective with impressions; it adds to the wonder of the world, so that the world's ugliness goes unnoticed.

(Kracauer 1995: 299)

The consumer is engaged by his or her own mobility and imagination: movement and incompleteness equally energise the imagination; fixity and solidity equally deaden it.

(Sennett 2006: 149)

A fictitious world, as illusion it contains more truth than does everyday reality.

(Marcuse 1978: 154)

Cities are fabulous with a soundtrack. They morph so easily – to becoming super-modern places if you're listening to, say, Belle and Sebastian, or a sexual playground if you're listening to some hot R&B. Or a melancholy wasteland if indie rock. People change accordingly. Rural landscapes are best appreciated with ambient stuff, or, in the case of America, good classic rock. Irrespective of what music you listen to, it makes your environment seem 'super-real' or more animated – charged somehow with the life of the music. Banal things seem more significant or poetic. You feel 'cooler' too, in your soundtrack cocoon.

(iPod user)

One set of strategies embarked upon by iPod users in their effort to deal with the contingent and chilly nature of urban space is to aestheticise it. This aesthetic colonisation of urban space is in part a technological tale whereby urban experience becomes synonymous with technological experience. This technological structure to experience is both pervasive and increasingly taken for granted in wide areas of daily life. The pervasiveness is simultaneously empowering and dependent for contemporary consumers. Technology as a medium of organisation seamlessly mediates urban experience for large numbers of citizens – whether it is through individualising technologies like the iPod, the mobile phone or the automobile or through the multitude of hidden technologies that enable everyday life to function.

This chapter focuses primarily upon the aestheticising potential of the most totalising of all of these technologies, the iPod. This aesthetics of the street is largely an audio-visual one in which iPod users are transported from one cognitive and physical space to another through the dominant organising potential of privatised sound. The aestheticisation of urban space represents one set of strategies undertaken by iPod users in their management of daily life. The use of an iPod enables users to create a satisfying aestheticised reality for themselves as they move through daily life.

The aestheticising strategies undertaken by iPod use differs from the traditionally accepted mode of urban aesthetics which goes by the name of flâneurism, which has become the romantic metaphor for city life in much urban analysis.[1] Flâneurism as a mode of urban appropriation is representative of the dominance of the visual in urban and cultural studies (Amin and Thrift 2002; Freidberg 1993; Jenks 1995; Tester 1994; Tonkiss 2005). The flâneur, in this literature, is understood as a rootless, displaced subject who places themself in the shoes of the 'other' – imagining what the world would be like from the position of the other. Flânerie is an act of alienated integration representing a quest to understand the other, albeit in imaginary terms, and is 'characterised by its very receptive disposition, a mode of embracing rather than of excluding external impulses' (Gleber 1999: 26). Benjamin understood the flâneur as representing the image of the outsider, yet in contemporary rhetoric flânerie has become universalised – we all become flâneurs in a sanitised image of urban relations in which flânerie becomes an integral part of the 'tourist' gaze.

Flâneurism is, however, an inappropriate concept for understanding the audio-visual world of the contemporary iPod user. The mundane and routine daily experience of the urban citizen is not primarily made up of the tourist gaze. Indeed, iPod culture embodies a directly contrary position to that of the flâneur. The aesthetic moment of urban experience within iPod use draws the 'other' mimetically into the users own imaginary realm – theirs is a strategy in which all 'differences' are negated to become one with the user. iPod culture represents the aesthetics of mimicry; it is an audio-visual mimicry.

Visual epistemologies impose a silent gaze upon the city in a manner that mimics the 'purely visual *agora*' of the city, which itself is thought to 'provoke mutual withdrawal' (Sennett 1994: 358). Visual descriptions of the city often resemble the snapshot – the fragmentary distillation of urban life as if through the aperture of a camera (Benjamin 1973). iPod culture, by contrast, concerns the seamless joining together of experience in a flow, unifying the complex, contradictory and contingent nature of the world beyond the user. The success of these aestheticising strategies depends upon the creation of an all-enveloping wall of sound through which the user looks. Users report that iPod experience is at its most satisfying when no external sound seeps into their world to distract them from their dominant and dominating vision.

The aesthetics of the street

Urban citizens frequently ignore the physical environment through which they move. The mundane journeying through the city invariably does not evoke the 'tourist' gaze (Urry 1995), with city dwellers rarely mentioning the spaces that they daily pass through. City spaces are, rather, experienced as habitual, not meriting mention. iPod use provides one way in which the urban dweller navigates through the mundane spaces of the city, frequently preoccupied with their own mood and orientation rather than the spaces passed through. iPod users' inattention to the visual is true both of crowded city centres and of quiet suburban streets. When iPod users do choose to look, their attentiveness is an auditory attentiveness facilitated by the rhythm of sound pumped directly into their ears. iPod users aim to create a privatised sound world, which is in harmony with their mood, orientation and surroundings, enabling them to re-spatialise urban experience through a process of solipsistic aestheticisation. iPod users aim to habitually create an aesthetically pleasing urban world for themselves as a constituent part of their everyday life. The aesthetic appropriation of urban space becomes one cognitive strategy as users attempt to create a seamless web of mediated and privatised experience in their everyday movement through the city, enhancing virtually any chosen experience in any geographical location at will. In doing so they create an illusion of omnipotence through mediated proximity and 'connectedness' engendered by the use of their iPod.

Jason is thirty-five years old; he lives in New Orleans and works in online media distribution. He is married, with one young child, and has owned an iPod for over a year, never having possessed a mobile music player previously. He regularly listens to music and audio books on his iPod, and employs both in his aestheticising strategies. Jason describes listening to a talking book on his iPod whilst drinking a cup of coffee in a local café: 'I love the experience of listening to a work of fiction and being in a public place like a coffee store. I like to watch people around me and imagine them as the characters in the novel.' The aesthetic impulse transforms the mundane space of the café into the scenario of the novel being listened to, with its customers as unknowing characters. The aesthetic impulse energises the mundane space of the café, creating an audio-visual drama in which Jason becomes its active audio-visual master. Listening frees up the eyes to observe and imagine, thus differing from the traditional reading of a book, in which the reader is visually engaged in the text. Jason can look around the café, the movements of his body unconstrained by the act of reading.

The text becomes a continuous flow of sound on to which he adds a level of physicality in the act of imagination. The sound print of the book is imposed on the silence of the world around him. Jason does not experience the café itself as an unpleasant environment – he chooses to enter and have refreshments, after all. The aesthetic impulse is triggered by the desire to heighten his experience. The mimetic character of iPod aesthetics occurs equally in music listening, as Jason explains, again in the café:

> My world looks better. I get more emotional about things, including the people I see and my thoughts in general. Sometimes I project the lyrical content of songs on to the people I see while I'm listening. For example, I can distinctly remember listening to U2's 'Stuck in a Moment' and I was looking at some of the people standing around me in a coffee shop, with the look of anxiety on their faces and general angst. It made me want to hug them and tell them it's OK ... I would look at other people and they would smile at me, almost like they knew what I was thinking .... It's like it polarised my world into these hemispheres of those who understood Bono's message and those who didn't. I'm not a Bono worshipper or anything; it was just the first time I had really listened to the lyrics of the song. That's a very private moment (in public) .... it's difficult to explain, but when he said the words 'I know it's tough, but you can never get enough of what you don't really need' it all just crystallised for me. I've had a lot of surreal moments like that listening to the music on my iPod and watching the world around me ... It's almost like watching a movie, but you're in it.

The reference to iPod experience as being like that of a movie is common, although its meaning varies (Bull 2000). In Jason's account it refers to the world in which he lives, appearing as if it were a movie in which he is also placed. The U2 song heightens Jason's mood. Listening to the song, he recognises the superfluity of the ethics of consumption as articulated by Bono and seemingly etched upon the faces of the hapless customers in the café. The lyrics of the song appear to describe the cognitive state of the others, visually imagined and interpreted by Jason. The aesthetic principle serves to elevate Jason beyond mundane concerns – placing him in a position of an empowered interpreter of the world whilst remaining distant. In the act of interpretation Jason remains silent, impenetrable to others.

City life is invariably about surfaces, the superficial reading and the transitory clues involved in our observations of others, hence the overriding dominance of the visual in urban accounts of experience. The presentation of self is a largely visual one – the presence of the other is largely a silent presence in urban culture, even in the urban world of the mobile phone. Silence protects the urban subject from 'the harsh realities of the world'. It is this silence which promotes both isolation and the flowering of self; the richness of interiority contrasted with the blandness of the outside world.

The flow of people moving through the street differs from that of those sitting or milling around a café. The café is also a place of talk, of snatched conversations, of potential exposure. The above account of iPod use re-imposes the purely visual on to the activity of others in order to construct them as significant, yet imaginary, others. Jason in drawing others into his 'enlightenment' vision is essentially saying, 'If you could hear what I hear, then you too would be transformed.' Jason's enlightenment, however, remains a mute and private enlightenment in which others are unaware as they move through space with their own unknown preoccupations. Jason's private revelations nevertheless cognitively empower him, heightening his sense of presence and purpose; his is an audio-visual mastery of the world:

> Sometimes I think I can calm people down just by looking at them when I'm listening to music. And sometimes, when they look at me, I think they do 'shift', because they recognise that I'm in a 'good place'.

Jason, in the act of private listening, imagines that he ceases to be a blank canvas, a mere surface that others look at uninterestedly. Meaning radiates from him, the internal becomes externalised, constructed through music and made transparent – immediate. He is transformed in the imagined eyes of others becoming the centre of a cognitive universe through which others reflect – his cognitive state becomes their cognitive state – though they are not privy to his sound world. The auditory 'look' is a sufficient tag, in the above account, for an 'imaginary' recognition to flow from the 'other'. Jason is not merely a part of this audio-visual world; he becomes its director, orchestrating meanings in which he imagines others as 'knowing' cast members. Jason is not alone in summoning up precise aesthetic re-creations through the creation of scenarios in which others play unwitting stand-up parts:

> For some reason, Talking Head songs seem to work best for this. Like, I will look at an old woman with a cane, and imagine her singing one lyric. Then move on to a hip-hop style teenage boy, and have him sing to the next line. My imagination really can take off. It sometimes makes me laugh and smile to myself – especially if a particularly amusing line comes up. It really does transform my surroundings. I sort of feel like I'm in my own music video.
>
> (Karen)

Underlying this virtual connectivity appears a playful narrative of invention in which users remain cognitively invisible. Alternatively, the personalisation of the user's sound world imbues the street and its atmosphere, indeed the whole world, with an intimacy, warmth and significance it otherwise lacks. The world mimics and moves to the rhythm of users. For iPod users the street is orchestrated to the predictable sounds of their favourite playlists:

> The world looks friendlier, happier, and sunnier when I walk down the street with my iPod on. It feels as if I'm in a movie at times. Like my life has a soundtrack now. It also takes away some of the noise of the streets, so that everything around me becomes calmer somewhat. It detaches me from my environment, like I'm an invisible, floating observer.
>
> (Berklee)

The process of auditory looking described above by the young Dutch user in Amsterdam mirrors that of users elsewhere. iPod users in their viewing strategies often describe themselves as 'not really there' The solipsistic viewer is shielded by their iPod from a truly reciprocal gaze. Jason's description above, for example, was of the imaginary gaze of the other; a constituent part of his own imaginative construction. iPod users frequently engage in non-reciprocal gazing whereby they don't receive the gaze of others at all – the iPod acts as a virtual pair of sunglasses from which the user stares imperiously. Susan, a manager from Toronto, describes this transformative power of the iPod over her urban environment:

> I find when listening to some music choices I feel like I'm not really there. Like I'm watching everything around me happening in a movie. I start to feel the environment in the sense of the mood of the song and can find that I can start to love a street that I usually hate, or feel scared for no reason.
>
> (Susan)

The solipsism of the user is frequently referred to in terms of general feelings of separateness:

> I'm living in a world where music is going on and things are happening and everyone else who can't hear what I'm hearing is not really in that world or slightly less connected to it. There's something going on in my head that's for me and only me.
>
> (Kate)

> I see people like I do when I watch a movie ... there is a soundtrack to my encounters ... music to accompany my thought about others. It dramatises things a bit, it fills the silent void.
>
> (June)

Streets perceived as silent are in reality a complex of sounds. June's observation that her iPod filled the 'silent void' is indicative of users' experiencing the world solely as a function of mediated sound. The unmediated sound world of urban society is a place where nothing happens – devoid of interest, throwing the subject back into the world of contingency, isolation and incompleteness.

Richard Sennett has argued that feelings of subjective incompleteness in urban space might be conquered through the mere act of movement. To move becomes an end in itself, whilst to remain still is to be reminded of 'self' as 'object' rather than self as activity; as Paris Hilton was heard to comment, 'I walk, I don't think.' iPod users, however, display no such completeness through the mere act of movement. They experience unmediated experience as threatening, silence is associated with falling prey to the unmanageable and contingent nature of their own cognition. In addition to this cognitive frailty they also become aware of the chill of city spaces, which are perceived as inhospitable, without the warmth of desired communication. Whilst the use of a mobile phone makes for a temporary respite, iPod use provides the user with the power to transform their environment seamlessly and continuously. A sense of completeness arrives through mediation – not movement.

Sound enhancement

To aestheticise, as Marcuse argued, is to simplify, to strip reality of its inessentials. The aesthetic principle is inherently one of transcendence. An essential component of this transcendence for iPod users is to replace the multi-rhythmic and hence unmanageable nature of urban life with their own manageable mono-rhythms. Mundane yet nevertheless unmanageable urban life is transformed through iPod use, creating movement and energy in the user where there was none before. Amy, a thirty-two-year-old who works in product design in Philadelphia, describes walking down the street with her iPod playing:

> My music drives my attitude as I walk down the street. If I'm listening to melancholy music my surroundings are a little greyer, a little more dismal, and the strangers I see on the street become a little more menacing. If I'm listening to upbeat music the strangers look friendlier and my surroundings are not as depressing. While living in a city is practical for many reasons, it can also be overwhelmingly depressing. Having cheerful music in my ears as I see a homeless person digging through garbage to find a meal is disconcerting. Sometimes the music acts as a buffer between me and the city, and other times the music draws such a sharp contrast between what I'm hearing and what I'm seeing that it's hard to take. Other times, when I'm walking through the city with a great song, one that's appropriate to my external surroundings and internal feelings, I feel like I'm the star of my own personal movie, strutting along to my theme song of the moment.

Common in iPod accounts of aesthetic experience is making the street mimic the mood engendered by the music playing on the iPod. In the above account the homeless that are observed are not so much aestheticised as recessed. The use of the iPod provides a 'buffer' between the user and the recognised reality of the city street, invoking Kracauer's observation that 'the world's ugliness goes unnoticed' in iPod culture. Negatives are transformed into positives as Amy describes her elation as she traverses the spaces of the city. Emily, a twenty-six-year-old worker in the advertising industry in London, paints a dystopian image of her experience of the city, highlighted by both her mood and her music:

> I'd just moved house, was going through a *very* rough patch in my life and particularly with my boyfriend. I decided to walk to a different Tube station, trying to find my way without the aid of a map. The song which came on was 'Roses' by Outkast. It's about a nasty woman whose boyfriend is fed up of her ... You can see the resonance – there's a sense of lonely resignation to the song, and this transformed the surroundings. (I was getting lost and moved from Little Venice, where I live, to the grittiness of Edgware Road.) I was into dull and hideous. Crossing a huge road – filthy petrol fumes, etc. – it all became more intense, thanks to the music. Another time was when I was in Paris for work, and was feeling less than good about work, and wanted to be home, and listening to familiar upbeat music (Basement Jax) made the surroundings seem even more melancholic and alien to me.
>
> (Emily)

Ironically the comfort of listening to familiar music whilst in Paris highlighted her alienation from the streets of Paris – acting merely to remind her of her wish to be home. The following respondent also highlights this colonisation of space in which one's surroundings take on the ambience of the cognitive state of the user, mediated through their soundtrack:

> I feel as though life is a movie and is playing especially for me. If I listen to sad music, which I only listen to when I'm down (boyfriend breakup, bad grade, just bad news) then everything sort of has a grey shadow over it, even when it's sunny outside.
>
> (Betty)

The world experienced as a movie script in which the user takes a central role is a common description of iPod use. The selection of 'sad' music to match the user's mood transposes those feelings to the streets passed through. The world and the user's experience within it gain significance through their enveloping and privatised sound world. iPod users invariably prefer to listen to their music loud, thus providing them with an overwhelming sense of presence whilst simultaneously blocking out any sound from their environment that might sully the heightened and empowering pleasure of use. In their world of aesthetic euphoria, experience is simplified, clarified – the aesthetic impulse provides an unambiguous sense of purpose and meaning for users, creating a 'space' within which to unwind and unravel their emotions. When attended to, the street becomes a function of their mood and imagination, mediated through their iPod:

> I like to crank angry, loud music at night; the city seems so much more dark and brutal in the dark if I do that. Walking home, I sometimes listen to more soaring, passionate melodies, and they make me see things differently. I listen to rhythmic and pulsating music sometimes, which makes me feel confident and secure – I don't have to do anything but 'following the beat', so to speak. Sometimes I listen to piano music, and because most of my piano music is kind of depressing/saddening (in a good way) it makes the world seem more fragile and on the verge of collapse. Delirium's music always strikes me in this emotional, soul-searching way, and elevates even the smallest details to some greater significance; every movement of the people in the streets seems spiritual and sacred.
>
> (Brian)

> If it's dark and gloomy and raining outside, I'll pick something that complements the weather, and that can alter the outlook on the world around me. I can take joy in otherwise gloomy, rainy, dank weather by putting on something wonderfully gloomy and dank, something I love to hear. It's a fine synergy of the visual and auditory environments. It makes me feel like I'm walking through my own movie, with my own soundtrack. The people around me look like extras on the set. Dark clouds look brighter and the smell of the rain gets stronger. I see myself in the third person.
>
> (Kerry)

> My iPod puts me in a place and time. It's very common for me to walk to the music, so to speak. What I am listening to affects how I see everything around me. I might listen to some classic soul while I walk and the city seems to have a very mellow vibe. On other occasions I might have on some Rage against the Machine or something like that, and the city seems chaotic, crazy, too fast. What I listen to always impacts the way I view my surroundings.
>
> (Freedom)

Aesthetic enhancement is a central strategy of iPod use. Times of the day or weather conditions are complemented by and enhanced through the use of music played on the iPod. This might be predetermined through the construction of playlists made for these occasions or found whilst scrolling through the contents of the iPod. The contents of the iPod represent a repository of sensory and environmental stimuli.

Some iPod users play music at random, rather than sorting through their playlists to find a suitable track to harmonise or illuminate their surroundings. They have their iPod on shuffle, thereby forcing a level of contingency upon the juxtaposition of sound and street. None the less, the aestheticising impulse continues to throw up interesting options for users in which the world continues to be brought into harmony with the music:

> I find that my iPod 'colours' my surroundings quite significantly; as it's on shuffle I don't know what's coming up next, and it often surprises me how the same street can look lively and busy and colourful one moment and then – when a different song starts – it can change to a mysterious and unnerving place. I like the sensation, though.

> (Andy)

iPods are non-interactive in the sense that users construct fantasies and maintain feelings of security precisely by not interacting with others or their environment.

Sound both colonises the listener and actively recreates and reconfigures the spaces of experience. Through the power of a privatised sound world the world becomes intimate, known and possessed. Imagination is mediated by the sounds of the iPod becoming an essential component in the ability of users to imagine at all. Users are often unable to aestheticise experience without the existence of their own individual soundtrack acting as a spur to the imagination.

In this ordering of cognition the user surpasses the disjunction that exists between their own soundtrack, the movement of others and the environment passed through. Without the iPod they experience the world out of sync. The polyrhythmic nature of the city relativises their own place within the world, making them just one more piece of an anonymous urban world.

Sound utopias

If movement is itself a potentially transformative activity, then moving to sound is doubly so. Movement itself embodies an element of ideology as the subject moves through the city. In the modernist urban world of the city it was the subject who was traditionally colonised by the enticements of the city, interiorising the utopian dreams fabricated in the electronic lights and billboards of the city of which the subject became a constituent part. The representational spaces of the city fill up subjectivity, so to speak:

> Illuminated words glide on the rooftops, and already one is banished from one's own emptiness into the alien advertisement. One's body takes root in the asphalt, and, together with the enlightening revelations of the

illuminations, one's spirit – which is no longer one's own – roams ceaselessly out of the night and into the night.

(Kracauer 1995: 332)

Kracauer's understanding of the urban colonisation of the subject is essentially Fordist, in which the dominant rhythms of the city create the cadences within which all citizens walk. Urban experience becomes mediated through the advertising technologies of commodity culture and the empowered dreams associated with the very act of movement itself. iPod culture reverses this phenomenon. The user is saturated with the privatised sounds of the iPod – the cultural imperative, fully commoditised, lies in the contents of the iPod itself. The world is drawn into the user's 'individual' narrative rather than the street drawing the user into its realm. The experiences of the city described by Kracauer and those of the iPod user remain mediated and commoditised. Both sets of descriptions are equally filmic. Kracauer's urban stroller lives in the polyrhythmic audio-visual world of the street, which presents itself to him as a spectacle in which the street becomes a commodified dream. iPod users, rather, construct a mono-rhythmic aesthetic narrative to the street deciphered from the sounds of the culture industry emanating from the iPod in their pocket. Theirs is a hyper-post-Fordist street of potentially multiple audio-visual scenarios – with each iPod user constructing their own singular mediated dream world simultaneously. Kracauer's subject is diminished, made smaller, by the scale of the street and its illuminated signs, whereas iPod users such as Sophie, a marketing manager from London, describes her iPod experience as

> making the world look smaller – I am much bigger and more powerful listening to music. The world is generally a better place, or at the very least it is sympathetic to my mood ... you become part of the music and can take on a different persona.

iPod use inverts the relationship between the user and the world. Sophie occupies the centre of her world. Empowered, she looms large against the horizon. The world, in harmony with her mood, is a better world. The world is brought into line through the privatised yet mediated act of cognition. A potentially perfect mimetic fantasy that denies the contingent nature of the world.

iPod users resemble both the imaginative city dweller who aesthetically recreates any chosen urban space at will, enlivening it as they move through the city, whilst also, and equally, appearing to represent an urban subject in retreat from a bland and alienating urban environment. Accounts of the blandness of urban experience are invariably accounts of the solitary subject confronting the 'non-spaces' of the city (Augé 1995). In these portrayals the city is portrayed as semiotically void, in which the subject, without the ideological props of commodity culture, remains 'transcendentally homeless'.

Aestheticisation has utopian imp[...] transcend the mundane world as it is [...] an active mode of appropriating the urba[...] making it the user's own. The desire to [...] processes derive both from the habitual pred[...] wider media use – for are not television and [...] positions of imaginary omnipotence whilst they wa[...] their own home? (Morley 2000) – and as a response t[...] space itself and the dislocation from it felt by the urban s[...] Sennett 1990).

In this process of aestheticisation iPod users transform [...] conformity with their predispositions. The world becomes part of [...] fantasy in which the 'otherness' of the world in its various guises is [...] This is an important strategy for iPod users, who subjectivise sp[...] consume it, as if it were a commodity. In the process, immediate experie[...] is fetishised. Technologised experience is fetishised experience. Experience becomes real or hyper-real precisely through its technologisation – through technological appropriation. The utopian impulse to transform the world occurs only in the imaginary: in its technologised instrumentality the world remains untouched. Users prefer to live in this technological space whereby experience is brought under control – aesthetically managed and embodied – whilst the contingent nature of urban space and the 'other' is denied. The concept of 'otherness' becomes increasingly redundant in iPod culture. Forms of urban reciprocity, of urban recognition, are denied within the very structure of iPod use. The empowerment of the subject implies an incipient crisis in the way in which users 'recognise' the other (Honneth 1995).

The aestheticisation of experience has traditionally been portrayed not merely as pleasurable, which it certainly is, but also as inconsequential in so far as the object of the gaze is left untouched – unsullied. 'Aesthetically, the city space is a spectacle in which amusement value overrides all other considerations' (Bauman 2000: 168). Yet, far from being inconsequential, this aestheticising mode of urban experience contains cognitive and moral resonances. The aestheticisation of experience remains relational, and, whilst the subjects of the aestheticisation process remain untouched, the aestheticising impulse highlights the underlying values of users in their relation to the 'other' and the spaces passed through. The aestheticising practices of iPod users contribute to our understanding of what it means to 'share' urban space with others from within an auditory bubble, immune to the sounds of others.

The audio-visual iPod 49

ːlications for users. To aestheticise is to
experienced. Aestheticisation remains
ɔn, transforming that which exists,
engage in these aestheticising
ːpositions of users located in
ɔ film viewers equally in
ːch from the comfort of
ɔ the nature of urban
ːbject (Augé 1995;

ːhe world in
ːa mimetic
ːegated.

me whilst walking or
the world during the
in my own head, so
ɣ community members
ɔf me, dancing ever so
ːning around them and
ːurly 'hello'.

ːce/the-age-of-shuffle/)

... ——— withdrawal; to the extent that silence can be
enforced, to that extent every person is free of the social bond. ... Here he
is learning that his codes for interpreting emotional expression are also
codes for isolation from others; here he is learning a fundamental truth of
modern culture, that the pursuit of personal awareness and feeling is a
defence against the experience of social relations.

(Sennett 1990: 212)

If physical proximity – sharing a space – cannot be completely avoided, it
can be stripped of the challenge of 'togetherness' it contains, with its standing
invitation to meaningful encounter, dialogue and interaction.

(Bauman 2003: 105)

iPod users never willingly interact with others whilst engaged in solitary
listening. The iPod is both a 'gating' and a 'tethering' technology. Gating
assumes a metaphysical stance in iPod culture – the drawing of circumscribed circles around the subject, both physical and metaphorical. This is
one of the historical legacies of the values of individualism and the concurrent demand for privacy – an overriding desire to be left alone whilst in
urban culture. The perception of face-to-face communication in public
spaces as a threat to this desired privacy has a lengthy cultural history
embodied in the use of communication technologies, which separate out,
and mediate, the subject from others. These technologies simultaneously
connect people together, enable them to socialise with one another in new
ways. Whilst the focus of this work primarily concerns the way in which
'solitary' individuals weave their way through everyday life through the use

of auditory technologies, the use of these technologies simultaneously fulfils the desire for, or management of, social proximity. The use of iPods in the domestic home, at places of work or used collectively in automobiles represents one moment of use: the transition from listening to talking as the iPod user receives a call on their mobile phone represents differential uses of these technologies in the construction of technologically mediated forms of interpersonal conduct.

Technologically mediated behaviour has become 'second nature to many residing in Western urban culture representing a dominant "mode of being in the world"' (Geurts 2002: 235) in which iPod users choose to live in an increasingly privatised and 'perpetual sound matrix', through which they 'inhabit different sensory worlds' (Howes 2003: 14) whilst sharing the same social space. In iPod culture users create a mobile and territorial identity for themselves as they move through daily life. In this chapter I discuss the variety of strategies whereby iPod users orientate themselves to, and respond to, the contingent incursions of the interpersonal into their privatised worlds, together with strategies for the mutual sharing of space, which are a significant whilst minor moment of use.

The desire for mediated withdrawal manifests itself in the design of houses, increasingly segmentalised into separate and privatised living spaces in which the geographies of living are increasingly segmented. This separation is furthered by the use of communication technologies whereby individuals increasingly choose the terms and conditions of their interactions with others within mediatised domestic spaces.[1] The home becomes a cognitive mirror to the urban street:

> The architecture of cities increasingly mirrors this division of domestic space in its creation of 'protective zones of distance around the individual', creating 'islands of undisturbed peace', for urban subjects.
>
> (Sachs 1992: 127)

Isolation is both a cognitive strategy operationalised by urban citizens and a structural constraint in the form of the design of cities we live in, and the roads we pass through (Newman and Kernworthy 1999; Sennett 1990, 1994; Urry 2006). These cognitive strategies of control and separation, together with the structural constraints of urban life, are filtered through a range of cultural expectations and responses – the desire for space, the desire to control one's environment and the desire to control and manage one's own cognition. The alienation of the subject from the spaces passed through and the subjects inhabiting those spaces is a product of urban design and cultural values embodied in, and furthered by, the social practices of iPod users. Sennett has noted that people living in 'urban high density structure[s] are inhibited from feeling any relationship to the milieu in which that structure is set' (Sennett 1977: 15). City spaces become immune to subjective intervention, becoming spaces of insignificance and indifference in which the subject is thrown back upon their own mediated resources. Whilst a cognitive move towards isolation derives largely from the structural constraints of urban space and place, it also acts independently whereby subjects desire to isolate themselves through technologies of movement and communication. The pleasures of mediated connectivity outweigh anything else that urban culture can frequently offer the mobile subject.

The public placing of, and consumer use of, technologies enabling the urban citizen to carry out most traditionally public tasks with little or no interpersonal contact further the architecture of isolation. Exchanges are increasingly taking place between subjects and machines in urban culture, making interpersonal exchange obsolete. Cognitively, consumers increasingly expect, feel comfortable with and desire no communication whilst out in public:

> Tracy expects to have wordless interactions with store attendants. When given a choice, Tracy will also use the 'You-check' line recently available in her neighbourhood's Fred Mayer, which allows her to scan her own purchases and credit card. 'I love it,' she says. In everyday life she wants to 'get in and out'.
>
> (Jain 2002: 394)

The normative foundation of the 'non-places' of urban culture becomes etched into the social expectations of consumers as they partake of 'public culture'.

The separation of tasks and spaces in the bourgeois home is an antecedent to contemporary urban gating practices – as is the manner in which the division of the tasks of everyday life in urban culture, represented by the geographical triangle which constitutes the movement of people between work, home and the shops, from where life's consumer needs are satisfied (Kunster 1998; Livingstone 2002; Putnam 2000; Stallabras 1996). 'Necessary' physical movement is mediated through the mobile technologies of the automobile, the iPod and the mobile phone. Physical and cognitive zoning becomes second nature in urban culture in which 'the basic idea of zoning is that every activity demands a separate zone of its own' (Kunster 1998: 120). Urban infrastructures increasingly complement the automobile, the mobile phone to the iPod. These technologies emphasise connectivity within circumscribed circles and spaces whilst simultaneously alienating subjects from the co-presence of one another in public space:

> I rarely even speak – I just hand them my credit card and say 'Thank you.'
>
> (Mark)

I tend not to notice people when I'm plugged in. I'm usually too preoccupied with myself to look at others.

(Elizabeth)

It removes an external layer. I see people and things as inanimate or not fully connected. It seems that I have an external connection they lack. It's quite odd, actually ... Yes. With the iPod and news talk radio files; I'm having an interactive session with the anchor. When I look at the people around me they appear to be two-dimensional and without significance.

(Jonathan)

Progressive withdrawal from the cosmopolitan city both motivates iPod use and furthers it:

I then started wearing it [the iPod] while shopping. I did it to control my environment and desensitise myself to everything around me. What I found interesting was that the more I wear my iPod the less I want to interact with strangers. I've gotten to the point where I don't make eye contact. I feel almost encased in a bubble. ... I view people more like choices when I'm wearing my iPod. Instead of being forced to interact with them, I get to decide. It's almost liberating to realise you don't have to be polite or do anything. I get to move through time and space at my speed.

(Zuni)

iPod culture represents a desire for uninterrupted and continuous experience as a central facet of the user's urban experience. This desire for a subjectively empowered sense of continuousness is enabled by, and facilitated through, iPod use, which enables users to link disparate places and moods through the temporal immediacy of iPod sounds. Sterne has traced this impulse to 'own' acoustic space to bourgeois notions of individualism and entitlement in which 'the space of the auditory field [becomes] a form of private property, a space for the individual to inhabit alone' (Sterne 2003: 160).

The role of the media in the privatising of public spaces is not confined to mobile technologies but increasingly involves the placing of fixed media technologies such as television screens in an array of public spaces such as airports, shops, in buses, aeroplanes and the like in which urban spaces become progressively privatised.[2]

The association of media segregation with physical urban segregation was noted by Douglas (2004) in her analysis of the role of the radio in American culture. In its efforts to cater for niche markets, Douglas found that radio stations in the post-Fordist era created taste ghettoes where consumers could rest assured with the certainties of musical programming that their selected radio station would deliver them. 'Audience research indicates that many Americans want this kind of safe, gated-in listening. It goes with our increasingly insular, gated-in communities and lives' (Douglas 2004: 348). The correlation of musical taste with the geography of living – gated-in listening habits to gated-in communities – implies a denial, or closing off, of difference in the everyday expectations of many domestic urban consumers. Douglas parallels the cognitive with the physical – a defensive strategy of urban living redolent of much of American urban culture (Ross 2000).

Most urban citizens, however, do not live in 'physically' gated communities, and even these are invariably not 'communities' in the traditional sense but merely accumulations of privatised dwellings whose inhabitants are merely doubly privatised (Gusfield 1975). The hyper-post-Fordism of iPod users takes 'gating' out into the public spaces of the city, but with one significant difference: iPod culture thrives on diversity of consumption. Whilst iPod users know the music contained in their iPods – its all theirs, after all – the variety of taste embodied in iPod collections often defies categorisation. The sequencing of music is frequently played at random on the iPod's shuffle mode, thus creating a sense of adventure among iPod users. This plurality of listening modes is, however, accompanied by the habitual gating of urban experience extending beyond the home into the public spaces of urban everyday life.

The use of mobile communication devices, to which the iPod is central, represents a reprioritisation of the relationship between direct interpersonal communication and technologically mediated experience. Cars, mobile phones and iPods now largely mediatize urban social space.

Managing the other: interpersonal iPod strategies

Social space is relational, making it potentially a moral space. How we inhabit and coexist in social space remains important, if co-presence remains significant as a social category in urban culture. In their desire for empowered and uninterrupted experience iPod users micro-manage their experience. In doing so users attempt to manage the interpersonal demands of everyday life through a range of strategies that combine the desire for solipsistic empowerment with the contingent demands of others. iPod users do not merely 'negate' the other – although that is one structural possibility – they invariably attempt to manage impersonal relations with others in shared public space.

Response to others is dependent on a range of mediating factors. For example, Ivan waits until the nature of the interaction becomes apparent:

> I usually don't switch it off, initially, I just drop the headphones on to my neck, or pull them out and leave them resting behind my ear where

I can hear them slightly. If it's a temporary street interruption I'll leave them there and put them in when I continue again. If it's a longer interruption, if I run into someone headed to the same destination, who decides to join me going there, I'll turn it off and shove it into my pocket.

(Ivan)

Ivan is relatively relaxed about interruption, and might well prefer the company of a friend on the way to work. On other occasions though, inter-action takes place simultaneously with listening, albeit with the earpieces placed behind the ear, enabling him to interact and listen simultaneously. In contrast to Ivan, the following user has some ambivalence about meeting up with colleagues on the way to work:

If in the morning someone wants to accompany me to the Tube I feel a bit 'Oh, I won't be able to listen to my iPod.'

(Emily)

Acknowledgement of the 'other' remains a matter of concern to many iPod users who develop strategies that conform to the recognition that the social world remains an interpersonal one:

I don't like turning it off if I can help it. I often will take out one of the ear buds if I have to interact with someone (ordering coffee at a coffee shop) so that I can listen to my music and interact with the real world at the same time.

(Paul)

I sometimes pause the music if I have to interact with someone else, although other times I just remove one earphone so that I can hear what they're saying. I never just turn the volume down.

(Fiona)

I take the headphones out altogether. I'd rather not be listening at all than have to try to concentrate on two things at once.

(Charlotte)

To keep both earphones in, even with the volume turned down, contravenes Fiona's sense of appropriate interpersonal behaviour, signifies a lack of attention to the other which implies that they are not worthy of the user's undivided attention. The removal of one earphone at reduced volume estab-lishes a visual and auditory norm of conduct for Fiona. Nevertheless, and despite her iPod etiquette, Fiona becomes irritated when interrupted. She regularly uses her iPod to modulate her moods whilst travelling through London on her way to work on the Underground system, playing her music loudly so as to block out the noise of the city. 'I do like to listen uninterrupted if possible. It can irritate me if I have to switch it off when I am in the middle of listening to something I want to listen to.' Interpersonal interruption diminishes the auditory pleasures of iPod use. Paul, equally, prefers to interact whilst simultaneously listening, noting the contrasting speed of his interior auditory world with the sounds of the world around him. Paul enjoys the multiplicity of this dual sound world, in contrast to users like Charlotte who prefer to switch their iPod off. Receptivity to interruption is often contingent upon what the user is listening to and the nature or cause of the interruption:

> Not having interruptions is naturally the best way of listening to longer mixes or albums. If need be I'll take my headphones off but usually don't stop the music when having a short discussion, buying train tickets, etc. This way I can easily jump back into the music without having to dig the Pod out of my pocket. I always remove my headphones if interaction is needed, as I consider it rude not to give your full attention when speaking face-to-face with someone.
>
> (Paul)

> At the supermarket or convenience store I'll sometimes turn the iPod off or take one ear-bud off (depending on the required length of interaction) when necessary. In most brief interactions I'll turn the volume down but leave it playing, like when I buy a pack of cigarettes at the newsstand at my train station. I don't need to talk to the woman there any more than to tell her what kind of cigarettes I want, and even that isn't necessary half the time, since she knows my brand.
>
> (Kerry)

> It really depends on how much I feel like being by myself. If I'm at the grocery store and I just want to buy things I'll turn it down but keep the headphones in. I'm a pretty social person, though.
>
> (Francis)

> I turn it off and remove the ear-buds – it would be rude not to. Of course, I wait until the last minute, keeping the ear-buds in and the music on while I'm in line at the supermarket.
>
> (Anne)

> I never remove the iPod if I'm just out for a day of shopping. I'll take it off, put it in a pocket if I'm having a conversation with someone I know. I'll leave it on if I'm having dinner at a restaurant alone. Also, I just let the music play if a sales clerk starts talking to me; I just point to my ear-buds and let them know I can't hear them. It's kinda rude but it's New York.
>
> (Janet)

Whilst Paul, a twenty-six-year-old graphic designer from London, desires uninterrupted listening, he nevertheless prefers to respond to the necessary interactions that embody much of city life, such as the purchasing of train tickets, even though automation has reduced the volume of such interactions in busy urban centres. Public space in the city is largely a space for minimal contact, the checking of a train passenger's ticket, and the purchase of a packet of cigarettes, which demand little or no 'recognition' of the other. Kerry paradoxically draws upon the prior recognition of her by the employee at the newsstand in order to engage in her regular daily mute transactions, whilst Anne remains listening till the last moment, when she turns her iPod off. iPod response varies in relation to whether the form of interaction is predicted, as in the supermarket check out, or sudden, as in a ticket inspection on a train. Janet, a twenty-nine-year-old New Yorker, extends her auditory solipsism to a lone meal at a New York restaurant. The use of an iPod provides her with a pleasurable auditory accompaniment to an otherwise potentially lonely experience. Whilst she recognises that others might consider her behaviour 'rude' she shrugs it off as something inherent in New York sociability. Verbal interaction is commonly replaced by visual recognition in the auditory world of the iPod user.

> If I'm doing something which involves speaking to someone, e.g. shopping, I pause the music – but if it's something I can do without having to say anything, such as getting on a bus with a bus pass [so not actually having to ask for a ticket] then I'll keep it going.
>
> (Chris)

Sometimes verbal communication is not considered a necessary component of interactivity on the street, or in the supermarket a mere visual acknowledgement becomes necessary. iPod relations tend towards asymmetry in which users define the nature of their interactive signs of recognition. Whilst users frequently switch their machines off or reduce the volume, the 'other' frequently has to guess whether attention is being paid or not. Many users simultaneously listen while interacting:

> If I'm shopping, and going from store to store, I won't take it off. I typically unplug one earphone when paying for my items so that I can interact with the cashier.
>
> (Tracey)

> Oddly enough, I'll use my cellphone over my headphones with the music on quite a lot these days. It really changes how you view your conversations, because the other person's voice is coloured by what you're listening to.
>
> (Ashvin)

Throughout this work I have analytically separated iPod use from mobile phone use. Mobile phone users whose phones contain MP3 players are unable to use the two functions simultaneously. Ashvin resolves this exclusivity of function by using his iPod and mobile phone simultaneously. The sounds of his iPod provide a background to phone talk and listening, the caller unaware that their discourse is in competition with a musical accompaniment. iPod users have a continuous auditory soundtrack through which they cognitively manage their time. Sound provides a constant background for cognition:

> I hate having to turn it off. It seems unnatural to not have something playing all the time.
>
> (Michael)

It is apparent that iPod use permits users to choose the terms and conditions of potential interactions, engendering feelings of power among them. Interactions can be avoided, feigned or engaged in:

> The iPod makes me feel like I can edit what I'm doing. If I want to talk to someone I can take the headphones off and talk, but if I don't want to talk I can keep on walking. The person will just think I didn't hear them because I'm distracted by my music instead of ignoring them on purpose.
>
> (Amanda)

> I treasure my commuting time as much needed private space. Having my iPod on decreases the chance that it will be invaded, so makes me feel calmer. You see, the risk of a work colleague 'bumping into me', especially on the way home, and wanting to TALK! is reasonably high. The iPod helps. In fact, this evening, I was at the station and aware out of the corner of my eye that there was a colleague on the platform. Having my iPod on made it possible for me to focus on the space in front of me (and so ignore him) without feeling that I looked disturbed! He's a nice bloke, of course. It's just that commute time is the only real private time I get.
>
> (Fred)

> It's a concrete visual sign that I'm otherwise engaged.
>
> (Emily)

The wearing of an iPod, with its emblematic white wires dangling from the user's ears signifies a 'fully engaged' sign to others, enabling users to feign avoidance whilst maintaining a level of interpersonal convention. Amanda would feel a level of discomfort if she felt that someone knew she had purposely avoided them. The iPod gives users an acceptable, to them at least, interpersonal get-out clause. The use of an iPod isn't primarily about the disregarding of others; rather, it concerns the reclaiming of the user's time in urban culture. In the busy and multiple schedules of iPod users commuting time represents time reclaimed in which users relax and enjoy themselves through listening to favourite tracks or yesterday's downloaded radio programme or a recently purchased talking book. Fred, like many other users, refers to the possibility of finding this reclaimed time in which he feels calm and in control 'invaded' by others. Fred, rather than seeing the city spaces of New York as anonymous, sees them full of work colleagues commuting to and from work as he does. The strategy of looking straight ahead is sufficient to maintain a sense of privacy without offending a work colleague, who might equally, of course, prefer not to engage in conversation. iPod users frequently do not realise that others may be trying to communicate with them:

> I prefer to be uninterrupted. Just now, for example (I'm listening to my iPod on a cross-country flight) a boy next to me had to tap me to ask me to get up so he could visit the rest room. I think he tried saying 'Excuse me' a couple times but I didn't hear him. I always try to be courteous, though. And if I predict that someone is about to interrupt me (e.g. the flight attendant is approaching for drink orders), I try to go ahead and pause it.
>
> (Annabelle)

In close proximity sound and vision become replaced by touch as a mode of communication. The possession of time is a significant motivation amongst iPod users, engendering a range of interpersonal responses as noted above:

> I do like to listen uninterrupted, and if I'm interrupted I feel slightly invaded. I listen to my iPod when I'm on my own. It's my time and in my space, and any interruption invades my time with myself.
>
> (Matt)

> I don't want anyone to bother me when I'm listening. I'm not interested in doing anything but listening to the song when my head-phones go on.
>
> (Wes)

Matt, a thirty-six-year old consultant from London, conflates the reclaiming of time with the reclaiming of space – both become his property in the ideology of iPod use. Equally, Wes desires total control over his interpersonal environment whilst listening to his iPod – a process accomplished by ignoring others. The immersion in a privatised sound world makes adjusting to the world beyond problematic and sometimes unpleasant. The collision of two sound worlds takes time to readjust:

> I don't like to be interrupted, as it can be a little jarring to pop back into the auditory experience of the real world, but I usually respond well.
>
> (Anne)

> I don't like having to switch it off quickly because it's not that easy to do.
>
> (Julie)

> I like deciding when to switch off. Announcements in airports irritate me for that reason. Stopping a song in the middle is like being rudely woken up.
>
> (Sarah)

This is in contrast to the following users, who, whilst wishing for continuity of their auditory pleasure, recognise the contingent nature of their activity:

> No problem with the act of switching the device off, although I do find my mental state doesn't usually switch the music off and on to whatever it is that needs my attention. I'm still in a relaxed frame of mind, and perhaps need to be more alert ... I'll usually unplug the headphones from my ears, as I'd find it annoying personally if someone else had earphones in their ears when I was talking to them, even if they did turn down the volume. By removing the earphones the track details and volume are unchanged and can be resumed after talking to the person.
>
> (Mike)

> I'll switch it off. The iPod is my personal entertainment but I don't want it to interfere in the way I interact with other people. So if someone speaks to me I don't mind switching it off. I consider it impolite not to.
>
> (Marianne)

Both Mike and Marianne refer to traditional modes of interpersonal conduct in which a Kantian mutuality of recognition becomes paramount. Personal preference becomes subordinate to interpersonal demands. Mike dislikes other users acting in ways that fail to recognise him. Whilst norms of social interaction are constantly changing in iPod culture, the norms regarding recognition of the other remain. Many iPod and mobile phone users dislike others treating them with a lack of regard – staking a claim to recognition that they often do not extend to others. The iPod, unlike the personal stereo that pre-dates it, permits the possibility of collective use, in the automobile, in the home and at work.

Sharing the auditory automobile

A family is driving 700 miles from northern Virginia to Chicago on vacation. In the car is a mother with her two sons. The mother has headphones on and is listening to her favourite jazz station transmitted via a portable satellite radio in the car. In the back of the car the boys watch movies on a small ceiling-mounted video screen. When they become bored with this they play electronic games via tiny consoles in the car. In the car are three mobile phones and a back-up entertainment package of a portable DVD/MP3 player to be used in any roadside hotel that they may stay in if the hotel happens not to have a cable television facility. The mother, when asked about the trip, says, 'I was at peace on that trip. I could listen to my music and concentrate on driving while they played their video games and watched their movies…Everybody was happy' ('Outward mobility', *Washington Post*, 31 July 2005).

The sharing of space in contemporary urban culture is a multi-faceted phenomenon – it no longer necessarily means the sharing of the same set of experiences with others, with even previously shared spaces becoming individualised, multiple and overlapping. The automobile as a site of media consumption sometimes reflects or mirrors the division of space in the home, with each room sequestered into entertainment space for different members of the family (Livingstone 2002; Spigel 2001). The space of the car is divided into multiple audio-visual zones in which personalised entertainment permits each person to pass away the time largely peacefully and pleasurably – an antidote to collective habitation within the intimate space of the auto, for it is unusual for members of a family to be locked into the same space for such a length of time, whether it be in their automobile or home (Putnam 2000). Frank, from Cheshire in the UK, is forty-eight and has three teenage daughters who frequently travel with him in his car:

> I sometimes use the iPod in the car with headphones. When the kids are in the car they used to listen to the radio or their CDs. Now that some of them have their own iPods it's great, as we can all listen to our own choices. My youngest daughter doesn't have an iPod yet, so she listens to her CD player and headphones. Two of my daughters sometimes try to synchronise their iPods to play at the same time so that they can sing along together!

The individualising of music choice is not necessarily incompatible with collective pleasure. Vicki, a thirty-five-year-old iPod user from the UK whose husband rides a powerful motorbike, describes her use of the iPod whilst riding pillion:

> The fact that it [the iPod] has no moving parts and has a remote control and playlists that can be very long make it ideal for a long ride. I set it

up before we set off, pop it in my pocket and use the remote to change the volume or skip to another track. It doesn't work too well at high speed because the bike is too noisy, which is quite annoying for me really, but he won't slow down much! On the bike I like faster stuff like Meatloaf or ELO. These tend to be louder as well.

Vicki is in close physical proximity to her husband yet inhabits her own mediated sound world, experiencing the elements through the sounds of her iPod as an exhilarating enhancement. The sequestering of space for individual entertainment is one possibility in the 'sharing' of the already privatised space of the automobile.

The sectioning of the automobile into separate and individualised consumption spaces is merely one increasingly available option for the users of cars. Whilst most car journeys are solitary journeys, the car remains a spasmodic site of multiple occupations for many families, and negotiation over the nature and content of its soundscape is frequent. School runs are frequent in which a parent shares the automobile with the children. Pamela is a thirty-seven-year-old management consultant from Boston, Massachusets, who takes her children to school as part of her commute to work. Pamela's iPod is a family iPod containing her own collection of music ranging from ambient to classical as well as containing her children's favourite music and some of their talking books. Pamela likes the flexibility of iPod use in the car. 'I used to have six CDs in my car and that was it. Now I listen to soundtracks one day and '80s music the next. The kids can choose between read-along stories and their favourite music too.' Pamela defers to the children in the morning, letting them listen to what they want. The car becomes a space of warm mutual interaction, with the children singing their favourite songs and Pamela joining in. Unlike the family above who were embarking on a long vacation trip, Pamela's journey to school is short and daily – the car is a space for family interaction. After dropping her children off at school she switches the music to suit her mood, the car becomes again a solitary auditory bubble, with her music keeping 'commuting from being too dreadful'.

Mike, a thirty-seven-year-old architect from Cheshire, also takes his children to school in his car:

I could listen to the same couple of songs over and over again, from driving into work of a morning to reading a magazine over lunch. For example, my youngest son will probably have Ozzy and Kelly Osbourne's 'Changes' on in the car on the way to school ... I might be thinking out changes at work and keep playing it after I've dropped him off as well as in work ... and then the Black Eyed Peas, as they remind me of the cool iPod adverts Apple has created. I only purchased the album after the advert came out! I can go deeper into moods/thoughts by listening to specific tracks ... and to also bring me out of moods. I could play the same track more than five times sometimes before playing something else, and then will perhaps come back to playing the same track some more.

Unlike Pamela he continues to listen to the music played. Music in the car is an interior activity for Mike, enabling him to focus on issues of concern and moods to be managed. Linda, a forty-eight-year-old secretary from Essex, uses her iPod to commute to London daily on the train and sometimes with her husband in the car. The iPod belongs to Linda, and it is she who drives. Journey time becomes one of auditory negotiation:

Listening in the car is very different from listening on my own, as I try to find things my husband would like – which isn't easy. I tend to move from track to track rather than listening to a whole album, and ones we can both listen to, like Darkness, Frank Zappa's 'Valley Girl', a lot of the White Stripes, Metallica's 'No-leaf clover' and so on.

Negotiating music choice is not always successful however, as the example of Roger, a fifty-year-old banker from London, illustrates:

I don't listen to my iPod in the car. My wife hates my choice of music, so if journeying with her, we tend to listen to a neutral radio station, or her choice of music. When travelling alone I take CDs which are part of my iPod collection.

Even for owners of iPods the sound in the car is frequently a mix of radio, CDs (if users have older models of cars, or no iTrip adaptor). Common to all these users as they negotiate the soundscape of the car is that the use of sound technologies to mediate their journey is habitual and taken for granted.

At home with an iPod

Whilst the Apple iPod mirrors the privatising tendencies of the earlier personal stereo, it also encompasses new ways to consume music that might be thought of as both more 'mobile' and as offering greater possibilities for collective music reception. The sharing of music files is often very social (Levy 2006; O'Hara and Brown 2006). Public spaces sometimes produce forms of collective recognition for iPod users ,who sometimes see themselves as members of an 'imaginary community':

I also like the sense of belonging. They [iPods] still enjoy a lot of cachet in London, and there's a sense of shared currency. You go out and meet someone in a bar who has an iPod – you can go through their playlists and build a musical profile of that person.

(Joanna)

The dynamics of home listening are potentially changed for some users through iPod use. iPods are sometimes plugged in to home stereo systems, working as home jukebox systems:

I port it to my home stereo system and use it to play throughout the house via the FM transmitter. When I walk from room to room the same music is playing.

(Jeff)

The home becomes colonised, with each room receiving the same sounds. Collectively this may or may not always be desirable, with issues of the control of domestic space coming to the fore in ways that solitary use avoids. iPods can also be added to the armoury of domestic yet privatised listening nodules:

I've gotten to the point that music portability is paramount to my day. I'll take my iPod into a relaxing bath. If my partner is watching TV I'll wear it whilst making dinner. I'll use it to go to sleep. It's also more polite to wear my iPod while doing yard work instead of blasting my home stereo.

(Ben)

At home I only use it with the FM transmitter over my stereo. I have used it for small and large gatherings (parties) as well as when I am home alone.

(Alison)

The iPod can be used to further secure both the user's private space but also that of other family members. Solitary use in the home might be construed as a way in which users respect the space of other members of the family. Equally, collective use of domestic technologies confronts the issues of the controlling of domestic space that is not apparent in privatised modes of use. Some homes are multiple iPod homes in which family members file-share and teach the skills necessary to download music.

Despite the collective potential of iPod use the silencing of the urban subject remains a structural condition of Western industrial nations. Silencing, the imposing and encouragement of a lack of verbal interpersonal communication in the public spaces of the city, feeds into the structure of iPod and mobile phone use which both reinforces the silencing of the subject and rescues them from it. For the most part iPod users successfully manage the interpersonal nature of the street – direct and unsolicited communication with others is relatively rare in contemporary urban life. The silencing of the subject creates a range of asymmetrical social relations through which users maintain control. The above users describe iPod use in London, Chicago, Paris, New York, Amsterdam and elsewhere. The structure of iPod interaction, that likes mobile-phone use, becomes increasingly similar across cultural divides (Castells *et al.* 2007). iPods, unlike the personal stereo, create new forms of social possibilities, primarily with others known to the user, in the home and in the car; they remain, however, the archetypal privatising technology.

6 Mobilising of the social
Mobile phones and iPods

I feel almost cut off from society if I don't have my mobile, whereas I feel like I'm cut off from a part of myself if I don't have my iPod.

(iPod user)

To understand changes in private life and personal relations, it is appropriate to examine the means by which people conduct those relations.

(Fischer 1992: 23)

Subjects mutually experience themselves to be loved in their individuality only in so far as they are not afraid of being alone. This mode of basic self-confidence represents the basic prerequisite for every type of self-realisation.

(Honneth 1995: 176)

Street walkers are so engrossed in their conversations that they do not apprehend what is going on around them despite their eyes being wide open ... the evidence does not suggest that these reductions in the human qualities of public space are likely to be mere transient adjustments.

(Katz 2006: 46)

All that separates desolation from elation is a phone call.

(Peters 1999: 201)

To attend alone is to expose oneself as possibly not being able to muster up companionship.

(Goffman 1971: 45)

iPod users also possess mobile phones. Drawing upon the themes of privatisation and the habitation of urban space identified in the previous chapters, I discuss the ways in which users mobilise their sense of the social through mobile phone use. The chapter does not set out to provide a comprehensive account of the social meanings attached to mobile phone use – others have attempted this task (Castells *et al.* 2007; Goggin 2006; Katz and Aakhus 2002; Katz 2006) – but rather to articulate the similarities and differences in iPod users' relation to 'others' and the urban spaces moved through, expressed through the use of mobile phones.

The urban subject draws the social into themselves through contacting selected others – mostly family and friends. A minority of users engage in regular work and business communication (Katz 2006), although iPod users frequently do not, for reasons which will become apparent in the following pages. The close-knit ties exhibited by earlier generations of traditional telephone users are repeated and extended among mobile phone users. Whilst Fischer (1992) found that most telephone users called, on average, five people regularly, recent mobile phone research confirms that the majority of 'voice' calls are made primarily to family and friends (Crabtree *et al.* 2003). The majority of mobile phone users today call little more than six people regularly on their mobiles, representing 'full time intimate communities' (Castells *et al.* 2007). It was this traditional focusing upon the few in American culture that led Richard Sennett to comment that the American individual 'rather than being an adventurer, is in reality most often a man or woman whose social circle is drawn no larger than family and friends. The individual has little interest, indeed, little energy, outside that circle' (Sennett 1990: 65). The selectivity of discourse appears to be heightened with mobile phone use (Matsuda 2005). The phenomenon of enclosed connectivity highlighted by Sennett as being primarily American shows similar traits among mobile phone users in the UK (Crabtree *et al.* 2003) and Japan, where phone use is referred to as 'a snug and intimate techno-social tethering' (Ito *et al.* 2005: 1). Heavy mobile phone use has also been interpreted as leading to a weakening of broader social ties beyond the small circle of intimates (Ito *et al.* 2005:1). This phenomenon, referred to by Hibachi as 'tele-cocooning', refers to the creation and maintenance of small, insular social groups maintained primarily through mobile communication. Habuchi points to common trends among Chinese, American, Japanese and European users. The increasingly global form of behaviour associated with mobile phone use is equally apparent in iPod use (Levy 2006)

Mobile technologies of the continuous and the discontinuous

Mobility is inscribed into both the iPod and mobile phone, as is their potential to reorder users' experience of time and space. iPod users possess mobile phones whilst expressing ambivalence towards their use. It is this ambivalence that I wish to probe in the first part of this chapter. The present study of iPod users primarily deals with early adopters of the technology. These iPod users are primarily from the higher socio-economic classes, and are aged in their twenties to forties, thus partially explaining why some of these users dislike the 'on tap' availability associated with the mobile phone, the paradigmatic mobile technology owned by virtually all Western citizens and the fashion accessory for teenagers.[1]

The two technologies – analytically separated in the present work – differ in their relational qualities, especially to time. The two technologies represent two distinct, and largely contradictory, modes of relating to the management of time, space and 'otherness' in urban life: the continuous and the discontinuous. The experience of continuity is most commonly evoked through the use of an iPod whereby users construct seamless auditory bubbles for themselves as they move through daily life communing with the products of the culture industry. In doing so users banish the contingency of daily life through immersing themselves within their very own private utopia in which they do not speak, but listen, silenced and silencing, through the spaces of the city, living in the continuous rhythm of unproblematic reception, shielded cognitively from the contingency of the world.

In contrast to this, mobile phone use punctuates daily life with the sound of absent others. Mobile phones represent the world of the discontinuous, of punctured time, a world in which the contingency of the world becomes apparent with each unexpected call, received or not. Mobile phones construct mobile sound bubbles of discourse – simultaneously private and public as the user both speaks and listens. In the act of speaking public space is transformed into private space, thus puncturing and intervening in that space. Mobile phones represent a different sound network from that of the iPod, one in which others have their own stubborn routines to live by in a mutual meeting of contingent voices. This openness to contingency is simultaneously functional and dysfunctional; 'It is worth noting that the issue of interruption and accessibility has as much to do with hampering mobility as the cellphone itself does with mobility, especially when the mobility itself is in the service not of one's own whim but of another's call' (Jain 2002: 397). The discontinuous poses problems both functionally and cognitively as users become accessible to the world.

One response to the ideology of 'total availability' inscribed into the rhetoric of contemporary mobile phone use is to rebel against it. Despite the manifold benefits of mobile phone use, even its staunchest advocates recognise the negative moment of the technology whereby 'employers may also use the technology to locate employees and control them, any time and anywhere, which is one reason why the mobile phone is blamed for the loss of leisure' (Katz and Aakhus 2002: 8). Whilst mobile phones are construed as a technology that enables users to reclaim and possess their time – the snatched moment of pleasure within work time to speak to a loved one – they are equally technologies that colonise and steal time away from users, subjecting them to potentially involuntary interruption and increasing the social demands made upon them (de Gournay 2002). Work and leisure become potentially intertwined and opaque with mobile phone use as employees use commuting time and increasingly home time to catch up on work, thereby potentially increasing stress levels as they try to juggle increasing numbers of tasks and arrangements. Permanent connectivity has the potential to drift into 'toxicity' when it 'spills over into homes and friendship networks' as large numbers of urban users increasingly live in 'phone-space' (Castells *et al.* 2007: 82).

The technological tethering of the urban subject to commodity culture, either through the mobile phone or the iPod, whilst they are 'cast adrift' in their daily movement through urban culture invokes multiple, and sometimes contradictory, responses by iPod users as the two mobile technologies vie for a place in the sound network of users. Users will frequently refrain from using their iPod in the street if they know they will be continually interrupted by work calls, or alternatively if they are arranging meetings with friends over the mobile phone whilst out on a shopping trip. The use of the two technologies is contingent upon the aims and activities of users. Availability to others frequently vies with the pleasures of solitary auditory immersion:

> I don't want to make myself available to others every hour of the day – my private time and quiet is important, and a mobile phone would threaten that. Whereas the iPod is a very private thing for me, a mobile is the diametric opposite.
>
> (Thomas)

The privacy engendered by the use of an iPod is an intensely guarded privacy. The two differing modes of connectivity – the one perceived of as private by Thomas, the other public – evoke differing responses. Connectivity sometimes enhances feelings of ownership over time as users connect with absent others whilst on the move, whilst for others 'quiet time' is time spent within a desired auditory space in which the privatised pleasure of their own auditory world takes precedent over the contingent, but potentially pleasurable, experience of being tethered to the voice of the absent other. Wes, a twenty-four-year-old American web designer who has a long history of mobile listening, describes this prioritising of the pleasures of solitary listening. He is a heavy user of his iPod and revealingly points outs his feelings when disturbed whilst listening:

> I don't want anyone to bother me when I'm listening. If I have to switch it off to answer a question at work, or because I've reached a point where I need to take off my headphones, you may as well have pulled the fire alarm at five in the morning and woke me up. I'm not interested in doing anything but listening to the song when my headphones go on.

Users often operationalise notions of a private/public divide in which the mobile phone represents an external intrusion into the private world and time of the user. A central motif of iPod use is to block out external interruptions whenever and wherever possible. The experience and desire for continuous and uninterrupted auditory experience becomes an issue of control, whilst the use of a mobile phone is perceived to threaten that control. For many iPod users 'free time' is equated with iPod listening, whilst negative feelings towards the use of mobile phones is frequently associated with passivity – an opening up of the user to unwanted interruption, thus contradicting a central tenet of iPod use: to remain continuously in control.

Mobile telephony, for these iPod users, is construed as time not experienced on their 'own' terms and is frequently unsympathically contrasted with the 'active' listening thought to be embodied in iPod use. From this perspective, mobile phone use represents a threat to the very space and time successfully reclaimed through the use of an iPod. The pleasures of global availability represent an uncontrollable contingency in the heat of these users' managed world.

Just as many iPod users become attentive to the syncing of mood to music, so they become hypersensitive to any other technological intrusion whilst listening. This response to interruption derives, not from technophobia – these are high-tech users themselves – but rather from the fear of the contingent in their auditorily managed world.

Mark, a thirty-six-year-old manager from London, is a heavy iPod user. He listens to music on his commute to work, in his office and at home. Mark takes great pleasure from iPod use, in contrast to his mobile phone, which merely represents a functional device for him, to be used in emergencies, and is invariably switched off:

> I do not understand why people want to be 'reachable' twenty-four hours a day. I have an answering machine. Leave a message and I will get back with you whenever I feel like it! I wouldn't want to be in that situation; therefore I never carry a mobile phone with me. I only use it as an 'emergency' phone in my car, where it stays 'turned off' unless I need to make a call ... I hate them! I hate when people use them around me .... It is a scary technology. I've never understood why people get so addicted to them.
>
> (Mark)

iPod users like Mark resemble many mobile phone users who also habitually have their phones switched off for much of the day (Crabtree *et al.* 2003).[2] They often reject the notion of round-the-clock availability whilst frequently disliking the intrusive sounds of other people's mobiles in public space. Complaining about the intrusive noise of mobile phones is common among iPod users. These users often point to alternative communication technologies which they prefer to use, such as answer-phones, that enable social contact to occur on the user's own terms. These users reject the view that mobile phone messages require an immediate response. Underlying this rejection of 'total availability' is an implicit desire to slow down the pace of urban life whilst simultaneously controlling it. Mark achieves a sense of empowerment precisely by not carrying a mobile phone, by not having to think about potential calls. His everyday movements are filled with his own chosen sounds and his day evolves to his own rhythm. The interruptive nature of mobile phone use is a recurring theme amongst iPod users:

> I hate my and all mobile phones. They interfere in life, so I have the ring off and just the vibrate on. Normally I ignore calls and phone

people back when I get a message . . . . It is an evil necessity. I prefer to use e-mail for business, as I can gather my thoughts and formulate a response. A mobile is a buzzer, which intrudes in every part of life. The principle of being connected in emergencies is good. The practicality of being a slave to the ring of the phone is appalling.

(Simon)

Simon, a thirty-one-year-old media consultant living in Ireland, describes feeling 'good' whilst listening to music on his iPod. He enjoys creating 'on-the-go playlists whilst travelling' and modulating sounds to mood and places. His music listening permits him to micro-manage his music to his fleeting moods of the moment. The auditory management of mood is a common strategy of iPod users whereby they prioritise continuous, uninterrupted experience in the construction of their everyday routines. The other capabilities of his iPod, some of which are replicated in mobile phones, also absorb Simon:

I also use the iPod when away for the contact and calendar details – an absolute necessity – plus it has the coolest applications – Pod2Go, which transfers news, stock info, web pages and a vast range of text to the iPod. Great to browse when you're on a train. You select the web sites you want and when you plug in the iPod to the Mac it syncs all today's stories/news to the iPod.

(Simon)

The iPod provides Simon with everything he 'needs' when he's away from home – both audio and visual, whilst, in contrast, the mobile phone is perceived as a 'necessary evil' whilst on the move, which he minimises by switching off his ring tone. For users such as Simon the mobile phone does not appear to be an intimate technology but merely an instrumental or invasive one.

Sound surveillance

The iPod and the mobile phone can both be construed as instruments of surveillance – the iPod user surveys themself, manages cognition through the mediated consumption of the products of the culture industry, whilst the mobile phone user is subject to the surveillance of others – family, friends, work, business and potentially government organisations (De Gournay 2002). Surveillance is built into the very structure of the phone, from the merchant bank employee who is not permitted to turn his mobile phone off at any time on pain of being sacked to the routine checking up by users as to the whereabouts of partners or their children (Williams and Williams 2005).

The mobile phone is potentially a portal for twenty-four-hour consumption and, unlike the iPod, is commonly issued by companies to their employees thus tainting the 'pleasure' object with the routines of work. The mobile phone joins other communication technologies such as fax machines and the internet that make workers subject to the regimentation of the global time of these technologies – increasing and intensifying the demands made upon workers in their everyday life, speeding up the pace of their lives and requiring the increased micro-management and multi-tasking of daily experience. It is unsurprising that surveys of urban experience describe urban citizens as becoming increasingly stressed in their daily life (Gleik 1999; Katz 2006). In the early days of mobile phone use it was thought that only the powerless would possess mobile phones precisely so that they could be contacted by those with greater power. It is hardly surprising that for iPod users who desire to be in control of their daily schedules there is such ambivalence towards that other mobile device, the mobile phone. The mobile phone becomes tainted goods in they eyes of many iPod users. This view is typified by Greg, a heavy user of the iPod, who works in a research station in Antarctica for seven months a year and in New York for the rest of the year:

> I loathe mobile phones ... I cut the cord on mobile phones about three years ago. Voicemail handles my information while I'm at home. It gives me the ability to pick and choose who I talk to and when. I don't have to act like 'Pavlov's dog' when the phone rings any more.
>
> (Greg)

Whilst it is not obligatory to answer phone messages, iPod users such as Greg embrace an ideological rejection of the mobile phone that questions the 'available any time' ethic that has moved from the business world to be integrated into the personal lives of many an urban dweller. The ability to be free from interference whilst on the move becomes paramount in Greg's embracing of the old voicemail technology of the fixed phone. The technologically sophisticated nature of many iPod users does not imply acceptance of all, and even the most popular, of communication technologies.

Functional sounds

The iPod and the mobile phone are both 'intimate' technologies. The mobile phone contains the user's most valued phone numbers, it is their portal to interpersonal communication, it contains potentially valued text messages, photos and connection to the world wide web, with all that that entails. Equally, the iPod contains the user's musical biography together with a similar inventory of personal items to that found in mobile phones. As repositories of the personal and intimate the two technologies are complementary and overlapping. iPod users, however, tend to report much higher levels of satisfaction from the use of their iPod than from their mobile phones:

> The size is brilliant – it fits in my coat pocket, the inside pocket of my coat too, my purse, luggage, perfect size on my waist at the gym and it's a portable tiny hard drive for files too. It fits into all aspects of my life due to its size and large capacity to store music and data files. Plus, I use it as a personal organiser. I also use it for work as a backup; projects that I am working on I will back up at the end of the day to the iPod so I can have an off-site record of my files. I also take it to clients' offices and other designers to pick up files.
>
> (Barbara)

> I love everything about it, to be honest. I'm a design nut, and a minimalist devotee, so I love the design (four buttons and a wheel, plus the all-white front). Integration with iTunes and automatic syncing make my life very easy, as well. Most importantly, though, I have all my music at hand, all of the time. Essentially, it lets me change or enhance my mood (which is what I use music for) however I want, whenever I want.
>
> (Jason)

iPods, whilst sometimes functioning as utility objects, are not perceived as items whose use becomes as routinised, in contrast to mobile phone use. The retrieving of their music collection through the use of their iPods appears to be a continual source of pleasure to users. Barbara runs a small advertising agency in Montreal, and uses her iPod continually:

> It makes it more fun. Especially when travelling in New York or somewhere. I don't see the grime and poverty. I can switch to a happy place in my head and everything around me becomes that much better ... it helps me to calm down, to relax me, to help me ignore others and especially tune out distractions.
>
> (Barbara)

iPod users successfully manage their experience through the creation of a personalised soundworld, which is intensely pleasurable. The intimacy associated with the iPod is one in which users manage their personal narrative as they move through space:

> Well, if I hear my phone ringing then I'll usually answer it. But if the music is on loudly then I might not hear it. I don't mind whether I answer it or not, I don't have this obsession with my mobile phone like many people seem to ... My mobile is important in the sense that

I wouldn't ever like not to have one. But I like to use it on my terms, e.g. for the convenience. If you forced me to choose between my mobile and my iPod though, it would be no contest – iPod winning hands down. I avoid giving out my mobile number if I can, especially to business contacts, as I feel it infringes on my freedom for them to be able to contact me wherever I am.

(James)

My mobile phone is important, but purely in a functional way. I don't have the emotional attachment that I do to my iPod – my iPod reflects my personality, my phone doesn't. The most fun I have with my phone is flirtatious text messages; otherwise I can take it or leave it. I don't want to be on call all the time and will quite frequently turn it off.

(Sophie)

The music my iPod contains adds a level of emotional attachment to the device itself for producing so many pleasant listening experiences. Strangely enough, this does not translate to the phone containing all of my numbers and text messages, and I only consider it to be a communication device used for calls, messages, and net use and as an alarm clock. If I lost my iPod I would be devastated but in the case of my phone I would just be annoyed because of all the contact numbers lost and would not think twice about it.

(John)

For John and Sophie the mobile is a useful, yet routinised technology, a communication device useful at times whilst used on the users own terms, whereby iPod use is enveloped in the intimate pleasures of the users own personal auditory narrative.

The iPod and mobile phones: complementary technologies

Many iPod users rely upon the mobile phone to maintain their communication networks. For these users the technologies are complementary, not oppositional. Brian, a thirty-year-old marketing manager from Washington, states, 'my mobile-phone is essential. I don't use it that much, but I've grown accustomed to having it available at all times. I can't really imagine being without either of them. They are complementary, not competing.' Brian, however, uses his iPod continuously. 'I feel I use my iPod the way it needs to be used – constantly.' His mobile phone is turned to vibrate mode so as to minimise the disturbance to his private auditory world.

Mobile phones are equally initiators of communication and not merely responses to communication requests. iPod users frequently keep their phones turned off, yet they nevertheless remain an important source of communication in daily life. Anthony, a forty-seven-year-old journalist in New York City, is typical of the dual use of both technologies, whilst still acknowledging the intense pleasure gained through iPod use. 'I check in as

I'm commuting home. If I'm on the road I use it more. I'm not a compulsive chatterer but the phone is a sort of security blanket for me, but the iPod is there by choice.' The use of these respective technologies is dependent upon the value placed upon the differential modes of communication – for those who prioritise 'being with oneself' in a continuous stream of personalised sound the iPod has greater normative power; for those who feel an overriding need to remain in continual contact with family, friends or work the mobile phone assumes greater significance. Most iPod users juggle their mobile technologies about to suit the contingency of their situation:

> Well, the phone takes precedence over the iPod. The iPod is for my leisure, that phone call could be life-altering ... My mobile phone is the most important piece of technology in my life. My girlfriend lives 200 miles away, so that's how we keep in contact during the week. Also everyone knows it's never off and always next to me. It gives me peace of mind to know that I can always be contacted in any emergency.
>
> (Matt)

Matt commutes 500 miles a week in his car; his life embodies an enforced mobility in which loved ones remain geographically dispersed. The use of a mobile phone is essential in the maintenance of his social network.

The mutual possession of an iPod and a mobile phone becomes, for some, an essential urban armoury acting as an urban digital Sherpa, helping them to navigate through the spaces and time of urban life. Sarah, a thirty-year-old freelance journalist who spends much time travelling between New York and London, is reliant upon her network of mobile communication technologies:

> It offers me the same kind of comfort and security as my iPod. Bit of company when I'm on my own, and the feeling of keeping in touch when I have prolonged periods of solo travel. And as someone who travels a lot my laptop, mobile and iPod really are my office/travel companions and friends ... my cell phone is very important to me. I can't really function without it. I feel stranded and helpless if I'm unable to make a call when I want to. I usually feel more anxious when I know I don't have it with me. It's my connection to my family and friends, and funnily enough, I feel anxious when I'm without it.
>
> (Chris)

> There is never a point in my day or night that I don't have my phone with me.
>
> (Sam)

> My cellphone is very important to me. I really can't function without it. I feel stranded and helpless if I'm unable to make a call when I want to.
>
> (Sarah)

When I'm on the bus or walking with the iPod I take the phone in my hand or in the pocket in the front side of my pants and I put the hand in my pocket so that I can feel if it starts to ring. The mobile phone is very important to me, as I do not have a telephone at home, so all my personal and business life is linked to the mobile phone number ... I do not switch it off day or night, as it's the only way my friends, parents and relatives can have news from me. I always carry my phone with me. If I go somewhere without my phone for a few hours I feel naked.

(Antonio)

I travel a lot – over an hour one-way to drive to and from work – so its great to know that if someone needs me, or I need them, I am not disconnected from them ... which, you're probably thinking, is strange, since I like the 'bubble' the iPod gives ... but what can I say? I'm a complicated person!

(Sarah)

The juxtaposition of a mobile phone with an iPod – representing the twin needs to commune with oneself and with others – poses a series of ambivalences concerning the management of time amongst users who use both with a mixture of enthusiasm and compulsion.

The toxic pleasures and tethered connectivity of mobile phone use

iPod culture is one in which users are increasingly tethered to their mobile technologies. The tethering of oneself to an iPod has its own relational consequences, as we have noted in earlier chapters. Mobile phone use concerns the mediated relations with others and all that that entails in terms of frustration, insecurity and pleasure:

I had this good friend who came down from London to stay with me overnight. I got really annoyed, as she kept phoning her boyfriend every five minutes as we were walking to go out. When she wasn't phoning him he was phoning her every ten minutes. I got so annoyed I said I thought she had come to London to see me and could she tell her boyfriend not to keep phoning. We went to the cinema and he didn't phone. As soon as we left the cinema she phoned him and didn't get a reply. She went on about it all the time. When we got back to my flat, she asked to use my mobile phone, as her battery had gone flat. She couldn't get hold of him, she was on the phone for three hours trying to track him down. Eventually she phoned her brother, and he was with him, drinking. He'd turned his phone off.

(Sarah)

Sarah, a thirty-two-year-old photo-journalist, describes the weekend visit of an old friend. It is a description of the compulsive nature of the desire for control and proximity; it is also a picture of the impossibility of achieving this in an interpersonal world of contingency. The subject's continual phoning of the 'absent other', her boyfriend, drifts into compulsiveness, engulfing her physical space and transforming her co-presence with Sarah, who becomes progressively involved in the drama of reaffirmation and search. The constant need for reassurance, and the possession of the technology to supposedly provide it, destroy the quality of the physically present, as the user is cognitively orientated 'elsewhere'. The invasive nature of mobile phone use, in this example, is mirrored in the asymmetrical nature of general media consumption in public (Bull 2000; McCarthy 2001).

Surveillance and compulsiveness become joined as each person takes sole possession of the absent other, as Chantelle de Gournay notes: 'one takes a part of the other person with one, sure of his or her availability for permanent and total possession' (De Gournay 2002: 210). The significance frequently lies in the very act of communication itself rather than in its content, with its implied simultaneity of response. The cycle of communication drifts into toxicity as the drama of perfect and constant communication breaks down into the contingency which lies at the centre of everyday life, thus spurring, in the above example at least, renewed and increasingly frenetic attempts at connection. Thus one mode of connectivity desires an exclusive round-the-clock availability as the norm in which users become voluntarily 'tethered'. In doing so the interpersonal context, in which users may find themselves, is denuded, stripped of life, as others become drawn reluctantly into the neurosis of constant surveillance. The technology of the mobile phone creates the structural possibility of total surveillance and hence submission whilst also rendering visible any act of rebellion against tethered subjectivity.[3] The tethering of the other is restricted to the few intimates through which users' social world assumes meaning:

> I've recently forced my mum to get one, selfishly, so that I always know where she is! Everyone in my family now has a mobile phone. I don't think I could handle not being able to get in touch with my boyfriend. It controls our lives to such a degree, if I call him and it goes straight to voicemail I get furious, and vice versa! I never feel alone if I have my phone with me. If I'm alone and feel nervous I write a text message or call someone just to reassure myself. It's like a friend is close at hand.
>
> (Martha)

As a rule the use of a mobile phone whilst with known others triggers an informal code to telephone etiquette which stipulates a 'rule of thumb' guide for interacting with absent others. I always think it's really rude when you hear people on theirs. I don't mind mobiles going off, but I don't like to listen to people talking into them in a confined space. So if someone does call you at a restaurant, or wherever it is, you move away, so you don't disturb everybody else. It depends who I'm with. If I'm with a large group of people then I will just say, 'Oops, sorry,' and I'll scoot off and take the call. If I'm with someone that I don't particularly want to be disturbed, then I'll turn it off. It's as simple as that. Yeah, and I'll pick up any calls or messages after I've finished. It's like going – you don't have it switched on when you go to the movies or go to the theatre or whatever.

(Jane)

Intimate face-to-face communication, whilst undergoing competition with mediated others, nevertheless remains significant. Indeed, the city becomes pregnant with potential meetings with valued others precisely through the use of mobile phones.

Urban connectivity and the mobile phone

Whilst the iPod is, in general, the favoured technology for those users wishing to remain in their solitary world, the mobile phone is the only technology that enables them to touch base with, or arrange meetings with, others. For some iPod users the mobile phone is the desired technology of communication whilst commuting. Caren is twenty-six years old, and works in central London for a large media corporation. She commutes daily into work on the Underground from an outer London suburb. Caren lives alone and uses her commuting time to organise social activities for later in the day or week. Her use of the mobile phone whilst commuting is continual and is made more pressing by her inability to use her mobile phone at work owing to the poor reception in her office. Commuting journey time is measured by the spaces in which uninterrupted mobile phone use is possible. Caren has become an expert on the geography of mobile phone availability on her routine journey to and from work:

I live in Woolston Green and I phone people from Finchley Road, as you get a signal practically straight away there. And I'll phone and say, if I'm meeting someone, 'I'm on my way,' or 'Where are you?' Sometimes I phone because a friend of mine lives by me, but I'd have to go a different way home to see her, so I use the phone to check if she's in or not, or if she wants me to get a take-away.

(Caren)

Caren micro-manages her arrangements and subsequent travelling route. The time and space of commuting become orientated around arrangements and the meeting of friends, checking on availability and acting accordingly – the purchase of a take-away meal to take to her friend's, for instance. The city becomes a space of localised meetings, a transforming of the cool spaces of commuting into the warm spaces of communication. For Caren, as distinct from those commuters who are going home to see their families, and whose daily life revolves around the predictability of social arrangements – and who are far less likely to use their iPods continually – she uses her 'free time' to generate social contact and to improvise her social arrangements with others. The mobile phone permits a possibility of near-spontaneous social arrangements:

> It [the mobile phone] gives you lots more opportunities. I probably would just go home all the time and never go out. I always think to myself when I'm on the Tube, well, maybe I do want to go out, and then I'll just phone to see who's in. It has opened up a whole new – I mean, I never would have stood at a pay phone and phoned four people to find the one that was in! So now I just sit on the train and then, because I can make plans there ... for those off-the-top, off-the-cuff, 'I just wonder if ...' things, a lot more of those happen now than ever would have.
>
> (Caren)

Urban space becomes a space of social improvisation, as a space orientated to future communication, orchestrated as a set of contingent possibilities, with routes changed and activities transformed. Caren might arrange to meet at a friend's flat in order to watch a DVD, she will phone the friend from the rental shop to ascertain which DVD to rent. Similar arrangements are made concerning the ordering of a take-away.

Arrangement is also made whilst out and about in the city itself:

> Well, I just say to a friend, 'Just call me if you're in town.' It's really nice to know you don't have to have a plan. If you both happen to be in town at the same time you can use the mobile to track one another down, which is great. It's like a homing beacon: 'Where are you?' 'I'm in M&S, where are you?' 'I'm in Starbucks.' 'Okay, wait there, I'm coming.'
>
> (Caren)

The experience of waiting is generally transformed through the use of mobile technologies. iPod users, for example, are conscious of the slightest gap in listening, using their iPods to potentially fill every second. The iPod responds virtually instantaneously, to any command, whilst the mobile phone offers users, at least, the updating of meeting times, enabling them to manage 'waiting time' more successfully. The expectations of instant connectivity embodied in mobile phone use vie with the contingency of city life. Caren realises that 'last minute' arrangements are fraught with potential disappointment: 'Well obviously, if you really want to go out you have to pre-plan, especially in London, because everybody has so many social calendars.'

Commuting time becomes a time and space for social arrangements: she rarely looks round at other people on the train, preferring to concentrate upon her mobile phone. When not arranging, she spends time talking, which she describes as 'just checking in' with friends. Mobile phone use mirrors traditional landline use in the sense that phone use is primarily concerned with augmenting local ties rather than extra local ties (Fischer 1992). It differs from landline use in its opportunities for social improvisation. For urban users such as Caren, using a mobile phone enhances her potential to lead a more spontaneous and active social life, organising meetings whilst she travels, whereas previously she would have phoned from home after her commute, thus making arrangement more difficult and reducing her 'free' time.

Every public space becomes a potential place of talk with intimate others. When not arranging meetings Caren uses the phone continually to 'keep up' with close acquaintances and family:

> I phone people on the bus or walking down the road, and so they're not really conducive to long phone calls. But because I've already spoken to them that day, I don't need a long phone call. I'll often phone people again when I get home, but the conversations don't carry much meat, just 'Hello, how are you?' or 'I'm fine, all right, bye-bye'.
>
> (Caren)

Superficiality of content does not imply superficiality of sentiment, but rather works as a form of continual reassurance. Whilst some communication over the mobile phone may well be 'emotionally empty [and] rather depressing' (Puro 2002), this in itself is not a necessary product of mobile phone use *per se*. Indeed, users such as Caren tend to 're-establish bonds over space and time', which strengthens the 'maintenance of deep bonds, not because of their content but because of the reassurance they bring and the trust they create or reinforce' (Licoppe 2002: 106).

Unsound expectations

Continual availability is something often demanded of others but not always succumbed to by users themselves. Caren sometimes uses the mobile phone to control her own time. Calls may be ignored or a response delayed till it is convenient to reply. Yet even unanswered calls demand some mental planning and thought in terms of feelings of guilt or future planning – 'When will I have time to call?'

> My mum is a case in point, because if she doesn't get hold of me in the morning she'll phone me every half hour – and I'm often not in the mood for her to phone me every half hour. It just annoys me, so it's just easier to phone her back.
>
> (Caren)

Caren never switches her phone off. 'I can't escape unless I switch it off, which is the worst thing.' When attempting to contact others she often gets a voicemail response:

> It can be really frustrating sometimes. I mean, that is, I think you set yourself up with a mobile because you assume it's instant access all the time. Then all of a sudden you get kyboshed and it's not instant at all. I mean, sometimes I have to call five or six people and all of them will be their voicemail, and I'm, like, No, I really want to talk to someone *now*! You can't all be on voicemail! I'm on the phone because I want to talk. I want to talk to people. If I'm waiting to confirm I'm going out, then I'm, like – Phone, phone, phone!
>
> (Caren)

Mobile phone use embodies a dynamic between the illusion of total connectivity and the inherent contingency surrounding the availability of others. Much of the time Caren spent on the phone was frustrating as she attempted to phone friends, attempted to make arrangements, waited for people to return calls confirming arrangements, and so on. Much of her time was spent fretting over unfinished or open arrangements. These frustrations also appeared to throw her back on herself, engendering feelings of isolation or rejection. 'Everyone other than me is doing something. They're all in cinemas or theatres or – I don't know.' Caren would not transfer her attention to her iPod but rather continue to use her mobile.

> Well, it can be frustrating, because sometimes I know that it would be really good if I could hook up with someone in Stoke Newington [a relatively short Tube ride from where Caren lives] and I know my friend lives in Stoke Newington but she's not at home, therefore she must be on her mobile and somewhere, and if I could just hook up with her then it would really be good! But her phone keeps going to voicemail or it keeps ringing and she doesn't pick it up. I'm, like, where are you? And then you have to conclude she either left it at home or just isn't answering it. But I'll phone five or ten times just to see if she'll pick up.
>
> (Caren)

Communication is also contingent upon place and situation. Calls are frequently interrupted by movement and geography and made less satisfying by the intrusion of the other noises of city life which surround users in public:

> I get really annoyed when you have to play phone tennis, where you have to keep going back because you lose reception or you get cut off or you run out of juice. I always find it's irony of ironies that you run out of juice just when you want to make a phone call.
>
> (Caren)

Caren frequently waits on her mobile phone, it is the object through which her social connectivity flows. She has no mobile reception in her work space in central London and she knows that her friends know that, so she looks forward to lunchtime, when she can walk out into the street outside her office to see whether she has any messages or texts:

> I get quite excited about going out and going 'Ooh, ooh, now I've got reception!' (Laughs.) I get quite excited! Sometimes I get obsessive or compulsive and I have to keep checking every two minutes just in case I haven't heard the buzz. If I'm expecting a call and haven't got it yet I'm, like, 'Have I got one?'
>
> (Caren)

Uncharged mobile phones are especially annoying to users – the technology in the hand pregnant with messages but unable to work. As Caren says, 'It's like not wearing a watch. You constantly want to use it and you know you've got messages in there and you're, like (bangs the phone), Come on! Please!'

Talking and texting

Whilst all mobile phone users talk down their phones, large numbers also use text messaging. The text message can also move the user whilst in chilly public spaces and often works to manage the contingency of communication in a manner not always available by talking over the mobile phone. Whilst the continual and everyday localised use of the phone is fully integrated into Caren's daily life, there are several factors determining whether she talks to someone over the phone or texts them. Texting becomes useful as a mode of communication which ascertains whether the other is available to talk or not.

> You can text people and say, 'Do you feel like talking tonight? Are you free? Can you talk to me?' And then they can phone you back, which I quite like. I do that quite a lot: 'Where are you? What are you doing? Have you got ten minutes? Give me a call' as a kind of initiator rather than the main thing.
>
> (Caren)

Texting is also perceived as being less intrusive for the receiver of the message. 'I tend to text people if it's relative early in the morning or if it's late at night. I'll text rather than phone so that they have the choice to either ignore me or not ignore me.' However, texting itself sometimes takes precedent as an ongoing mode of communication:

> Sometimes I can have conversations for an hour by text. So, instead of actually picking up, instead of actually speaking to the person – I don't know why, but you can just, and do things where you watch TV and then

say, 'Did you just see that bit?' and then … yes, and then they say, 'Yes, I'm watching that too. I saw that bit,' and then do that kind of thing. I can, I might text that kind of – it's almost like having someone in the room with you with passing commentary rather than a conversation.

(Caren)

Texting is an alternative way of confirming relationship whilst not wishing to engage in conversation:

There are some people who, that I would text because I wouldn't necessarily want to speak to them, so it's quite, it's quite a good way of saying 'I haven't forgotten about you. I've just been kind of really busy. But I just wanted to say Hi, let's catch up later.'

(Caren)

Texting is frequently used for friends that are seen less frequently, giving greater control over the timings of response:

You don't always have to reply, so even in the middle of a conversation you can sometimes go away for a bit and then reply again later. I quite like it for that, sort of being able to pick things up and put things, put them down again. I think you sort of, you feel less offended if they don't reply to you. You think, that's all right, they're obviously doing something else, so it's not too bad.

(Caren)

Texting enables users to further improvise on their mobilising of the social, in a manner, which works some way to protecting both the privacy of the other and the demand for a response.

Privatising space

The use of mobile phones has permeated all areas of social life (Castells *et al.* 2007), rearranging the meaning of, and relations between, work and home, of leisure and sociability itself. Mobile phones have become an integral tool in the management of everyday life. In doing so the nature of public space has been transformed. Connor has argued that the very meaning of social space is 'very largely a function of the perceived powers of the body to occupy and extend itself through its environment' (Connor 2000: 12). The sound of the voice colonises the space it inhabits, and mobile phone talk is everywhere. Local customs of reserve become progressively eroded as individual mobile phone users become more assertive in their public demonstration of talking to absent others (Castells *et al.* 2007). The mobilising of public space for the engagement of technologically mediated and 'private' intimacy warms up the space of the street for users as they commune with small numbers of intimate others. Urban space becomes decontextualised as the intimacy of the home is recreated in the public spaces of the street.

Mobile phone use transforms representational space into a very specific form of vocalic space – a space of potential intimacy and warmth whilst all else that occupies that space is recessed, transcended. A denuded public space is transformed into a privatised intimate space in which 'private' life gains greater visibility in a 'public sphere emptied of its substance' (De Gournay 2002). One in seven urban citizens on average uses a mobile device at any one time in urban space, thus transforming its meaning (Katz 2006: 4). This privatising of public space is endemic in urban culture:

> With a *keitai* [mobile phone] a girl can turn any space into her own room and personalise paradise ... The *keitai* is a jamming machine that instantly creates a territory – a personal *keitai* space – around oneself with an invisible, minimal barricade.
>
> (Fujimoto 2005: 97)

Geographical space becomes recessed, as the speaker inhabits 'another' space. As Bassett has noted, 'phone space is often prioritised over local space' (Bassett 2004: 349). This very prioritisation has relational consequences and speaks to the inherent prioritisation of private space over shared social space.

The use of mobile phones represents an alternative way of filling up users' time as users habitually phone others in the public spaces of the city:

> When you're walking to and from, I like to utilise my time so there's no dead time or down time. I'll do a quick fifteen-minute call to my mum, or to my brothers of friends.
>
> (Samantha)

The street is turned into a utilitarian space of interpersonal discourse. Time is accounted for in terms of its 'usefulness' but also in terms of an ethic of 'waste', stemming from users increasing desire to multi-task on a wide range of social activities (Gleik 1999):

> I'm not very good at doing one thing at once. I always feel that if I can do two things then its better.
>
> (Samantha)

Streets walked through become secondary to the act of talking over the mobile phone. Lucy, a thirty-two-year-old charity organiser from Brighton, describes the following scene:

> It was a Monday night. It had been a lovely day, and I thought, 'This is crazy, I've been in the flat all day doing bits and pieces. I'll go out for

a walk along the seafront.' Well, I spent almost the entire time walking along the seafront and back again talking on my mobile phone. It was almost as if just walking wasn't enough for me. There was an element of wanting to tell people that it's ten o'clock at night and I'm walking along the seafront, aren't I a lucky girl?

(Lucy)

Lucy ended up not looking out to sea as she had intended but rather talking to friends about looking out to sea and enjoying the experience. Experience appears to derive meaning through communicating it to others and in doing so negates the very experience originally sought. Lucy does not notice who is in close proximity.

When I'm on the phone it's my ... my concentration is ... I'm talking to this person and what's going on around me is of secondary importance ... I don't notice other people when I'm talking on the phone ... I'm in my own little world.

Neither is she inhibited about talking about private or intimate issues over the phone whilst in public space:

I work on the assumption that those people don't know me, I don't know them. So they can only hear half the conversation and it's not particularly going to be interesting to them anyway ... I'm not aware of any reaction I might be causing.

Public space becomes a blank and neutral canvas on which to write one's personal and intimate mobile messages.

Being cast adrift – 'cut off', has different meanings for mobile phone iPod use. The mobile phone connects to others, the iPod to the self. Both mobile technologies act as digital sherpas to urban users, helping them navigate their way through their day, through the spaces of the city, in communion with themselves (the iPod) and absent others (the mobile phone) – the one continuous communication, the other 'discontinuous'. Together they form a formidable armoury for the urban user. Some simultaneously make use of both technologies:

I have my phone set to vibrate, and then when it rings I take out an earbud and chat away. It's not as bad as you think, listening to a person and music as long as you don't focus too much on the music and ignore the caller.

(Adam)

I have my mobile phone on all the time. I have my iPod on me maybe 75 per cent of the time, but I have my phone with me 100 per cent of it ... I'll generally pull out one earphone, but lately I've taken to keeping the volume low and just holding the earpiece over my headphones ... My phone is my life. I don't have a landline, and because I have free long-distance, and I travel between cities a lot, it's essentially my only marker of 'home'.

(Ashvin)

My mobile phone stays in my pocket and is always on vibrate. I find ring tones in public obnoxious, so I always keep it on vibrate. So it doesn't bother with the iPod at all, since it doesn't make noise ... The phone goes with me everywhere. The iPod and the phone interact really well together, since the phone is on vibrating. That way I never have to worry about missing a call because of the music, and if it's a call I don't want to take, or just a text message, I can respond to it without the use of my ears. I don't have to interrupt my music.

(Matthew)

The above users maintain continuity of listening whilst talking over the phone. Music acts as a backdrop to discourse on these occasions, enlivening the discourse and providing a musical backing for pauses in the dialogue. Sound acts as an accompaniment to discourse and in doing so produces an asymmetrical relationship with the 'other' that is potentially in competition with the soundtrack of the user.

The continuous and the discontinuous in urban experience are personified by the mobile technologies of the iPod and mobile phone, which sit in uneasy alliance as users move through their daily lives, juggling the need for control with the desire for contact. Turkle describes this mediated connection as a 'tethering' of the subject, arguing that, just like an umbilical cord, we are joined continuously to the processes of mediated communication. To be 'tethered' can be looked upon either positively or negatively. To be tethered is to be constrained, held down, yet this tethering is often experienced as pleasurable and desired, enabling the urban subject to function better both in terms of cognitive control and in terms of arranging daily experience. One might also look upon tethering as a form of intimacy – of a connection that warms up the hostile spaces and times of daily life. In a world in which physical mobility is the norm, the connectivity engendered in the mobile phone is emblematic of both, the desire for intimate contact with others and the end of shared social urban space.

7 Contextualising the senses
The auditory world of automobility

The car becomes a comfortable platform for the boomin' on-board sound system ... The car emerges from this as a place of listening, an intrepid, scaled-up substitute for the solipsistic world of the personal stereo, a kind of giant armoured bed on wheels that can shout the driver's dwindling claims upon the world into dead public space at ever-increasing volume.

(Gilroy 2001: 96–7)

In the monad of the car the bourgeois dream of personal autonomy is partially realised; the more the outer world is excluded, the more this dream seems to be realised.

(Stallabras 1998: 127)

Ours is an automobile-driven isolation so pervasive that its implications seldom surface.

(Kay 1997: 50)

Automobility is ultimately impossible *in its own terms.*

(Böhm *et al.* 2006: 11)

Motorised traffic enables people and objects to congregate and mix without meeting, thus constituting a striking example of simultaneity without exchange, each element enclosed in its own compartment, tucked away in its shell; such conditions contribute to the disintegration of city life.

(Lefebvre, quoted in Inglis 2004: 208)

The automobile is intimately tied to the twentieth century's narrative of urban space. It is credited with contributing to the liberation of the subject from the ties of place and simultaneously with the destruction of habitable urban space. Indeed, the twentieth century is sometimes interpreted as the century of the automobile (Brandon 2002; Sachs 1992). The same has often been claimed in reference to the moving image. What better than to juxtapose these two flows of experience, the actual movement of people through space, with the spectatorship embedded in everyday consumer practices? This juxtaposition of the moving image with the moving automobile has been taken up in the few existing commentaries that discuss the meaning of automobile use (Baudrillard 1989, 1993; Bull 2001, 2004;

Morse 1998; Thrift 2004; Urry 1999). In doing so, the voyeuristic and the phantasmagorical nature of automobility, frequently employed by the advertising industry itself, has become a dominant and recurring motif in the description of and understanding of automobility in social and cultural studies. Discussions of driving have therefore largely focused upon its visual element. Cities are said to float by as some kind of filmic embodiment.[1] The daily act of television viewing shifts to the everyday mobile spectatorship of the occupants of automobiles, who are thought to watch the world through the transparent barrier of the automobile's windscreen, hermetically sealed off from the duress of the world beyond the screen. The interior of the automobile is likened to a moving living room from which to view the world. This 'phantasmagoria of the interior' is thought to produce forms of 'mobile privatisation' (Williams 1977) enacted through the privatising 'bubble' of the automobile. In doing so, it is claimed, automobility increases the conceptual distance between the interior (for this read private or domestic space) of the automobile and the world beyond; the public spaces through which the inhabitants travel. The windscreen and television screen increasingly make the world as one, isolating the urban citizen from their surroundings (Kay 1997: 33). The screen itself assumes prime epistemological status in the redrawing of spatial relations:

> The automobile ... is connected to the world outside via the very glass and steel which encloses the driver. However, the dualism of outside/inside within these separate realms means that a connection with 'outside' drifts between a 'real' outside and an idealised representation. A sheet of glass is enough to provide a degree of disengagement from the world beyond the pane.
>
> (Morse 1998: 110)

Drivers are thought to become spectators through the simple act of looking through the automobile's windscreen. The looking through a shop window or the watching of television become foundational elements of automobility and hence a central tenet of urban experience itself. This visual epistemology of urban experience tends to objectify that which is gazed upon as a function of the aestheticising process of a Western consumer culture in which automobility takes centre stage (Bauman 1993; Debord 1977; Denzin 1995).[2] 'It is only within the frame of the windscreen that places coexist, that they become animated along the continuous narrative through which you drive' (Cross 2002: 255).

The outside environment suffers degradation both materially in relation to the automobile and cognitively in terms of the occupant's relationship to the outside world. A sensory reorganisation occurs: one of sensory enhancement (private automobile experience – often sonic) and sensory diminishment (the outside distanced, flattened, imaginary). This diminishing and enhancement of sensory experience relates to both the controlled sensory experience within the interior of the automobile and the experience of movement itself. The experience of movement is diminished as the driver sits motionless, comfortable in the hermetically sealed space of the automobile. The driver inhabits not the road but the interior of the automobile. This alienation from the world beyond the automobile screen has ramifications for the subject's sense of social space: 'Individual bodies moving through urban space gradually became detached from the space in which they moved, and from the people the space contained. As space became devalued through motion, individuals gradually lost a sense of sharing a fate with others' (Sennett 1994: 323).

Whilst drivers necessarily look and are attentive to the world beyond the windscreen they are often invariably and simultaneously immersed in an interior world of sound. Cognitively, sound contributes as much to the privatising experience of automobility as does the visual nature of automobility. The interior 'soundscape' of the automobile can produce feelings of protectedness, security and confidence in a manner that the physicality of the automobile or the visual aspect of automobility tends not to do on its own.

The theoretical visualising of automobility, to the exclusion of sound, has led to a misunderstanding of the nature of automobile habitation, its pleasures and the management of contingencies involved in the everyday use of the automobile. Focusing upon forms of sound habitation permits an analysis of the way in which automobiles are used to mobilise forms of social contact and connectedness, issues which visually based explanations of automobility are unable to address. In doing so I primarily investigate the automobile as a solitary space of habitation within which driver's experience the pleasures of aural habitation.[3] Whilst drivers invariably have a wide spectrum of potential user situations, many report that they either prefer or gain greatest satisfaction from driving alone. Sole occupancy makes the automobile a potential space of solitude, of mediated social contact through an increasing number of technological accessories and as a deeply privatised space of experience. The use of sound technologies enables drivers to mobilise distinctive forms of the social in their daily lives. These technologies make the automobile more 'habitable' and the journey potentially more pleasurable. Pleasure and sound increasingly appear to go together as drivers use their car radio, their music system and their mobile phone; these technologies enable drivers to mobilise their experience of the social in new and novel ways.

The automobile has been extensively discussed in terms of its appropriation of urban space, yet this reappropriation also occurs within the automobile itself. It is this relationship between the interior soundscape of the automobile and the world in which it is situated that is the present chapter's focus. The auditory habitation of the automobile furthers the separation between the interior of the car and that which lies beyond it:

> It's an extension of my space when I'm on the road.
>
> (Susan)

When you're in your car you don't notice the pollution, even though you're in your car, which is polluting the atmosphere. Somehow you don't notice it. And I do find when I'm in London and I'm on foot and I'm having to walk and get the Tube I'm much more tired at the end of the day and actually have a headache. It does get to me a bit more, the chaos of the city. Whereas in my car I can be stuck in a traffic jam for three hours and it doesn't affect me. I stay calm.

(Jo)

I think you're in your own little bubble. You're in your own little world and you have a certain amount of control and you don't have so much interruption.

(John)

When I'm in my car with the radio on, nothing outside seems to matter. It's like I'm the only one who's really there, and everyone else – the drivers, the people walking by – are not, kind of, real. I suppose it seems like that because I'm shut off from other drivers. They don't seem real.

(Alex)

This hermetically and aurally sealed form of living in privatised public space affects the driver's relation to the act of driving. Driving is invariably described as more pleasurable when accompanied by music or radio sound. While some drivers report avoiding certain kinds of music, as they feel they might drive too quickly, or get 'carried away' by the sweeping or emotional force of the music, this is by no means universal. Many drivers report moving or manoeuvring through traffic in a dance-like manner, as if the relation between the driver and the act of driving were essentially aesthetic. Descriptions of driving often take on a romantic or filmic resonance in the literature:

Who can resist keeping the station tuned to 'Born to be wild' whilst racing down the interstate. Crankin' it up. Firin' up a cigarette. Rollin' down the windows. Exceedin' the speed limit ... Dreamin' of automotive decadence.

(Loktev 1993: 206)

The following driver, more typically, describes the simultaneous nature of listening and driving in which the private experience of listening is seen as paralleling the public occupancy of the road:

It's very strange, what happens. You're driving on a very low level in terms of your awareness of your driving, and you drive on this low level ... This whole conversation is going on in your head with the radio which is on a totally separate level and you're absolutely, you feel

100 per cent aware of both. You're quite capable of taking in information from both, but they're both separate.

(Sharon)

The sounds of the interior of the automobile contrast with the silence of the suburbs where many of us now live, and act as an antidote to the noise of the engine and to the traffic beyond the confines of our private piece of habitation and to the multi-rhythmic nature of the everyday world.

Sonic bridges and automobility

Since the 1960s automobiles have increasingly become sophisticated mobile sound machines, equipped with CD players, digital radios, multiple speakers, iPods and of course mobile phones. Yet the use of sound technologies in automobiles pre-dates the 1960s. Significantly, the beginnings of mass ownership of the automobile in the 1920s were also co-terminus with the growth of many domestic media of cultural reception – the radio, the gramophone and the telephone. Just as the home was becoming transformed into a space of aural pleasure and recreation for many, so the car was becoming the emblem of individualised freedom of movement. Yet privatised and mobile listening pre-existed the car radio, as it had been possible to use portable crystal radios many years earlier. Earlier still the city dweller could plug in to early jukeboxes located outside railway stations and in cafés from the turn of the century. Even home listening was often privatised, as listeners to the radio often used headsets to listen to the sounds emanating from the ether (Kracauer 1995). As early as the 1930s American motor manufacturers associated the radio with individualised listening in automobiles. In the space of five years, between 1936 and 1941, over 30 per cent of US cars were fitted with radios (Butsch 2000). The use of sound in the car furthered the increasing mobility of sound use in Western culture in general:

> The invention of the transistor in 1947 meant that by the mid-1950s increasing numbers of Americans were participating in what the industry called 'out-of-home' listening. At work, in the car, on the beach, people – especially the young – brought radios with them and used it to stake out their social space by blanketing a particular area with their music, their sportscasts, and their announcers. With transistors, sound redefined public space.
>
> (Douglas 2004: 221)

The rise of the cassette deck in the 1960s further revolutionised the nature of automobile habitation, whilst today many cars are fitted with digital radios and sophisticated sound systems that work with push-button efficiency, enabling the driver to switch seamlessly between media at will.

Most recently an increasing number of car firms such as BMW and Volkswagen have introduced sophisticated interfaces permitting iPod users to slot their machines into a dock on the car dashboard, permitting drivers to control their music through their existing audio system and multifunction steering wheel. The introduction of the iPod into the automobile differs from its use in the street in so much as whilst iPods have replaced the older technology of the personal stereo, many car drivers still listen to a mix of the radio and their iPods – the one connecting them to the ongoing world beyond the car, the other to the individualised schedule embedded within their iPod.

The introduction of audio equipment in automobiles transformed automobility from an experience of 'dwelling on the road' to one of 'dwelling in the car' (Urry 1999) and in the process has transformed not only the driver's relationship to the car but also their relationship to the world beyond the windscreen.

For many contemporary drivers the proximity of the aural now defines car habitation. Drivers often describe the discomfort of spending time in their car with only the sound of the engine to accompany them; driving without the mediation of music or the voice qualitatively changes the experience of driving. Many drivers habitually switch on their radio or sound system as they enter their automobile, describing the space of the car as becoming energised as soon as the radio or music system is switched on:

> In the mornings I feel relaxed when I get into my car. After rushing around getting ready it's nice to unwind, put on my music and the heater and get myself ready for the day.
>
> (Jonathan)

> I suppose I feel at ease. I put the radio on, put the keys in the ignition and I'm away. I've had new furry covers put on the car seats, so they are really comfortable and snug. In a way too, I suppose, after getting out of the house, getting into Ruby [the car] is a way for me to relax and unwind.
>
> (Alexandria)

> It comes on automatically when I switch the ignition on. Like I never switch the power off, so it automatically comes on as soon as I start the car.
>
> (Alicia)

> Well, it's on anyway. When the car starts it switches on. So it comes on automatically.
>
> (Gale)

> I can't even start my car without music being on. It's automatic. Straight away, amplifiers turned on. Boom! Boom!
>
> (Kerry)

It's lonely in the car. I like to have music.

(Joan)

I put it on to Radio 4 [a talking news and current affairs channel], because I knew I had a long drive. So it depends what kind of drive. Radio 4, I wanted someone talking to me – yes, I need someone talking to me, so I put it on Radio 4. I want to be listening to a voice telling me about various bits of news.

(Sharon)

It connects me to the world because you've got someone talking to you, to connect you.

(Ben)

Mediated sound thus becomes a constituent part of what it is to drive. The sound of music competes with the sound of the engine and the spaces outside the automobile. The use of personalised sound helps to produce a seamless web of experience from door to door. Automobile use mirrors iPod use in this context, with users describing putting their earphones on as they leave home. Equally, both automobile users and iPod users often report that the first thing they do on arriving home is to switch on the television or radio. The we-ness of sound use in automobility is thus contextualised by the use of the mediated presence of sound in domestic contexts.

iPod automobiles

The technologisation of the sound environment of the automobile has furthered the privatisation of the listening environment as drivers increasingly use the automobile as a private space of aural habitation. The acoustic environment of the car has continued to become increasingly sophisticated through the digitisation of sound in the form of digital radio and MP3 technology, which further contributes to the potential perfection of the audio environment of the car:

The iPod has replaced tapes completely. I have it plugged into the car stereo. I use it most driving from home to work and back, a three-hour journey. I have selected about four hours of my favourite music that I listen to on the way. Alternatively I will just listen to an album of music – really, it all depends on my mood. I don't think I could drive without it any more. It is now as much a part of my driving as filling up with petrol is.

(Matt)

Now I have my own little personal radio station that knows what I like and don't, and can also tell me my hairdresser's phone number and let me know if I have plans this coming Friday. My iPod is my music in the car!

(Rebecca)

I bring my iPod everywhere I go. I use an accessory that lets me transmit my iPod's signal to an open FM frequency on my car radio. This has completely changed my forty-minute commute. I haven't used my car stereo in six months. Since the purchase of my iPod and the iTrip accessory, my iPod *is* how I use music in my car. It has completely revolutionised my commute, and made it more enjoyable. Rather than lugging around a hundred CDs with me each day, I just throw my iPod in my pocket on the way out of the house and that serves as my musical commute choices for the day.

(Frank)

Jim, a thirty-year-old American computer technician, seamlessly links his use of the iPod in his car with its uses elsewhere:

My iPod's day starts with my commute to the city where I work. I utilise the iTrip accessory, which allows me to transmit my iPod's signal to an open FM frequency on my car stereo. When I arrive at work I take the iPod with me and usually hook it up through the audio input of my work computer, or if I'm out in the field I'll use the earbud headphones – this is only if I'm at jobs where I know I'll be there for an hour or more. If I'm doing lots of service orders that don't require much time I just put it in my desk drawer ... Once I'm home I'll hook it up to my Powerbook for library maintenance, moving tunes back and forth, purchasing new songs from the iTunes Music Store, etc. ... Then, I use it while I do any work for my graduate classes. At bedtime I take it upstairs and will listen to it for about a half an hour before I go to sleep.

Jim has 2,500 songs on his iPod and describes it as having reinvigorated his music listening. Like many American users, Jim tends not to use his iPod in the street but at work, at home and in the car. The iPod is a continual companion to him as he drives to work, at work and at home, where he reorganises and updates the contents, purchases new music and listens to it late at night. At work listening takes place if it is appropriate to the type of task undertaken – short jobs with interruptions make iPod use redundant owing to the interruptive nature of the task – iPod users desire uninterrupted seamlessness. The flexibility and increased choice of the use of the iPod in the car is commented upon by many users:

When I get in my car for school in the afternoon there is no plan, just mood! As I use my iPod mostly in my car, where I drive, the weather, how I feel are the most important factors in choosing my music. I often change music while I'm driving or waiting at a signal. If I feel sleepy I change to up-tempo music to wake myself up. If it's heavy traffic I change to slower music to calm myself down. For long drives, songs that I can sing along to work well for me.

(Norita)

Norita, a twenty-nine-year-old student from Los Angeles, demonstrates the ease with which iPod users can modulate the music to mood and place, to how she 'feels now', through the use of the iPod in her car. The iPod responds immediately to the transitoriness of her moods or desires. The very choice offered by the iPod changes users' listening patterns in their cars and elsewhere. So whilst Samantha, a twenty-three-year-old user from Cincinnati, habitually uses her iPod in her car on the way to work, to shop and to visit her boyfriend, using music to 'get in the mood', she now fiddles continually with her music choice as she drives, unable to listen to any song all the way through. 'There are so many songs, so many types of songs, that I find it hard to listen to one all the way through.' Samantha listens to music from the time she wakes up until she is at her desk at work. On leaving her car at her company's car park she is picked up by the company mini-bus whilst still listening:

It's funny. Where I work you have to park in the parking lot and catch a shuttle to the office. The shuttle is a Toyota mini-van which seats six, including the driver. I laugh to myself while I listen to my music, which is sometimes obscene and vulgar.

Samantha chooses not to talk to her work colleagues, preferring to continue her privatised listening even in the confines of the work minibus. She also listens to music during her breaks at work and at the end of the working day. 'Instead of pairing up with a fellow employee and walking to my car I clip on the iPod and start walking to my car with music blasting in my ears.' Samantha doesn't listen to her iPod in the street, as 'I don't do much walking in the streets, I'm mostly in my car. And if I'm not in my car I'm walking a very short distance.' The use of the iPod acts as a perfect complement to a privatised urban life in which everyday life consists of moving in an automobile between privatised nodules of activity.

Radio sounds in iPod culture

iPod users, whilst listening to their iPod in the car, will often continue to use their radio, or sometimes the car CD player. Not all cars are able to integrate iPods into their sound systems successfully. The iPod in the present analysis is used as both an empirical example and a metaphor for individualising and privatising tendencies within contemporary consumer culture. The relationship of radio use to iPod use, however, differs in its relational qualities. Car users tuning into radio programmes are communing with the world beyond their automobile – keeping up to date with the events of the world, local traffic reports, weather forecasts. Through the radio they tune in to certain facets of everyday culture. Through radio use they are buying into the polyrhythmic nature of the media day which structures much of daily life. Through the use of an iPod car drivers are individualising their listening, transcending the orchestrated rhythms of daily life whilst often being firmly entrenched in them as they commute to work or take the children to school.

Whilst some car users prefer the sounds of their iPods or CD players, others prefer to use the radio. The radio represents a specific connection to the body politic – often a conversation with the presenter or DJ. Sharon is a thirty-six-year-old scientist and mother who commutes to work each day from a London suburb into the city centre. She begins driving before she puts the radio on to BBC Radio 4, a talking news and current affairs channel.

> I listen to Radio 4 on the way to work because I like to wake up to Radio 4 as well. So I listen to talking because it gets my head into things.

Sharon demands a certain cultural connection, a specific type of 'we-ness':

> Talking stations are very much to key yourself into the world – to engage with it.

On long drives she needs 'someone to talk to me', so 'I put Radio 4 on ... I want to be listening to a voice telling me various bits of news ... It connects me to the world, because you've got someone talking to you, to connect you.' At times listening becomes interactive:

> I'm quite happy with it blaring out at me and chatting back at it. I'm sitting there mouthing off to it. You talk, as you would any time when you're on your own.

She likes to have the sound up, so as to cancel out the noise of the car. Sound in the car structures Sharon's work day. On the way home it is not a current affairs channel but a music one:

> I'm more likely to listen to music after work on the way home, because it's much more relaxing. I'll listen to a dance station, such as Kiss or Radio 1, if they've got some good dance music on, and that will make me feel good.

The week is still played out traditionally via radio programming. She visits her mother every Friday after work:

> I always go at a certain time, so I always listen to the same programme. I look forward to it. The relax programme.
>
> (Sharon)

Sharon also possesses tapes which are reserved for those times when there's nothing on the radio.

> I've got my selection of tapes, and, for long journeys, tapes are a way of recording how far I've got. I change tapes every forty-five minutes, and, especially when you're on your own, I say, 'That journey will take four tapes.'

The tapes go on the seat next to Sharon as a supplement to the radio and her mood. Many of the tapes are old ones, ten years old, dance compilations that she no longer listens to at home. Sharon doesn't daydream in the car 'I just sing. It energises me. I don't daydream.'

Yvette, a thirty-five-year-old teacher from London, never uses her iPod in her car, preferring to listen to the radio:

> In the mornings it must be Terry Wogan and in the evenings Johnny Walker. My drive to work takes over an hour. When Terry or Johnny are not on when I'm in my car I have a CD changer, so use that. I usually play my own compilation CDs.

For Yvette the radio is imbued with the intimacy and proximity of the soothing voices of her favourite radio presenters, through which she structures her commute. For other users the radio assumes a more functional role in the management of their commute within a more general pattern of iPod use in the car:

> Prior to the iPod, listening to music in my car involved either being trapped listening to what the radio station wanted me to hear or changing the tape or CD every forty-five minutes or so. The latter not only takes time but also involves deciding exactly what I want to listen to. Going anywhere in my car, I start the engine, make sure the stereo is tuned into my 'iPod station', and start the iPod. If the weather is bad, and it's morning rush hour, I'll leave the iPod off and scan the radio stations until I get a traffic report. Sometimes I'll listen to a local talk radio show, but if they're in commercials I'll switch on the iPod and stay there. In the car I'll listen to any of my playlists.
>
> (Cathy)

Cathy, a forty-year-old American software developer, demonstrates both the flexibility the new technology provides as well as the potential persistence of radio use in the car. The iPod transforms listening in the car in very much the same way as listening in the street is transformed. Drivers can micro-manage their auditory mood through the use of an iPod. Drivers no longer have to carry CDs and tapes back and forth from home to car or change tapes or CDs whilst driving. The car radio remains the driver's contact with the world beyond the car, together with their mobile phone, and drivers often continue to use the radio for a variety of reasons whilst invariably becoming increasingly intolerant of information they don't require such as advertisements:

> In my car I sometimes have the radio on for music, and still hear news, weather and traffic. You can hear new music on the radio, but it all goes back to what you're in the mood for. With my iPod I have choice. I can play what I want when I want. With the radio you have to listen to what they're playing.
>
> (Cathy)

Some iPod users object, not merely to the structured patterns of radio stations but their content, especially advertisements. American iPod users frequently complain about the quality of radio programmes, both current affairs and music channels. In response to this they programme their own 'channels' through their iPods. Bernard, a fifty-four-year-old artist from Vermont, typifies this ideological rejection of US radio stations:

> Most days I plug my iPod into the car's cassette adapter and listen to BBC4 or BBC7. In the US decent radio is virtually non-existent, it is either Jesus Radio or pop and shock junk run by large corporations. I prefer to listen to verbal radio when I'm travelling long distances. Before travelling I'll download eight or ten hours of BBC4 and 7 then play it back in the car. It's fresh enough that it's like listening live in terms of news.

Steven, a New York scientist, concurs:

> On any trip over fifty miles the iPod is playing and streaming in my car through the stereo. It allows me to escape inane commercials and the computer-programmed music of Clear Channel owned stations in America.

The use of an iPod in the car adds a hyper-post-Fordist moment to the auditory habitation of the car, in so much as users are able to construct their own individualised listening package. The iPod, however, does not necessarily replace the radio in the car. The radio still provides drivers with a live connectivity to the world beyond them, connecting them to the mediated rhythms of daily life.

An ethography of sound interiors

The metaphor of the car as home has a long anecdotal history in cultural theory. The root of this is discerned in the automobile as metaphor for the values of individualism, freedom of movement and private property. The cultural meaning of the automobile as a privatised entity is inscribed into its very origin. This 'home', however, is a noisy home:

> The car is one of the most powerful listening environments today, as one of the few places where you can listen to whatever you like, as loud as you like, without being concerned about disturbing others, and even singing along at the top of your voice – the car is the most ubiquitous concert hall and the 'bathroom' of our time.
>
> (Stockfeld 1994: 33)

More recently the car as 'home' is described as becoming increasingly filled with gadgets, from Apple iPods to GPS systems, making drivers feel even more at 'home'. Automobiles themselves have changed in recent years from 'utilitarian means' of moving people to actual living spaces – rooms on wheels. As a commuter 'you may spend more time in your automobile than in your living room, especially if you are commuting in a dense metropolitan area' (Blesser and Salter 2007: 192). Automobiles are increasingly represented as safe technological zones protecting the drivers from the world beyond and, paradoxically, from themselves:

> 'Dwellingness' has changed from 'dwelling on the road' to 'dwelling in the car' ... car drivers control the social mix in their car just like the homeowner controls those visiting their home. The car has become a 'home from home' a place to perform business, romance, family, friendship, crime and so on ... The car driver is surrounded by control systems that allow a simulation of the domestic environment, a home from home moving flexibly and riskily through strange environments.
>
> (Urry 1999: 16–17)

The historical turning point between 'dwelling on the road' and 'dwelling in the car' is located in the development of audio technologies in the car. The symbolic status of the automobile as a 'mobile home' is empirically complex, as the following descriptions indicate:

> Being inside my car is like, This is my little world, it's my car, it's getting away from work, any hassles I've got ... It's an opportunity for me to let my mind focus on all sorts of different things. I might be thinking

about work, I might be thinking about relationships, I might be thinking about family. Its because I'm in my own little bubble, in my car that's an environment, and I'm in complete control of all the distractions around me.

(Lucy)

When I get in my car I turn on my radio. I haven't got a journey to make before I get home. I'm already home. I shut my door, turn on my radio and I'm home. I wind the windows down so I can hear what's going on and sometimes as the sun's setting and I'm in town I think, 'Wow, what a beautiful city I'm living in', but it's always at the same time when that certain track comes on. It's a boost.

(Jane)

Picture this: smoking a cigarette, texting my friend on my phone, fooling around with my iTrip adapter, and switching songs like a madwoman. I swear I'm doing too much ... My phone is the only lifeline I have. Without it I'd be lost. I do a lot of long-distance travelling and I feel very safe with a phone in my car, being a young female.

(Fali)

All these car drivers habitually drive to music, whether it is the radio, CD player or iPod. Lucy's description represents the car as an escape, 'a getting away' from the vicissitudes of daily life, a heterotopic space beyond surveillance. The car becomes a space, through music, within which cognition is clarified – a space of no interruptions. Cognition is permitted to flow, precisely through the non-intervention of others. Home is a space where she is free to be herself precisely through the physical separation from others. Home is a space of total control:

I've always had people around me, so to have some space and time to myself was not always something I was able to get ... so the car is a little bit of a refuge, although obviously, you know, people always say people can see into a car and see what you're doing, it's almost as if this is my little world and nobody can see what I'm doing, and if I want to – if I want to sing loudly to music or talk to myself, or whatever, I don't have to answer to anybody. I don't really have to consider anyone else. I can behave in exactly the way I want to.

(Lucy)

For Jane, automobility transcends movement – the interior of the car is redolent of feelings of home. She's home as soon as she gets in her car – it is both an extension of her home and a mobile home. She looks out on to the world in the manner of Baudrillard, constructing an aesthetic of the city – with the windows down, listening to music.

For Fali the automobile is a solitary space of multiple communication and activity. It is a space in which she smokes, eats and plays continuously with the communication technologies in the car. These technologies provide a 'lifeline', a substitute for the warmth of contact from which she is divorced in her daily suburban life on the move. Fali's is a reluctant mobility in which communication technologies replace that which is desired. Her car is a messy, anarchic home, yet denuded of physical interpersonal proximity.

To inhabit a car is to inhabit an intense sound environment. Automobiles are potentially one of the most perfectible of acoustic listening chambers. Unlike living rooms, where manufacturers cannot control room size, furnishings and the number of people, it is possible for acoustic designers to create a uniformly pleasant listening environment (Bose 1984) for the three metres of acoustic space that make up the average automobile. Speakers in the front, rear or in the seats themselves produce an aurally satisfying listening booth. As Trudy describes listening to music in her automobile:

> I'm in a nice sealed, compact space ... I like my sound up loud; it's all around you. It's not like walking around the kitchen, where the sounds are not quite as I want them.

The car is a totally separate environment – outside:

> You and the car are one thing and that's it, it's your space. Outside it's different. You're in your time capsule. It's, like, your living room, and you're mobile living room.

Driving without sound is often considered to be boring:

> I don't want to go on a journey in a car without a radio or music ... I like driving. I love driving on the road and I like driving on my own, because it's a totally separate environment. It's a total indulgence. It's your environment. You control it. You can do whatever you like in it. It's like time off. You're travelling from A to B, but it's the ultimate idleness, really. You're not doing anything but listening. It's great.
>
> (Emily)

The automobile becomes a successful and personalised listening environment that is difficult to replicate in other domestic or public spaces unless one uses an iPod. The automobile offers the advantage of a skin of metal and glass for the driver, in contrast to the use of an iPod in the street, which offers a conceptual barrier for users. Acoustic design permits even the drivers of convertibles to experience the immersive qualities of sound in the car:

> I don't like not having music. I love driving my car. I've got an MXS [convertible]. It's the only way to drive ... I change the music. If it's a

nice sunny day it's more old-time jazz or something quite up and happy, some really good chirpy classical. It's nice and loud – in my car I've got speakers in the headrest, so although it's quite loud it's not very intrusive for everybody else.

(Jane)

The more sound the more immersive the experience. Nathan, a twenty-four-year-old American living in Britain, has installed a twenty-two-speaker sound system throughout his car interior. Nathan enjoys driving down the local motorway with the sound system going full blast, preferring the motorway to the town, as he feels less concerned with others on the motorway. Nathan enjoys the thrill of driving in a sound-immersed world. He doesn't actively look out at the world – he is in his own saturated mobile bubble of noise. Sound, unlike vision, is a bodily sense, as Nathan describes:

> After a time I have to stop the car and get out. I lean against the car, as I can't stand properly. My legs are limp and it takes a few minutes for me to regain the equilibrium of my body.

Nathan's body is affected by the volume of and intensity of the sound to such an extent that he can no longer stand. In North America Nathan's automobile would be referred to as a 'boom car', the interior louder than that of a typical clubbing interior, 130 dB. Music that loud can be heard up to 100 metres outside the car with its windows shut! Boom cars such as Nathan's reside on the edge of the spectrum of automobile sounds yet point to the power of sound over cognition. The following driver, unlike Nathan, is more aware of the seepage of sound, which in this case has a technological fix in the form of speakers in the headrests of the seats:

> I quite like driving to dance music, because it's quite mindless in quite a nice way. I tend to tune into some fairly intense, particularly in London, techno-oriented dance music, which are the kind of tapes I would play as driving music. I also like sort of classic rock band sort of stuff, for a similar type of reason, it's not very challenging, but it's immersive.

(Kate)

Drivers are increasingly able to co-ordinate the soundscape of the automobile to match their mood or their journey. The automobile becomes a perfect listening booth for drivers, who thus deny the contingency involved in their traversal of these routine spaces and times of daily life.

Mobile solipsism and sound

The management of experience through sound technologies is tied to implicit forms of control – control over oneself, others and the spaces passed through. Hence it is unsurprising that drivers often prefer driving alone. In this way they are able more successfully to re-appropriate their time. Time possessed is more likely to be time enjoyed. The experience of immersion in sound is thus enhanced by sole occupancy, which also permits the driver to have enhanced feelings of control and management of their environment, mood, thoughts and space beyond the gaze of 'others':

> I can sit back in my car, enjoy the drive, listen to my sounds, and not have to talk.
>
> (Trudy)

> I don't think there's anything pleasant about being in a car with somebody else … For me it's quite a solitary thing. You just do it. You're not thinking about – it's quite – in many ways it's quite like doing sport: you just switch off … . You're just thinking little thoughts, you're not really thinking about … It's really quite contemplative, and having to make conversation whilst you're doing that … Sometimes you want to make conversation but then you'd sooner not be driving around. I just like to get there.
>
> (Sarah)

> Yes, because I can do all the driving. I can concentrate on the driving. I do really get quite absorbed in driving. I can listen to the radio or have the music on as a sort of atmosphere-provoking thing. Whereas if someone else is in the car I feel I shouldn't have the music on because you can't hear him or her, and I can't stand that – fighting for noise or quiet. I also find it more relaxing driving on my own, because I don't need to worry about them being uncomfortable and feeling that I'm going too fast.
>
> (Lisa)

> I do a lot of thinking in the car. I find it quite a good time to be by myself and to sort of think things through and work out lists of food that I need on the way to the supermarket … I drive more safely when somebody is not distracting me. I find that, when there's somebody in the car, I feel that I have to talk to him or her. It's not so much looking at them; it's more that I find the mere listening to what they're saying is making me less aware of the things happening on the road. I don't like not to have that complete control.
>
> (Sara)

The automobile offers drivers a space to be alone with their mediated thoughts, a space which is pleasurable, precisely because it offers no contradiction to the preoccupations of the driver. Automobiles thus become spaces of temporary respite from the demand of the 'other' whilst the driver is often sitting in gridlocked unison along with all the rest of those living in illusory control of their environment.

Sound performances

The car is a space of performance and communication where drivers report being in dialogue with the radio or singing in their auditised/privatised space. The car becomes a site of intense pleasure as the driver sings and gesticulates to music whilst potentially being looked in on from beyond the confines of car. The space of a car is both one to look out from and to be looked into. It is simultaneously private and public. Drivers lose themselves in the pleasure of habitation yet may also become increasingly aware of the 'look' of others:

> Actually, that's one thing I love about my car – she's all mine. I don't have to share her with anyone. I can do what I like in my car – within reason. I can turn the radio up full blast and have a good singsong without anyone looking at me. Actually, sometimes I suddenly realise that I'm merrily singing along and the person in the next car is having a good laugh at me, but I forget that people can see in and I get really embarrassed.
>
> (Alexandra)

> I'll sing along at the top of my voice and I always worry what people in other cars think when they see me. They think I'm talking to something or myself ... I just sing along all the time. I don't stop, like every song that comes on. Cause I watch a lot of music channels at home, so I know the words to a lot of songs. If I'm listening to the radio I'll sing along to practically every song that comes on.
>
> (Alicia)

> The car is a little bit of a refuge. In a way, although people can see into the car and see what I'm doing, it's almost as if this is my own little world and nobody can see what I'm doing, and if I want to sing loudly to the music, talk to myself, or whatever it is, I don't have anyone else to answer to. I don't have to consider anyone else. I can behave exactly the way I want to.
>
> (Avril)

The space of the car becomes a free space in which the driver feels free to indulge their aural whims with no inhibitions. Houses have other occupants or neighbours to inhibit any such desire:

> The louder the better. In fact I use my car; I use it more than in the house, because I don't want to annoy the neighbours. But in the car, traffic is very noisy, so nobody can hear you. I sing incredibly loudly, especially on the motorway. In fact I have certain cassettes that I'll put on to sing incredibly loudly to.
>
> (Susan)

The sound of music, together with the sound of their own voice, acts so as to provide a greater sense of presence as well as transforming the time spent driving. Mediated sound thus becomes an opportunity for interactive dialogue, of a personalised performance. Drivers even in the act of singing are not of course hermetically sealed from the outside world.

Talking technologies

Automobiles are also increasingly being used as spaces of interpersonal communication between drivers and 'absent' others. Paradoxically, whilst many drivers prefer to be alone in their automobile, increasing numbers also report using their driving time to communicate directly with others:

> I hold the phone to my ear ... I often use it to catch up with people that I haven't spoken to for a while. It's a time when I know I'm going to be in the car for a while. I have had journeys that the journey may have been three hours long and I have spoken to three people during the journey, one for forty-five minutes, another for half an hour, so I may have spent virtually the whole journey talking on the phone ... It's a time when I know I'm going to be in the car for a while and I might as well phone my family, my friends, just to have a chat.
>
> (Lucy)

Using a mobile phone permits drivers to maintain social contacts during 'road' time. Time and journey are thus transformed into an intimate 'one to one' time:

> It's a good way to spend your time, talking and catching up. If I get bored I'll just put it on to my list, list of numbers. I'll just flit through and ... say I haven't spoken to that person for ages ... so the people at the beginning or the end of the alphabet do quite well!
>
> (Jane)

If users of mobile phones in the street transform representational space into their own privatised space as they converse with absent others, then this scene is replicated in the everyday use of mobile phones in automobiles. The automobile becomes a mobile, privatised and sophisticated communication machine through which the driver can choose whether to work, socialise or pass the time.

Sound technologies provide a form of accompanied solitude for consumers. Just as the technologies that make us feel secure on the street are also to some extent illusory forms of security, so 'automobile self-sufficiency' is equally an ideological or virtual self-sufficiency. The disjunction between the interior world of control and the external one of contingency and conflict becomes suspended as the occupant develops strategies for managing their experience of travel mediated by music or voice.

The empowerment of and possession of the road as a form of private space mediated through the power of the automobile was highlighted by Adorno's early description of road rage, 'and which driver is not tempted, merely by the power of the engine, to wipe out the vermin on the street, pedestrians, children and cyclists' (Adorno 1974: 40). Adorno's description of urban intolerance fuelled by the technology of the car is highlighted in the well publicised case of a US baseball player who demonstrated his disdain of others during an interview undertaken whilst driving:

> During the bigoted diatribe, the culprit was driving a large SUV and speeding down a massive multi-lane freeway. Whilst venting to the reporter his disdain for New York's subway, he yelled obscenities and made gestures at other motorists from within the speeding cocoon. He held the steering wheel in one hand and a cellphone in the other, continuing to speed, and he said the thing he hated more than anything else in the world was traffic ... Everyone else on the road was in his way.
> (Henderson 2006: 298)

Henderson points to the spatial secession of automobility in which the city is divided up not just physically but normatively as well. The automobile keeps its occupants separated from those on the street. The illusion of total control over the environment is maintained solely in the interior of the vehicle. The use of music in the interior of the car can be used either as a pacifier or to heighten aggression towards others (Brodsky 2002).

The daily strapping of the individual to an engine has been sold to consumers as the epitome of individualism and freedom – gridlocked culture, a culture that makes it apparent to drivers that are caught in the polyrhythms of daily culture. In response to this, drivers progressively retreat into the interiority of their automobiles, surrounded by their personalised intimate sound technologies of the iPod, radio and mobile phone.

The pleasures of driving are in part ideological and require dissembling. The freedoms attached to driving become increasingly circumscribed as more and more drivers are obliged to drive in daily gridlock with others to and from work – prisoners in their cars, often forced out of living in the city by the cost or in search of space and the domestic and privatised life of the suburbs, itself a form of anti-urbanism, yet necessarily tied to the city as a place of necessary work. Urry has pointed to the structural ambivalence of driving in which the driver is simultaneously controlled and yet potentially free:

> Automobiles coerce people into intense flexibility ... The car, one might suggest, is more literally Weber's 'iron cage' of modernity, motorised,

moving and privatised ... Automobility thus develops 'instantaneous' time to be managed in highly complex, heterogeneous ways. Automobility involves an individualistic timetabling of many instants or fragments of time.

(Urry 2006: 20)

Automobile habitation provides the driver with their own regulated sound-scape that mediates their experience of these non-places and manages the flow of time as they drive accompanied by their own regulated soundscape. Drivers choose the manner in which they attend to the non-places of urban culture, transforming these spaces into personalised spaces, making the space of the automobile into one which reflects their desire for accompanied solitude.

The use of sound communication technologies in automobiles demonstrates a clear auditory reconceptualisation of the spaces of habitation embodied in users' strategies of placing themselves 'elsewhere' in urban environments. Users negate public spaces through their prioritisation of their own techno-logically mediated private realm. The uses of these technologies in automobiles enable users to transform the site of their experience into a technologised 'sanctuary' (Sennett 1994). Drivers habitually exist within forms of accompanied solitude constructed through a manufactured industrialised auditory, either through mediated music or the voice of the 'other' accessed through their mobile phone. The preferred exclusion of many forms of intrusion constitutes a successful strategy for urban and personal management. Drivers reclaim representational space precisely by privatising it. The aural space of the automobile becomes a safe, pleasurable and intimate environment. The mobile and contingent nature of the journey is experienced precisely as its opposite, in which the driver controls the journey by controlling the inner environment of the automobile. Drivers feel empowered for as long as the sound of communication is turned up.

The consequence for any notion of shared urban space appears serious as the warmth of privatised and mediated communication produces the 'chill' that surrounds it. Proximity and solitariness are increasingly dialectically linked in the mobilisation of contemporary forms of sociality in such a way that in the future we may all become like Paul Gilroy's driver, shouting out, impotently, into dead urban space.

8 The auditory privatisation of the workplace

> Life is an invention of the haves, which the have-nots try to imitate to the best of their inability. Since it is in the interest of the propertied classes to maintain society as it is, they must prevent others from thinking about that society. With the help of their money, they are able in their free time to forget the existence for which they slave during the day. They live. They buy themselves an amusement, which allows the brain to take time off because it keeps the other organs so completely busy. If the dance clubs were not already fun in themselves, the state would have to subsidise them.
>
> (Kracauer 1995: 296)

In chapter two I introduced the reader to Adorno and Horkheimer's analysis of the meeting between Odysseus and the Sirens. I argued that the passage represented the first description of a privatising of auditory space in Western culture whereby Odysseus has the oarsmen of his ship block out the seductive sound of the Sirens with wax, enabling them to steer their ship on a safe course whilst Odysseus, tied to the mast, hears the Sirens' song. Paradoxically, Odysseus empowered the oarsmen's ears by ordering them to insert wax into them; their ears were no longer 'naturally' open to the seductive sound of the Sirens. Both the ambient environment of the ship and the Siren's sounds are abolished. Nothing replaces their sound world: the oarsmen row in silence, effectively deprived of choice. Odysseus has constructed the aural conditions of their work environment through an act of creative deprivation. The representational space within which they work is transformed and determined by the power of Odysseus. No matter how they may orientate themselves to their task, they remain mute. The passage in question is a tale of inequality, Odysseus is at heart a tourist, and the oarsmen's work is a function of Odysseus's project. The construction of aesthetic experience and the ability to control the world are Odysseus's domain, not something the oarsmen are permitted to aspire to.

The tale of Odysseus contradicts the historical notion of hearing as invariably 'passive' (Simmel 1997), an account that portrays the sounds of the world flooding in unhindered into the subject. The intervention of the wax reorientates hearing – in this case, the abolition of external sound completely. We do not know what the oarsmen may have been thinking about, but they probably would have focused upon the hard physical work necessary to perform their onerous task.

With the rise of mechanical sound reproduction in the late nineteenth century, and the concurrent development of the culture industry, the domestication of the potentially subversive power of sound extended into the workplace of 'industrialised' oarsmen. Factories, in the twentieth century, were engulfed with the 'Fordist' sounds of music, enabling the workers to work in time to the music – a symbiosis of machinic and musical rhythm. The rhythm of music chimed with the rhythm of work in the brave new world of the Fordist production line (Korczynski 2003). The seductive and utopian sounds of music were harnessed for practical and instrumental ends.[1]

With the advent of MP3 technology iPod users frequently report listening to music at work for the first time. Not for them the Fordist sounds of the workplace. These iPod users are not factory workers but skilled professionals possessing considerable autonomy in the workplace. In the following pages I analyse the use of iPods in the workplace to discover whether contemporary iPod users are more like Odysseus or the oarsmen in their use of sound at work. The 'democratisation' of auditory power hinted at by the use of individualising technologies like the Apple iPod are far from clear. Three related issues require investigation: the role of music as a form of aesthetic experience in the workplace; music listening as a form of instrumental rationality, and the power of the listener to define his or her own space and interaction.

Work in contemporary urban culture increasingly takes place everywhere – in the office, in the car, on the train and at home – so the following analysis requires a greater sense of fluidity than merely analysing the work space traditionally defined (Laurier 2005). In effect the whole world potentially becomes a workshop in iPod culture.[2]

Existing work on earlier generations of mobile sound devices such as the personal stereo took for granted the rationalist ethos of the role of music in productivity. Marginal benefits in productivity accruing to individualised use of personal stereos in the clerical professions were measured. These experiments consisted in giving personal stereos to workers who did not normally use them, predetermining what was to be listened to, thus replicating traditional modes of managerial control over the auditory terms and conditions of the workplace (Oldham *et al.* 1996). In contrast to this Fordist mode of music use, the following iPod users choose to, and are free to use their iPods at work – the soundscape of the workplace becomes individualised. Many users had a history of mobile listening, having previously owned a variety of personal stereo devices but very few had used these earlier generations of machines at work due to the limitations of duration and content intrinsic to the earlier non-digital technologies.

The fluid sounds of iPod culture

The desire and ability to control one's experience through the use of music is not restricted to the workplace – indeed, iPod use embodies a range of control strategies that potentially embody any social space or time frame. The desire for control is not merely a response to the work environment for many users, but rather a habitual and desired way in which to occupy large segments of their day. iPod use confounds the traditional distinction between work and leisure time as users construct a seamless auditory experience from home to work. Users might consecutively aestheticise the street through which they move, manage their various and changing moods through privatised listening, avoid thinking about the tasks of the day ahead of them, or use the iPod to enable them to move through the street more satisfactorily, their feet in step to their music. The desire for managing the workplace through music is premised upon the use of music prior to work.

The iPod as digital Sherpa

iPods have the ability not merely to store songs in a machine considerably smaller than the size of a cigarette packet but also contain the capacity for transporting the user's computer files, personal photos, address book and other personal information with them wherever they go. Kathy, a thirty-six-year-old director of a small creative agency in Ontario, typifies the functioning of the iPod as a digital urban Sherpa:

> I used to have tons of CDs all over my car. Now I use the iPod, along with the iTrip FM finder, and when we travel we have music everywhere. Same at the office – no longer do we have a stereo, we now just listen to the iPod through the computer and have good speakers hooked up to it. It has also changed how I travel. When my daughter and I were in France a couple of years back I needed to send out some postcards and I simply used the address book/contact function of the iPod and found all the names and info I needed and sent the postcards. Then I lay back down on the beach [south of France] and continued listening to the iPod. I also use it for work. I use it as backup – projects that I am working on I will back up at the end of the day to the iPod so I can have an off-site record of my files. I will also take the iPod to clients' offices and other designers to pick up files.
> I went to NYC in November and had all my active files (two gigs of data), all my music (fifteen gigs) and all my contacts with me (485). At the airport I got into the cab, looked up my friend's address in Brooklyn and directed the cabbie to her place. At the same time I used her number in my contacts to call her to let her know I was on the way. During the weekend I used the iPod to listen to music on the subway. One day

I checked my e-mails at the Apple Store and found out we were missing a file. I had it on my iPod, so I borrowed a Firewire cable from Apple, hooked it up to the computer and copied the file to the desktop, then e-mailed it to my office. Problem solved – and I didn't have to have any external extra stuff. It was all on the *one* iPod!

Connectivity is central to the above account, coupled with a seamless movement from work to leisure, enabled through iPod use. iPods enable users to weave the diverse elements of their daily life together seamlessly. Portability is inscribed into the very design of the iPod, yet it differs from earlier generations of portable music devices in as much as it can be played via automobile radios in the car, can be plugged into home stereo units and played as a jukebox, or can be plugged into a computer and played via its speakers. The iPod, unlike the previous generation of personal stereos, is both a privatising technology and one that permits the possibility of collective use. The user can negotiate which form of use he or she desires.

The ability to take their music collection to work and play it at will is often a function of the worker's occupation and authority within the workplace. The present sample of iPod users primarily occupies social classes 1 and 2, having managerial positions, often in new media or the creative industries. The following pages point to the possibilities of privatised music use at work by these users, who have sufficient authority to use their iPods at work. Many of these workers gain much satisfaction from their job and often do not draw a strict distinction between work and leisure. The examples derive from benign management structures in which these iPod users have much autonomy. However, it would be a mistake to assume that these workers are stress-free or necessarily feel secure in their work organisations (Sennett 2000).

Traditionally music at work has been discussed as a form of collective experience. Music as a privatised listening experience at work has rarely been investigated in a work setting. The following workers have a high degree of autonomy at work, or work in an environment where their managers perceive the virtue of using music in this way at work. Music use largely embodies the rational model of music at work, which aims at making work more efficient. The utilitarian motive behind this form of music use doesn't exhaust its subjective meaning. It can also work to maintain or enhance mood, to punctuate the working day or to act as a form of private reverie. The structural possibilities of managing work experience, including work space, and the interpersonal nature of work through iPod use, are analysed below.

iPod use and the sole office occupant

John is thirty-five years old and works in web development for a major international bank in New York. He lives in Manhattan with his wife and daughter. John, like many iPod users, has a long history of listening to music but describes the iPod as having enabled him to rediscover the pleasures of listening to music and has downloaded all his CD collection on to his computer and then on to his iPod. John travels to and from work listening to his iPod whilst also using it in his office at the bank:

> I now listen to music while I work...at work. I suppose this would be possible with a tape or CD player. But there are a lot of hours in the day, so the hassle of changing media and carrying it around in the first place means that it just isn't practical. With the iPod it is...When I arrive at my desk inside my building the iPod goes immediately on to my desk. Although I don't listen to it right away at work, I know I will at some point during the day (when I need its magical protection against interruptions).

So, whilst John had been able to use music at work previously, it had never come in a suitable form to make it attractive to him. What he desires is ease of use, seamless listening and his own music on tap. The iPod on the desk also signifies a 'Do not disturb' message to other workers. This is similar to iPod use in the street, where the earpieces signify much the same to others. The iPod works as a kind of territorial preserve, a boundary marker for others within the office space of the bank. The earphones also signify the user's status in the organisation. Their appearance indicates that he can listen whenever he wants. This signifies not leisure but rather efficiency:

> By listening to music at work I'm now using music (or rather the fact and act of listening to it) to (*a*) block out distractions, (*b*) send out a signal to co-workers that I'm actually busy and so their interruption had better be work-related, rather than just casual chat, and (*c*) prevent myself from distracting *myself* [*sic*]. I find my attention easily wanders to surfing the web or doing 'other stuff' unless I have music on. It's as though listening to music focuses me in on the task at hand.

Music use, in this example, represents a 'rationalisation' of work practice. John can only be disturbed if it is a query about work. Thus music reception enables him to function better in terms of his perceived tasks by helping him to focus upon his work rather than have his mind 'wandering off', as he puts it. Music as a form of cognitive control is centrally important here. Rather than being distracted at work by music, it enables John to work in a more concentrated and focused way. iPod users often describe having to stream 'appropriate' music at work, by which they mean that music should match their perception of the type of task to hand. Music in these examples is often described as background and 'non-interruptive'. Music fitting this bill differs from one user to the next. It is not the type of music listened to that is significant but the role that music structurally plays in the auditory ecology of the user. What unites most work users is their desire for the mediated sound of music to accompany them through their working day. iPod technology appears to produce the correct seamless environment for working to music, unlike CD players that need continual attention or the radio, over which the user has no control of content.

Work tasks often vie with the user's fleeting moods, personal thoughts, tiredness or lack of concentration. iPod use permits users to manage these changing cognitive states effectively. John, for example, listens to his music through headphones at work rather than plugging in his iPod to his computer, thus producing his own aural cocoon within his office, a space already inhabited by him alone. The space of the office itself acts as a boundary marker, yet his use of the iPod in his office demonstrates his authority to transform his work space into a privatised space of audition. The tell-tale white headphones signify to others 'Do not disturb' unless absolutely essential. Office space is transformed into an auditory and hermetically sealed space for his own work and thoughts. He works whilst listening to a variety of rock music, classical, opera, choral and 1960s Motown chosen at random by his iPod. He describes his feelings at work as follows: 'I feel insulated from what's happening around me and that there is less chance of anyone invading my private space. This gives me a sense of invulnerability.'

Privatised music listening reduces the subjective experience of contingency, enabling users like John to feel empowered over their immediate surroundings, people and their own cognitive processes. For John this appears to be real control. Yet, within this private bubble, John pragmatically recognises the necessity for interaction at work:

> I'm realistic about what it means to actually live in the real world, especially at work. What I mean is, I understand that there are going to be interruptions and so there's no point in getting visibly upset. If an interruption has been particularly pointless, then I'm as likely to be frustrated by it if I was listening to my iPod as if I was just sitting at my desk with no music on... When interrupted I always switch it off (using the remote) and take an earphone out. I just think it's rude not to. In these circumstances you've got about ten seconds' interaction with the person. You can't leave them wondering for the first eight seconds whether or not you're listening to them. It's a question of respect, really.

iPod use requires attentiveness to the expectations surrounding workplace sociability and traditional modes of courtesy that may well be undergoing change in iPod culture. The obligation to interact with work colleagues is far stronger than the fragmenting rules of recognition that exist in the street or in the supermarket check-out. John, however, extends his environmental control to commuting to work and back. Commuting for most represents an extension of work – dead time – which iPod users reclaim through their use of music. John describes his experience as 'film-like' and 'insulated':

> Blocking out other sound is pretty important. Especially on the subway, where people are sometimes – particularly in the evening – talking loud enough to be heard over the roar of the train. I like to read while travelling, though, so I tend to listen to the music slightly less loud while I'm actually on the train (reading) and then turn it up as I walk along the street so I can appreciate the music a little more.

The use of personalised music listening permits John to reclaim his commuting time as his own 'special' time. The music creates a space that permits him to read successfully on the Underground.

Choice over the terms and conditions of interaction is a central feature of iPod use, whether it is in the street, on the Tube or at work. John's use of music is not merely a work phenomenon but a way of approaching daily time and space through the personalised use of music. Experience is modulated through the construction of an auditory bubble, rendering the world a pleasanter place to move through and be in. In iPod culture mediated sound represents a continual presence in the daily experience of many users – becoming second nature to the experiencing of urban culture. It is also symptomatic of a day filled with too many commitments in which users such as John eke out their own private space.

The sounds of contested office space

Amy, a thirty-two-year-old development manager from Philadelphia, differs from John in so far as she shares office space with others whilst listening to music on her iPod. She, like many iPod users, is listening before arriving at work:

> If I'm off to work I tend to listen to something upbeat but not too overpowering, such as someone within my singer/songwriter category. Once I get to work I usually choose something I've heard a million times so I don't mind if I'm interrupted. If I have a particularly difficult task ahead of me I tend to choose something with a driving beat, like Soundgarden, the Matrix Soundtrack or Rob Zombie. If I'm the last one to leave I put on something I can sing along with, take off the headphones and attach the iPod to my speakers.

Amy getting into the desired frame of mind prefaces the workday. Work tasks are then synchronised to music. Working in a busy office brings certain restrictions for Amy, as evidenced by her singing along to her music whilst listening through speakers rather than headphones when nobody else is in the office. Equally, the contingent nature of interaction in the office is understood, as is the nature of her tasks, which determine whether she listens to music or not:

> When I arrive at work I take it off for a bit until I've spoken to my staff about the day ahead, or worked out any personnel issues...[At work] I listen to it as much as I can without letting it interfere with the course of my work. On rare days I prefer silence, or don't want the feel of headphones/earbuds, so on those days I leave it off. Also, if my day is filled with meetings and/or phone calls, I'll leave it off, as it doesn't make much sense to me to keep turning it off and on.

Interruptions disrupt the benefits of continual privatised sound offered by iPod listening, rendering its use dysfunctional. Dysfunctional because users prefer to settle into a mood through uninterrupted listening. This limits the use of privatising technologies like the iPod to certain types of task and particular work spaces. As a rule, Amy experiences the office as a free and continuous space of listening:

> One of my favourite moments was when I was listening to a really great song that put me in a perfect mood, and I wanted to get some more water to drink. I started taking my headphones off, when it hit me: I can take the iPod to the water cooler and not miss a note! It was such a great revelation.

The space of the workplace is thus transformed through the user's ability to reinvent it as a privatised space over which she has, temporarily at least, total auditory control. The movement from one place to another accompanied by headphones appears as an aestheticising moment of the workplace, and an empowerment over the user's space of habitation. There is, however, very little evidence of iPod users constructing aesthetic narratives within the workplace as contrasted with their strategies of the street, where many users describe their experience in filmic terms. This may well be a function of their knowledge of the people around them whom they interact with on a daily basis. They are not the anonymous people inhabiting the street, or alternatively may well be a function of the rational purpose of music listening at work – to instrumentally enhance the working environment.

After work Amy maintains her mood through her use of the iPod. The rhythm of her day matches the music that she listens to and her step as she moves through her day:

> If I'm walking home I'll put on something to either de-stress me, or something to cheer me up if it was a rough day. If I'm in the mood to take a walk around the city I put on faster music to get my blood moving. When I'm wearing it and walking down the street I find that I match the pace and cadence of my steps to the music. I also find myself

setting distance markers and timing my arrival to the marker to the music. For example, I'll say to myself, 'I'll reach that corner by the end of this song.'

iPod use not only regulates the day for users, it creates an alternative linear sense of progression to the day. From the enervating music in the morning to the wind-down music after work, daily experience becomes increasingly mediated and modulated by their chosen sounds. The world becomes mimetically 'in tune' with the user's desires and movements.

Contested office sounds

The post-Fordist office is also a potentially contested space of sound in which competing soundscapes vie with one another for supremacy. Marianne, a thirty-eight-year-old web engineer from Berne in Switzerland shares an office with another worker who plays commercial radio all day in the office, filling office space with 'unwanted' sound. Marianne responds by wearing her iPod in the office for most of the day:

> During working hours I will wear my iPod as soon as I need to concentrate on something, and I don't want to listen to my office mate's boring radio station! This radio station plays the same songs all day long, and that's really boring. I have more choice within my iPod.

This example demonstrates the stark contrast between the post-Fordist taste ghetto of the office radio user, reminiscent of Douglas's analysis of radio use, and the hyper-post-Fordist iPod user who desires her eclectic mix of privatised sounds (Douglas 2004). Marianne varies the volume of her iPod in relation to the amount of noise being made in the office:

> If my co-worker is on the phone and talks loudly I'll increase the iPod's volume so that I won't have to hear what he's talking about – especially if it's personal. But most of the times I'll just have the music on a normal volume.

iPod use for Marianne is private both in terms of protecting the co-worker from being overheard in conversation and in creating a cocoon of sound within which she works. It is also reactive in relation to the unwanted sound world of the shared office space. iPod use thus empowers her in relation to other workers – it is a hyper-post-Fordist use of sound within a post-Fordist sound space in which one worker is being fed a diet of commercial radio, the other her randomised yet personal playlist on the iPod. The office space becomes two simultaneous privatised environments – one existing in radio sounds, the other in iPod sounds.

Once the iPod is 'running' I will barely touch it. I let it play in random mode. If I'm in the mood for a special kind of music [i.e. more 'rock' or, on the opposite, more 'relaxing'] I'll select a specific playlist and let the iPod randomly play through the songs.

Music enables Marianne to manage her work space and work but in general also makes her feel better about herself and the world around her:

I have sometimes the feeling that music lets me see the world around me in a 'happier' or 'brighter' light. I have the feeling that I'm happier when I listen to music. But I don't always 'need' that to be happier. It's just that music lifts the spirits when one is a little down.

The power of a privatised auditory world enables Marianne to transform time and space into a warmer set of hues. The world increasingly becomes one with her cognitive disposition. iPod use permits an extension of this mimetic role of music into increasing areas of daily life.

Mitch, a graphic artist from Bradford in the UK, also has to grapple with the generalised sounds of the radio at work. Whilst he doesn't mind the use of Radio 2 till midday he dislikes the use of Radio 1 after twelve, so uses his iPod as a means of drowning out the unwanted sounds of that channel. He feels that it is acceptable to wear the iPod whilst he's at his desk but not when he's walking around the workplace:

I take my iPod off when I need to converse with someone or leave my desk [at work], as I don't think it would give a professional image, walking around the company wearing it.

The rules conditioning the appropriateness of use are fluid and subjective. Whilst Mitch feels it inappropriate to move through the office wearing headphones, Amy, in a previous example, experiences a sense of excitement and empowerment moving through office space with her headphones on. Mitch is also, like many other users, ambivalent about being interrupted whilst listening. The pragmatics of the situation is that at work one will be interrupted:

I do prefer not to be interrupted, and I find it mildly irritating if I have to switch it off, though as most of my listening takes place at work I don't let my irritation show, as that would be unprofessional. As I am so absorbed by much of what I listen to, being interrupted can often make me feel as though I have been rudely awoken from a great dream.

The power to create a privatised auditory world of the user's making cannot be overestimated. Users often describe feeling divorced from the sound world and activities of others around them. Mitch's analogy with a dream is instructive here. At times users have described being briefly disorientated as they are brought unexpectedly back into the random sounds of their environment. Yet despite potential disruption Mitch thinks that listening to his own music makes him feel better about both work and others:

> When I am exposed to the type of music I love I feel more relaxed, more optimistic and more stimulated. This is reflected in my whole view of life, and I am generally more positive, co-operative and tolerant of everybody and everything when I feel like this.

The mood created in the mind of the user is transposed on to their feelings for those around them and on to the work process itself, precisely through the auditory privatisation of the workplace.

Open plan offices pose particular difficulties of auditory control. Charlotte, a twenty-three-year-old civil servant from London, describes how she uses iPod listening to regain control of her work space so as to enable her to work in a more concentrated fashion:

> I sometimes use it at work if the open plan office is exceptionally noisy and I need to concentrate, or if I'm alone in the office and want something other than silence.

Use is contingent of the sound levels of the office and the work tasks embarked upon. Yet it is also a foil to the isolation of the office when empty, enabling Charlotte to create her own auditory company and intimacy. John, a thirty-six-year-old systems analyst from London who uses the iPod to drown out the general noise of the work space, also describes the instrumental management of the contingent soundscape of office space:

> I use it at work. The Networks Operation Centre can be loud with background sound. The iPod comes in handy when I want to 'zone out' and focus on the work at hand.

Whilst most users of iPods who were permitted to use them at work reported high levels of satisfaction from their occupation, some users drowned out the very experience of work through the use of their personalised music:

> I like the way it can seal me off so I feel I can be alone in an office environment where I really don't want to be.
>
> (Sarah)

iPod users also suffer the stresses associated with the requirement to work and the need to meet ever quickening deadlines.

Sharing office sounds

Whilst the use of iPods in office space is primarily a solitary exercise it is also a potentially shared piece of technology to be used as the music system for the whole office, connected to the speakers of the user's computer:

> It has become the office sound system. I have a set of computer speakers hooked into it, put it on random and everyone listens to it…In the office it can be anything that takes my fancy. I think during the day at work the most played stuff is probably the 80s music, but that's more to do with the age of the people in the office.
>
> (Frank)

This demonstrates how technologies like the iPod have a potential for collective use, unlike the personal stereo before it. It can be used for general office use. Yet collective use brings up issues of negotiation. In this example it is also dependent upon the authority and disposition of the iPod user. Frank brings his machine into work and tends to decide what to play. There is no evidence of file sharing or collective creation of playlists, although this would be a structural possibility of use.

The iPod is a dependent technology, dependent upon both the organisational practices of the workplace and the desires of individual workers in relation to their work colleagues, their office space and the type of work undertaken. The present analysis of iPod use at work is based on user accounts and, as such, there is no quantitative evidence that the use of these technologies actually makes users' work more 'efficient', unlike in Oldham's study of personal stereo use in the office (Oldham *et al.* 1996). However, users invariably report high levels of satisfaction at work. The dominant rationale for using iPods in the workplace appears to be a combination of the role and power of sound within the user's life world and the desire for instrumental control over their own work space and pace. Work is described as increasingly pleasurable and efficient, precisely by shutting out the existence of others through the creation of a hermetically sealed aural bubble. iPod users impose their own codes of silence upon office space, not by controlling the sounds of others, but by absenting themselves from the auditory world of the office.

The use of music at work operates more restrictively, or has greater focus, than general iPod use. There is little evidence of users aestheticising the work situation, for example. Primarily iPods fulfil the function of providing a continuous and controlled soundscape through a shutting out of the external sounds of the office, thereby minimising the user's sense of contingency in the workplace. Whilst the desire for a seamless and fluid auditory experience remains paramount, the use of iPods appears as more restricted than use either in the street or at home, although there remains a strong potential overlap. The desire for an accompaniment to their work day provided by the iPod was common, appearing as the first technology to successfully provide for the needs of the hyper-post-Fordist worker. Life indeed appeared better through the creation of their own soundtrack, and whilst most workers appeared not to be disillusioned with their work, the use of an iPod did permit users to manage those parts of the day that were more routine.

Occasionally some workers, to distract them from the mundane reality of their job, also used the iPod. All iPod users interviewed used their iPods in a wide variety of contexts at work, travelling and sometimes at home. The split between work and leisure identified by the rise of industrialisation appears to be reversed by iPod users, who reintegrate music reception into everyday life, albeit in a commodified and highly individualised form, a form in which the worker chooses the terms and conditions of their aural working environment. The use of these sound technologies also casts doubt on the assumption that identity work is merely associated with leisure pursuits rather than with work. Identity work is potentially carried out in all spheres of life.

I began this discussion of iPod use with Adorno's and Horkheimer's use of the Odysseus myth in relation to the Sirens. I did so in order to foreground the role and use of music in daily life and the seductive role that it appears to play in much experience. The question becomes one of the role and significance of the democratisation of sound worlds brought about by contemporary technologies of sound reproduction like the Apple iPod. Simply put, are contemporary iPod users more like Odysseus or like the oarsmen in their working lives?

Music itself appears domesticated and made safe in the work world of iPod users. Yet they control their auditory environment in the manner of Odysseus – but not so as to savour the aesthetic delights of music but rather to work more efficiently to music. In their individual use and creative manipulation of their sound world they appear in the image of Odysseus. There remains, however, a qualitative shift in the use of individualising technologies such as the Apple iPod and the use of music in the Fordist work and leisure environments described by Adorno and others. iPod users do not appear to be passive consumers of the products of the culture industry, although they live firmly within the matrix of consumption. Equally, whilst iPod users often appear to have a social position resembling that of Odysseus in their ability to control their auditory environment, they appear, paradoxically, to use music, at work at least, in the manner of the oarsmen. In effect, work space becomes a domesticated but effective siren song. Odysseus goes down to the galleys and rows with the oarsmen but with his headphones on.

9 Bergson's iPod? The cognitive management of everyday life

[With music] one enters the 'dark world' in which language and daily structures of time and causality no longer reign supreme, and one finds the music giving form to the dim shapes in the darkness.

(Nussbaum 2003: 269)

There is no state of mind, however simple, which does not change every moment, since there is no consciousness without memory, and no continuation of a state without the addition, to the present feeling, of a memory of past moments. It is this which constitutes duration.

(Bergson 1998: 72)

Masses of people are concerned with their single life histories and particular emotions as never before; this concern has proved to be a trap rather than liberation.

(Sennett 1977: 5)

In the morning when I first put on my iPod, I walk through a residential neighbourhood, comprised of mainly low- to middle-class homes, to the bus stop at the edge of a small public park. I like to listen to music with faster, driving beats, so my pace quickens as I walk to the bus stop. Things look clearer and my outlook for the day is more positive, even if I know I'll have an incredibly busy day at work or a long commute due to traffic. I find that listening to the iPod helps to calm me, and lets me modulate my moods according to the morning's circumstances. The same goes for walking in the streets during any point in the day: I don't mind the jostle of the city so much, and the stress I feel is dissipated.

(Mia)

Tia DeNora has commented, 'the role that music plays in ' "the constitution of the self" has been insufficiently analysed, (DeNora 2000: 46)'. Music is intimately linked to our deepest strivings and most powerful emotions. iPod use appears to offer a glimpse into the internal workings and strategies engaged in by users in their management of themselves, others and urban space through engaging in a series of self-regulatory practices through which they habitually manage their moods, volitions and desires. In its inherent fluidity music appears to correlate with a Bergsonian model of consciousness based upon duration in which the notes of a tune melt into one another to produce an organic whole. iPod users appear to be embracers of a Bergsonian world of free consciousness, a world in which consciousness is inherently mobile, fluid and in flux – and, hence, ultimately uncontrollable by others, the culture industry or society in general. In a Bergsonian world the 'intuitive' and 'non-quantifiable' self stands apart from any rational and external critique.

iPod users, in describing their attentiveness to the flow of experience, appear to intuitively tune their flow of desire and mood to the spectrum of music contained in their iPods. Beyond the scrutiny of others, they believe they exist in a naturalised heterotopia (Foucault 1986). The presumption of subjective significance is supported within a Bergsonian framework. Bergson believed that as the body moved through space so it was indeed the centre of the experienced universe. This centrality of world view is replicated technologically by iPod users who experience all before them through the mediated and privatised sounds of the iPod.

> ...It's as though I can part the sea like Moses. It gives me and what's around me a literal rhythm, and I feel literally in my own world, as an observer. It helps regulate my space so I can feel how I want to feel, without external causes changing that.
>
> (Susanna)

On a Bergsonian world view, what is essentially creative in a person resists mechanical repetition – consciousness is essentially unpredictable (Boym 2001: 50). Yet in the present age of instantaneous digital reproduction iPod users manage their flow and flux of experience precisely through the technology of the iPod. Technologically mediated behaviour increasingly becomes second nature to iPod users: habitual and unrecognised. This entails the presupposition that everyday behaviour is mediated by, and constructed through, the omnipresent sounds of the products of the culture industry in some form or other. Mediated behaviour is transformed into an ideology of directness – of transparency – like so much in consumer culture in which appearance masks the production process. Transparency is suggested by the technological enclosing of the ears by headphones, enabling music to be played directly and immediately into the ears of users.

Adorno *contra* Bergson

Bergson's understanding of the innateness of free consciousness works in direct opposition to the colonisation of consciousness thesis portrayed by Adorno, Baudrillard and others (Adorno 1991; Baudrillard 1993; Marcuse 1964). From an Adornian position the use of consumer technologies like the iPod, rather than signifying a free and uncontrolled consciousness, highlights the fetishising role of music in the management of contemporary urban experience. From this viewpoint the contemporary consumer appears increasingly unable, or at least unwilling, to organise significant portions of daily life independently or autonomously. iPod users, from this perspective, rather than being 'free', become imbued with the need for mediated experience in order to remain cognitively 'in control'. In contrast to a Bergsonian free spirit, iPod users represent a hyper-form of one-dimensionality in which they mimetically embrace the culture industry in order to remain 'free':

> They need and demand what has been palmed off on them. They over-come the feeling of impotence that creeps over them in the face of monopolistic production by identifying themselves with the inescapable product ... The fetish character of music produces its own camouflage through the identification of the listener with the fetish.
>
> (Adorno 1991: 288)

The following comments by iPod users represent, from this perspective, a form of 'one-dimensionality' (Marcuse 1964):

> I can't overestimate the importance of having all my music available all the time. It gives me an unprecedented level of emotional control over my life.
>
> (Terry)

> I love the freedom to have any music I want to listen to in my pocket, wherever I am. I find that music really helps to change my mood, so it's nice to have the ability to get a quick 'pick me up' in my pocket.
>
> (Frank)

Music represents an especially powerful ideological aphrodisiac in Adorno's analysis of commodity culture owing to his interpretation of the existence of an archaic utopian remnant of non-commodified, direct communal experience embodied in music itself. The 'happy consciousness' of the iPod user becomes, from this perspective, an intensified form of conformism in which users intuitively manage their social behaviour in tune to the increasingly sophisticated dictates of consumer culture. The fulfilment of the iPod user is increasingly administered to them through the multiple options available to them through the use of their iPod.

This contrasts with a Bergsonian world view in which consciousness, by its very nature, resists total colonisation. From a Bergsonian position the fluid nature of music itself, coupled with the structure of choice offered by digital technologies like the iPod, complements the very nature of the user's consciousness, enabling them to construct an 'individualised' relationship between cognition and the management of experience. Contra to the colonisation of consciousness thesis, the choice offered by the iPod would work to create a conceptual distance from the structural organisation of these products. In effect, iPod users become free, transcendental consciousnesses in contrast to being tethered to the fetishised products of an all-encompassing culture industry.

Whilst the idealism of a Bergsonian world view is attractive to users, and is replicated in many descriptions of use, it suffers from an historicism in which consciousness is always structurally 'free'. Much of the repetitive or compulsive behaviour associated with consumer culture sits ill at ease with a Bergsonian world view. iPod culture rather appears to sit somewhere between the parameters of freedom and those of constraint. The choices engendered in iPod uses have, as we will see, potentially rebellious underpinnings as consumers distance themselves from the hyper-commodification embodied in much of the media. As they construct their individualised consumption packages there is a sense in which consumers have progressed from the Fordist tendencies of popular culture critically encoded in the work of Adorno and others. Yet this distancing strategy of the subject – the autonomous resistance to the predetermined schedules and rhythms of the mediated day – sits uneasily with the increased dependence upon the use of technologies like the iPod through which their cognitive states are managed. The following pages investigate this conundrum through an analysis of iPod cognition.

Sound cognitions

Mobility, fluidity and flux are the condition of subjectivity in contemporary urban experience. This is accompanied by a ratcheting up of the pressure, speed and demands made upon consumers (Gleik 1999). Communication technologies themselves further the experience of flux, transitoriness and fluidity whilst simultaneously providing a buttress against these tendencies. Users commonly describe themselves as bereft without the mediated auditory presence of their iPod. Experience unadorned by the immersion of experience through the intimate sound world of the iPod is often described with apprehension:

> It [the iPod] removes the internal dread. For example, when I needed to do yard work I used to become depressed because my mind would wander. Now, with the iPod, yard work is a positive experience because I know I have hours of uninterrupted listening, exercise, fresh air, and no business worries … Sertab Erener's 'Everyway that I can' stirs me for some reason. As a consequence, when I confront larger problems, I play it several times in a row and it seems to help. Also, Coldplay's 'Clocks' has a strange, positive effect upon me when I play it.
>
> (Sam)

Non-mediated experience creates a sense of vulnerability in many users. This sense of vulnerability refers to the perceived uncontrollable nature of their own streams of consciousness and the cognitive states associated with it. Users often recognise their own sense of cognitive contingency, which the use of the iPod negates. Routine, often pleasurable activities like gardening may threaten the user's sense of cognitive control with the introduction of 'uncontrollable' thoughts, or with feelings flooding in, engulfing the subject left to their own unmediated cognitive state. Cognitive control comes with technological mediation in iPod culture. iPod use permits users to saturate periods of 'non-communication' with their own intimate, familiar and comforting sounds.

Strategies of mood maintenance

Sound loops

One strategy for mood maintenance is the repeat – the listening to a music track repeatedly in order to maintain a specific cognitive state in contrast to the ebb and flow of time. Users are often unable to articulate just why certain songs enable them to manage their experience is the desired way or why the same repeated song permits them to maintain their required mood. It is 'as if' consciousness becomes the equivalent of and, in contradiction to Bergson, a tape loop:

> If I'm in a particular mood then I will repeat the same five or six songs for a very long time, basically until my mood changes or I have to go talk to someone.
>
> (Rosa)

> There are times I'll listen to the same song, two or three times in a row. And this relates to my mood as well as to the place I'm in. If I'm in a good mood, and I'm listening to a song that I just love, I'll repeat it. If I'm working out, and a song really gets me moving and raising my heart rate accordingly, I may well play it two or three times.
>
> (Donna)

> It usually happens when I feel that I am 'in' a certain song so much that I couldn't think of listening to anything else. The song becomes sort of a mantra and I just want to hear it over and over, absorbing it.
>
> (Sean)

> I often play the same song repeatedly back to back. When I do, it's more because the song strikes a chord within me, or fits the moment so perfectly, that I want to extend the feeling or moment longer. The best way to do that is to play the song again and again.
>
> (Amy)

> I play the same song repeatedly – for example, the [non-traditional] song we used to walk down the aisle at our wedding – when I need to

improve my mood – and lower my stress level! Also, if I'm playing it at work as background music, and I miss some of it while I'm in other parts of the office, I let it repeat.

(Michelle)

The rationale for the repeating of songs varies from the maintenance of mood, the syncing of mood to place, the maintenance of a mood engendered by a specific memory, to the maintenance of body movement and rhythm. A particular song or rhythm may also act as a 'mantra' into which all experience is channelled.

Bauman has argued that the need to have time filled with sound implies that 'it is [the] fear of silence and the seclusion it implies [that] makes us anxious that our ingeniously assembled security wall fall apart' (Bauman 2003: 98). Modern consciousness is conditioned to experience daily life through the mediated sounds of the culture industry – the habitual presence of radio sounds, television and the like. The silent vistas desired by a Thoreau, who required spaces of silence in order to think clearly, is clearly not a desire possessed by iPod users. Rather, iPod users describe needing the throbbing personalised sounds of music in order to think clearly – or, alternatively, to take them away from themselves so as not to be subject to invasive and undesirable thoughts and moods. iPod use is transcendent precisely in its capacity to take users away from 'the conventional confines of time and space' (Boym 2001: xiv). This 'happy consciousness' is dependent on the technology of the iPod – contingency is invariably controlled successfully as users manage the rhythms of their mood and desires, creating a successful cognitive congruence between emotion, music, technology and experience:

If I'm angry I'll put on something dark and angry. If I'm happy, upbeat happy music. If I don't want to be brought down from a good mood I'll avoid depressing music. If I'm not sure how I feel I'll put it on shuffle. That sometimes leads me to listen to a whole album, or I'll just skip over the tracks I'm not in the mood for until I find something that fits the way I feel that moment. Or, if I want to change the way I feel, I'll choose music accordingly. I never plan... My choice of music isn't determined by time of day but how I'm feeling or want to feel.

(Elizabeth)

I like being able to listen to any song, any artist, any album, and any genre that either fits my current mood or that can change my current mood.

(Juno)

iPods become strategic devices permitting the user to shape the flow of experience, holding contingency at bay by either predicting future experience – the next song on the play list – or by shaping their own sound world in tune with their desire. Users are also able to adjust their privatised soundtrack whilst on the move, thus micro-managing their mood with great precision and skill. iPod users demand an instantaneous response to the nuances of their mood, signifying a ratcheting up of expectations demanded of new technologies such as the iPod.

The technology of the iPod appears to further promote the development of an 'attentive' or 'listening' self embodied in rudimentary forms in previous analogue technologies. Earlier portable sound technologies such as the personal stereo provided less capacity for users, often requiring prior and precise planning for the day's listening. For some users this was not a problem, as they would play the same tape each day for long periods of time – forcing their environment to mimic the straitjacket of their own auditory mind set. For most users, however, a hastily bundled selection of tapes or CDs would be carried in the hope that it would contain appropriate music (Bull 2000). The development of MP3 players such as the Apple iPod provided a technological solution to the management of the contingency of aural desire. Users now habitually take large portions of their music collection with them in their iPods. As one user describes, 'It gives me the ability to carry my entire music collection in my pocket instead of a steamer trunk.'

From Walkman to iPod sounds

The iPod expands the options available to users for customising music to mood and environment. It is rare for iPod users to resort to switching off their machines for lack of appropriate music, unlike the world of Walkman users, where no music was often preferred to the 'wrong' music:

> It has completely revolutionised how I listen to music. Before it I had to decide what I felt like listening to and then be restricted to one CD at a time. Now I let the iPod choose, or use specific playlists.
>
> (Helen)

> I can now carry all my CDs with me and listen to whatever I want whenever I want. I don't even have to think about it any more – what should I bring, how do I feel today, I wish I had that one... Not to mention now I can bring songs that I don't particularly like, the whole CD as well. I've not had that since I used to have mixed tapes on my Walkman... There's no need to plan any more, because I'm bringing all my music with me all the time. I used to have to plan with the Walkman or Discman. I listen to whatever I feel like. I listen depending on mood and what I'm doing and where I am.
>
> (Susan)

John, a thirty-year-old US computer technician, points to the seamless technological infrastructure that provides the backdrop to his mobile listening habits:

> Between the iPod itself, iTunes software and the iTunes Music Store my relationship to music has been changed for ever. Due to the hassle of carrying CDs around with me I had begun to lose touch with my music collection. That has all changed since I bought the iPod. For example, the Beatles are my favourite band. Sometimes, I will want to hear a particular song from the eighteen Beatles CDs I own. Now I simply reach into my pocket and the song is there. I don't need to carry a duffel bag filled with CDs.

iPod users fully embrace the ideology that 'more is better'. The carrying of large slices or perhaps all of one's musical library in a small piece of portable technology appears to liberate users from the contingency of mood – they no longer have to predict what they will want to listen to or the vagaries of potential future moods.

Whilst the personal stereo was commonly used as an 'in-between' device – from door to door – the iPod expands the possibilities of use from the playing of music through attaching it to the user's home hi-fi, plugging it into the automobile radio, and by connecting it to the computer at work, thus giving users unprecedented ability to weave the disparate threads of the day into one seamless and continuous soundtrack. In doing so, iPod use extends users' field of aspirational reorganisation to include many more segments of daily life. The dream of living one's life to music becomes for some users a reality. With the increased power of the technology comes the ratcheting up of consumer desire. What was previously acceptable for the personal stereo user is no longer acceptable for the iPod user. The iPod permits users to control time continually and in microseconds.

> I used to listen to one album at a time, or multiple albums from one artist at a time. (I'd keep an entire group's back catalogue on a single mini-disc.) Now I spend a lot more time listening to playlists I set up in iTunes. It's a painless process to create a new playlist for every conceivable mood or situation.
>
> (Kerry)

The iPod permits users to be more attentive to the vagaries and changes of mood, seeking either confirmation of mood or transformation into an alternative mood via their choice of playlist. Playlists are created precisely to cater for a wide spectrum of moods or times of the day, as the following young US user demonstrates:

> When I'm going to work I like loud, energetic music to get me going. The same for when I get off work. I want to listen to something as

non-work-related as possible. Probably some rap music. A lot of times at night I go visit my boyfriend, and on my way to his house I throw in some 'get in the mood' music. Something slow and sultry that makes me feel good inside. At the gym I like high-energy music ... I feel as though life is a movie and is playing especially for me. If I listen to sad music, which I only listen to when I'm down – boyfriend break-up, just bad news – then everything sort of has a grey shadow over it, even when it's sunny outside. Music is like a drug to me, and not just one drug that does one thing but many different drugs that magnetise your existing mood, or even sometimes the music is so powerful that it changes the mood you're in. Music can make you feel happy, horny, sad, wanting. It can do wonders.

(Fali)

iPod use permits unparalleled micro-management of mood, environment and sound, permitting the successful management of the self through the contingencies of the user's day. iPod culture is a culture that habitually controls experience:

I tailor my music and content by activity. 'Playlists' allow me to create subsets of music that I can easily call up. I create 'playlists' to tailor my music to my different moods. I label them as 'Quiet' or 'Exercise tunes' or 'Contemplative'.

(Jeremy)

Digital technology, with its storage and organising potential, has enabled users to fulfil their dream of control over mood, time and surroundings, permitting them to live in a dream of auditory control:

Music tastes are largely a function of environment and mood, both of which can be hard to anticipate when you're out and 'on the go'. Since music listening in public is essentially a form of isolation, I find that I especially depend on the iPod during phases of my life where I'm depressed or needing encouragement or energy or reinforcement. Sometimes that will mean finding a particular song that matches – or influences – my current mood and thought patterns, and putting it on repeat for an entire day.

(Ivan)

There are times where I will put on one song, and then half-way through it I will change my mind and switch to another song because my mood changed or the song wasn't capturing my mood correctly.

(Heather)

The fleeting nature of cognition is often hard to manage. Moods vary in consequence of users' response both to the environment and to the internal flow of experience. The Bergsonian iPod becomes the tool used by the listening and attentive self. The expectation that there is something in the iPod to suit any circumstance becomes increasingly taken for granted:

> Mostly the sheer amount of music constantly at my fingertips changes listening habits, as access is always instant.
>
> (John)

> I have lots of music that to me evokes a feeling of either peace and calm or even melancholy. I use the soundtracks to *The Piano* and *Schindler's List* for those. Both instrumental, but really emotional and powerful... I almost always keep the setting on 'shuffle' so that the songs come up randomly. If a songs starts that doesn't suit my mood at the moment I just hit 'Next'.
>
> (Karen)

> Most importantly, though, I have all my music at hand, all of the time. Essentially, it lets me change or enhance my mood however I want, whenever I want.... I usually listen to my iPod on my way to work, and have it set to my 'Most played' list, which ensures that I start my day in a good mood...Sometimes I'll just have a random song day, but then I flip songs every time I hit one I'm not in the mood to hear. If I'm on a random by artist or genre mode I usually don't flip past a song. On my way home I'll pick something that suits my mood. For example, if I'm heading out to a club I'll throw on some trance.
>
> (Ashvin)

The music on the iPod provides a stimulus for mood matching as users treat their music collection as a 'magical' prompt for cognitive management. Central to these strategies of control is the enhancement of mood.

Sound reinforcements

Music listened to on the iPod invariably enhances the experience of the user, colouring their relation to the environment passed through. The following is a description of a user moving through the city wearing their iPod:

> It is usually a mood elevator or, at least, a mood intensifier. For example, if I'm wearing it on a crowded city street the crush of people seems like an obstacle course and a fun challenge to wend my way through. Without it I would be annoyed and frustrated at my lack of progress through the crowd, but with it it's almost as if I'm dancing. If I'm frustrated or angry, intense, driving music makes me feel like I have company in my mood. Pleasant weather seems that much more pleasant with music to accompany me. I am aware that, even when I'm not

singing along, the way I walk and move and my facial expressions are affected by what music is playing.

(Malcolm)

I commute into Paris for the week and sometimes, when a desire to hear something in particular occurs, it's to reinforce the mood of the moment, happy after a success at work, or thoughtful or depressed as per the events of the day. Having the huge song library in my pocket makes this possible.

(Eric)

The mundane world of the city becomes more adventurous to privatising sound. The contingency of the street in which one moves with the others, dependent upon the ebb and flow of others, becomes manageable and potentially pleasurable. The subject is simultaneously 'passivised' and 'energised' as they wend their way through the street. Walter Benjamin, in his analysis of city life, was attentive to the role that technology played in the navigation of the urban subject through the city. iPod users become reminiscent of the urban subject whom Benjamin described as plunging 'into a crowd as into a reservoir of electric energy…a kaleidoscope equipped with consciousness' (Benjamin 1973: 171). The iPod user has moved on technologically, and is accompanied by music, which drives both their mood and their relationship with the spaces passed through. Enhancement relates to the mood of the user or, and sometimes also, the environment passed through, which in turn feeds back into the cognition of the user. iPod users describe the pleasure of mood reinforcement:

I use it as a mood enhancer all the time. If I'm depressed I'll throw on some Leonard Cohen or Nick Cave to bring me down even more. If I'm happy I'll use upbeat music to put a smile on my face. And sometimes, when I just want to think, I'll use a familiar classical piece (I use Vivaldi) so I can enjoy it and still think about other things simultaneously.

(Damien)

Whether subjects live in New York, London or Paris there is a similarity of description as to how the iPod functions to manage mood and experience, a similarity of desire to micro-manage experience through the use of the iPod and to construct a mediated and privatised auditory world through which experience is seamlessly filtered. This filtering aims not just at enhancement but also at mimesis, to bring the world in line with cognition through music:

If I'm feeling depressed I'll often try to match that with suitable music, quite often to achieve an insularity.

(Ryan)

Users habitually require the iPod to orchestrate their day functioning as a cognitive Sherpa, accompanying them and directing them through the cognitive and physical spaces of their day. The nature of this mediated experience varies according to the activity and purpose of the user. Whilst music is invariably listened to loudly, it is not always experienced as such. Remember the user who played music in search of peace and quiet: 'I didn't realise how much I yearn for control and probably peace and quiet. Strange, since I'm blasting music in my ears.' Music functions in this instance as a clarifier of experience, enabling users to 'clear a space' for thought:

> If I want to be with my own thoughts I'll use the iPod.
>
> (Rosa)

> If there's a specific mood I'm in, especially if it means contemplating a situation fairly deeply, I will pick music that seems conducive to that kind of thought. It's odd, because once I'm fairly well lost in my thoughts I can't really hear the music any more. I'd notice if it was gone, though. The right music can help isolate me from the things going on around me. I use the music on my iPod as a buffer between the outside world and me, giving me a more secluded environment to think about whatever needs my mind's attention.
>
> (Kerry)

> Frequently the iPod is more of a contemplative device than the actual thought 'Let's listen to music now.' Music is such a huge part of my life that it's almost imperative that I have *something* happening all the time. I have music stuck in my head almost non-stop for the same reason. In certain moods the iPod serves to extend and accentuate the mood rather than being a source of something to *listen* to. In fact, unless I'm listening to something specific, like a new artist, it's usually just there to have something playing in the background...to help my thoughts along.
>
> (David)

> The iPod allows me to drown out everything and everyone else. This is important for me. I am a thinker, and the iPod allows me my time to do that free of interruptions. I pick and choose my songs in accordance with how I'm feeling. It can either bring me down or pick me up, depending on what I select.
>
> (Freedom)

> Sometimes it's wonderful to have so that I can block out everything else and concentrate on the things I need to think about.
>
> (Donna)

Clearing a space is used both metaphorically and physically in the above descriptions. Users clear cognitive spaces for themselves in which music assumes the role of a clearing mechanism, providing a platform for the users' thoughts, uncontaminated by the vicissitudes of their own cognition. Equally, the privatised auditory world inhabited acts to cognitively passivise the spaces passed through.

iPod users exclude or transform their spaces of habitation, managing 'duration' in the process. All the above strategies point to the potential and powerful transcendent possibilities entailed in iPod use.

The fragility of, or contingent nature of, cognition in relation to external (the world) or internal factors (cognition) is kept at bay through iPod listening. The exclusion or transformation of the world beyond the user, coupled with the transformation of the user's 'inner space', permits a restructuring of cognition, creating a free and orderly mobile space in which the user is able to successfully manage experience. Situations of cognitive conflict are avoided through a process of compartmentalisation through which users focus upon the immediate task of control. The control of the self is managed through technological mediation in which the subject gives themselves over, albeit actively, to the technology of the iPod as a form of higher control. The iPod user resembles Lasch's 'minimal self' in which the user withdraws into a world small enough to exert total control over it.

iPod culture is also a culture in which users successfully manage the potentially oppressive nature of routine, of the day stretching ahead, of the unwanted journey, the unwanted meeting, the decisions to be made at work. In everyday life, users may not wish to think about the day ahead, the relentless routine of going to and from work. The drudgery of the everyday and the lack of freedom in the daily rhythm of consumer culture is success-fully mediated, and put at a distance, through the use of iPods. The iPod delivers. It is a strategic device permitting the user to shape experience in a manner they are unable to accomplish on their own. In iPod culture, success-ful experience is invariably mediated experience. Structurally this micro-awareness – this listening self – constitutes both a heightened invasion by the culture industry of the auditory self and a distancing strategy through which users attempt to reinforce a sense of presence – self-mastery. Enclosing the user's world between the earphones of the iPod monumen-talises the significance of users' cognitive processes, making them loom larger in the mind's eye as more immediate and pressing. With the subject's attentiveness to the micro-management of cognition comes the increasing realisation of their contingent and unpredictable nature, resulting in the mediating influence of the iPod becoming more pressing, more necessary. Users wish to remain at the centre of their universe – they do not embrace a decentred subjectivity, as postmodern thought would have us believe. They embrace a Bergsonian ideology of cognitive freedom precisely through a tethering of cognition to the auditory products of the culture industry. Yet it is the very fear of dislocation and decentring that provides a powerful motivation for continuous listening.

10 The nostalgia of iPod culture

Time is projected on to space through measures, uniformising it and emerging in things and products. The apparent reversibility of time through products in the everyday gives us a feeling of contentedness, constructing a rampart against the tragic and death.

(Lefebvre 1991: 31)

Nostalgia inevitably reappears as a defence mechanism in a time of accelerated rhythms of life... The nostalgic feels stifled within the conventional confines of time and space.

(Boym 2001: xiv)

Records are possessed like photographs: the nineteenth century had good reason to come up with phonograph record albums alongside photograph and postage-stamp albums, all of them herbaria of artificial life that are present in the smallest space and ready to conjure up every recollection that would otherwise be mercilessly shredded between the haste and humdrum of private life.

(Adorno 1927, in Leppert 2002: 278–9)

Don't we all have a certain number of images that stay around in our head, which we undoubtedly call memories... and which we can never get rid of because they return in our sky with the regularity of a comet – torn away also from the world about which we know almost nothing?

(Augé 2004: 18)

I have always believed that certain songs play as a musical timeline for your life. So, now that it's easy to listen to anything and everything that I want, I'll have a song for just about every happening in my life.

(Fali)

Nostalgia is a dominant mode of address in contemporary urban experience. Nostalgia helps to locate the subject in the world – it gives a semblance of coherence, it warms up the space of movement in a mobile world in which users increasingly deflect away from the spaces and time traversed. iPod users often report being in dream reveries whilst on the move – turned inward from the world, living in an interiorised and pleasurable world of their own making, away from the historical contingency of the world into the certainty of their own past, real or imagined, enclosed safely within their very own auditory soundscape. Nostalgia bathes experience in a warm glow of 'personalised' and privatised experience.

Nostalgia itself is a contested and culturally loaded concept often equated with simulated forms of sentimentality – a view of the past viewed through rose tinted glasses, the cracks polished over, the product of individual fancy and collective ideology, representing a trivialisation of experience invariably associated with popular culture as contrasted with the view of nostalgia as an authentic mode of experience, 'a travelling back with pain – and aching' in search of a past more authentic than the present (Seremetakis 1994: 4).

The dominant view of nostalgia is, however, a negative one where it is treated as a structural and contemporary disease of the present – as a set of *ersatz* experiences (Appadaurai) promoted by the culture industries, intent on stealing not just the present but also the past from consumers. From this perspective, contemporary consumer culture is thought to be awash with simulated forms of nostalgia in which 'the past has become part of the present in ways simply unimaginable in earlier centuries' (Huyssen 2003: 1).

If consumer culture attempts to commodify all experience, colonise as much of the daily lives of consumers as possible, then the production of mobile technologies like the iPod and the mobile phone would appear to signify this 'colonisation' of our life world on an even more pervasive level. We have seen that through these technologies experience is increasingly mediated and constructed – for example, users find that they are largely dependent on their iPod for the operationalisation of many of their nostalgic reveries. What better than to sell mobile technologies to consumers that enable them to tap into the dreams of commodity culture virtually anywhere and any time?

Yet this 'one-dimensional' view of the relationship between the consumer and commodity culture may well obscure the way in which individuals actually reappropriate these products of the culture industry. The status and meanings attached to forms of auditory recall remain deeply problematic. Are they repositories of utopian desires, or are they reified fictions of an imaginary past? Do they open up the past to the user or do they foreclose it? In the following pages I suggest that the culture of nostalgia embodied in the personalised auditory recall of iPod users should be treated as a significant 'practice of everyday life' that, despite the workings of the culture industries, permits potential creativity within the everyday routinised consumption process. From this position nostalgia and the workings of memory are not merely the product of a culture striving to sell people memories at all cost, but also a utopian moment in daily life whereby consumers attempt to transcend the present.

Practising nostalgia

Nostalgia can be triggered by a sense of smell, touch, a sound or image. The first clinical study of that very particular form of memory, nostalgia, invoked the sounds of home as instrumental in conjuring up bouts of nostalgia for the patients. Swiss solders stationed in France in the eighteenth century were the first clinically defined victims of nostalgia (Boym 2001). Supposedly, bouts of nostalgia among the soldiers were triggered by the Alpine melodies of Switzerland: 'the sounds of a certain rustic cantilena that accompanied shepherds in their driving of the herds to pasture immediately provoked an epidemic of nostalgia amongst the soldiers' (Boym 2001: 4). The troops were treated with leeches or alternatively and probably preferably a swift return home. Auditory memory for these soldiers was represented by the sounds of home. Their memory of the sounds of the village was frequently communal – as was their plight: fighting in a war far from home. Yet the way in which the soldiers articulated their sense of longing was also individual, whereby remembered sounds formed part of their own personal narrative. Their traditional sense of life's slow rhythm was in contrast to the experience of the speed of a bullet and the swift nature of the battle that they unfortunately found themselves in. The memory of home invoked by the soldiers – one of slowness and community – was epitomised by the ringing of the village bell. The soldiers would remember the timbre of the bell to evoke images or a sense of presence in their lives. Alain Corbin argued that in rural France people's sense of presence was a largely auditory one, with the sound of the bell invoking stronger memories than the image of the village. Bells were 'invested with an intense emotional power' (Corbin 1998: 80). Memories were simultaneously collective and individual, yet memories were invariably rooted to a particular geographical space, with the bell symbolising a strong sense of community. In contrast to the sound of the bell in the eighteenth century, in contemporary iPod culture the technology of the iPod provides the auditory mnemonic for the contemporary nostalgic.

Jerome is a Swiss national who has lived and worked in the United States for seven years since meeting Claire, his American wife. Jerome is thirty-seven and works in Indianapolis as a senior partner in a law firm. Jerome's life has been inherently mobile, having lived not just in Switzerland but also in France, Australia and now the United States. Like many urban dwellers, Jerome's life has been one of chosen displacement, movement and transitory abodes. Movement is also inscribed into his working day by his sixty-minute solitary drive to work each day. Jerome uses music as a form of auditory mnemonic, stating that he uses music as 'as a kind of diary'. Music plays a central role in the life of Jerome and the use of the iPod enables him to operationalise his nostalgic reveries at will:

> The iPod is pretty much the diary or soundtrack to my life. There is a song for every situation in my life. Even if I might have forgotten about a certain time, person or place, a song can trigger these memories again in no time.

Jerome has a music collection of over 5,000 CDs and LPs. At the time of the interview Jerome had downloaded 9,800 tunes on to his iPod, divided into twenty-five different genres and multiple playlists. Jerome, like many users, is tethered to his iPod, which he describes as his regular companion in the activities of his day – 'There hasn't been a day since I bought my iPod in 2003 that I haven't used this little device' – describing the iPod as acting as his 'time machine'. Memory recall itself is contingent on the music played – Jerome might consciously recall a memory by choosing a specific tune or play list or, alternatively, rely upon the iPod randomly choosing something from his whole collection. The iPod becomes a 'kind of diary' providing instantly accessible data to hand. Memories are evoked most predictably from his 'all-time favourites list' of 113 'five-star' songs. Nostalgia is most commonly evoked by Jerome whilst listening to his iPod on the drive to and from work:

> Driving in the countryside of Indiana does not quite take as much concentration as driving through the rush-hour traffic in London. I usually set my car on cruise control and just keep an eye on the traffic in front of me (which is not too heavy here in Indiana). The songs transform me to all kind of places in my life.... . And that is what I love about the 'shuffle' feature. Whenever a 'childhood' song comes on I 'feel' like I am back in my parents' house. Then a track from an Australian band might bring me back to the two years I spent in Sydney. I sometimes don't even remember that I've passed certain 'points' on my drive from or to work. This thing is a wonderful 'time machine' and is better than any diary.

Driving becomes primarily an auditory experience, with the shuffle feature of the iPod picking music at random. Jerome has placed all of the 9,800 tunes contained in the iPod there – the unpredictability of the randomness of choice is prefaced by the certainty of what is contained in the iPod's memory. The unpredictability contained within the random mode of the iPod differs significantly from that of a favourite radio programme, for example. The iPod has supplanted the radio and the CD player as the auditory companion of the driver, as Jerome explains: 'I don't want to have to listen to a song I don't like.' The iPod 'drives me wherever I go'. Jerome is 'gated in' by his music preferences, experiencing the pleasure of random access to his music whilst simultaneously isolating himself away from traditional auditory technologies, which are perceived as either limiting or unpredictable. The iPod permits him to successfully micro-manage his mode of nostalgia:

> Sometimes I am in a certain mood (homesick for Switzerland, melancholy – thinking about my childhood or certain events in my life etc.), in which case I choose a specific playlist that has all the songs that relate to this specific situation. Sometimes I just want to hear all my favourite tracks and I only play 'five-star' songs.

Jerome is precise about the way in which certain songs go to make up his 'auditory diary':

> I have a lot of music that I use as kind of a 'diary'. As an example, when I grew up in the '70s in Switzerland I was a huge Smokie fan. In fact, the very first record that I bought was 'Bright lights and back alleys' from Smokie. I saved all my money for months, just to get me that album. So I have music on my iPod that reminds me of a very specific part of my life (Smokie = childhood, Status Quo = my teenage years, Jesus and Mary Chain = my first love, Wham! = the very first time I went to London and absolutely loved it there, REO Speedwagon = the very first time I went to Indianapolis and met my wife...). I left Switzerland seven years ago and moved to the United States. Hence I have some 'Swiss folk' music on my iPod, which I usually wouldn't listen to, but whenever I get homesick it's the perfect soundtrack to my mood. This is where playlists come in.... This feature is simply great!

Nostalgia might then be represented by a 'mood', the music played representing some notion of home – very much in the manner of those eighteenth-century Swiss soldiers. For Jerome it merely means Swiss music that he otherwise would not listen to. Other music appears to represent either generalised times of life or more specific situations. Jerome can access these through specific playlists that can also be played randomly by the iPod. Auditory recall thus works both in a generalised way to periods of his past and to specific occasions, as the following very specific list illustrates. He describes these songs as his five-star list of perennial favourites which all hold specific and 'very deep meaning' for him, meaning which he habitually conjures up whilst listening in his automobile. Whilst Jerome listens to much music at home, stating humorously, 'my wife sometimes jokes that I spend more time with my iPod then I do with her', nostalgic reverie appears to take place primarily in his automobile – a solitary exercise:

> 'Thirty-nine' (Queen) gets me back to my happiest childhood memories.
> 'Hook' (Blues Traveller) gets me back to the first time I met my wife in the States.
> 'All torn down' (the Living End) brings me back to the great days I had in Sydney, Australia.
> 'Bang-a-boomerang' (Abba) gets me back to the days when my mom used to sing along to this song while cooking us dinner.
> 'Oh, oh, I love her so' (the Ramones) gets me back to the time when I got my first car and I drove all round Zurich.
> 'Break the silence' (Climie Fisher) gets me back to the times with my best friend in the '80s when we went out on Saturday night, went dancing, and then drove home at 4.00 a.m. in the morning with this beautiful song playing.

'All I want is you' (U2) gets me back to a time when my heart was broken into a thousand pieces.

The act of listening becomes a journey through the iconic moments and periods in Jerome's life – a private and domestic narrative of both specific childhood experiences, of his mother singing along to Abba whilst cooking, for example, to the sentiments of lost love. The music may have actually been played – Abba – or may merely remind Jerome of his feelings at that time. The power of being transported out of his time and place by specific songs is vividly recalled:

> A song can transport me to any time and place in my life in a matter of seconds. It plays 'Wake me up before you go-go' by Wham! and I am immediately walking down Oxford Street in my mind. It plays 'For a few dollars more' by Smokier, and I am back in my room at my parents' home, looking out of my window over the city of Zurich. It plays 'Unbelievable' by EMF, and I am back with my best friends in Serfaus on our annual ski vacation that we used to have during the '90s. It plays 'Happy when it rains' by Jesus and Mary Chain, and I am immediately back in the Swiss army, the time that I hated the most, but which also brings back some of my most treasured memories, because my girlfriend was waiting for me at the train station every time I got back home for the weekend.

Sound is a powerful aphrodisiac when it comes to evoking memory. Memories are largely mediated memories in iPod culture – a mediated life through which to filter one's personal narrative. This coupling of the personal to the commodity is a hallmark of iPod culture, with users in potentially constant touch with their narrative past.

Musical pasts also become reconfigured and rediscovered in iPod culture. Musical identity is inscribed onto a portable memory bank, giving the user instant access to its contents. George, a forty-nine-year-old teacher with two teenage daughters living in the north of England, both of whom have iPods bought by George, keeps musically up to date by downloading his daughters' music. He also uses his iPod to excavate his own musical past:

> There are the favourites that were favourites at particular times in your life. You have forgotten them, and hearing them again brings back a particular memory. Hunting them down is part of the fun. Friends, family and libraries can now be searched in order to put a track into iTunes, on to the pod and back into your memory banks to refresh them! Perhaps rekindling or reliving a moment, a memory, emotion, albeit more faint and distant from the original effect that a particular tune had on you at the time of hearing it. This could be a very old memory for you or a recent one...I keep Tampa favourites – Johnny Bristol,

Barry White. Songs from my teen days as well as modern black artists' music such as Black Eyed Peas. I can now select a particular piece of music from a CD and put it into the relevant Favourites folder. Now I can hear them at any time rather than relying on the radio to occasionally throw one up.

George describes living in a poor rundown Liverpool neighbourhood as a child, describing his house as having no garden and only an outside toilet. George describes how the Harry Belafonte song 'Oh, island in the sun' became firmly entrenched in his media reveries: as a child as he dreamt of an elsewhere that would take him away from the bleak, cold environment in which he lived. The Belafonte song evoked an idyll – blue sky, blue sea and white sand ironically displaying the mediated power of orientalism even on a young child. As an adult he recalls the shock of visiting the Bahamas and hearing a group of musicians playing 'Oh, island in the sun'. Paradoxically, he recalls being taken back to his childhood, to the cramped and damp Liverpool house of his childhood, by the sound of the song.

The successful retrieval of time – of a past brought to a vivid present through the construction of a complete and personalised archive, as hinted by George's description of his auditory search into the past, taps into a consumer dream of omnipotence – that there exists in fragments one's musical past which is 'out there' ready to be found or completed.[1]

Sarah, a thirty-year-old freelance writer who travels regularly between New York and London, shows that the retrieval of one's musical past need not be the preserve of the middle-aged:

It's reacquainted me with my old 'back catalogue' of music that I only have on vinyl or tapes and had therefore not listened to in years. Now, with file sharing on line, or borrowing from friends, I feel like I've got a lot of 'old friends' back. That is, music that really means a lot to me in a nostalgic way, I guess, that I hadn't got around to repurchasing – and maybe wouldn't have. It's like having all your books with you wherever you go – or, better still, a library of your own creation at your fingertips.

Whilst the practice of nostalgia is commonly a solitary exercise for iPod users, the gathering in of one's musical past is frequently a social exercise involving friends, family or acquaintances. The virtuality of the process of collecting music breaks down the considerable physical barriers to potential retrieval associated with music stored on tapes or vinyl. Whilst Jerome's flights of nostalgia are primarily located in the automobile, nostalgia can, in principle, be evoked virtually anywhere. Jim a thirty-year-old American technician, describes working out at the gym:

At those times I focus on the music so I will not think about how fast I am walking, how far I have gone, etc. ... I guess I just forget everything and think about the music I'm listening to – remember events in my past related to the particular song I'm listening to.

Auditory mnemonics also cultivate generalised memoryscapes for users in which the sensory landscape is transformed through evoking a mood or memory of the listener's:

> Sometimes, if the music has a particular memory associated with it, the world takes on the characteristics of the time and place the memory evokes. Listening to an old Beatles track, for example, brings back memories of my father listening to that music when I was a kid, and the world can sometimes feel like it was still in the late '70s and early '80s, even though that isn't the time of the recordings themselves.
>
> (Brian)

Auditory mnemonics work directly as users literally reimagine the experience through the song or through association:

> My favourites are normally my favourites because they remind me of a specific time or feeling. Some of those favourites are Tori Amos's song 'Winter' because it reminds me of words my dad would say to me before he passed away.
>
> (Heather)

Anderson has noted that auditory memory might often be involuntary – or embody a practice of intuition that 'embodies a form of sensual mimetic remembering' (Anderson 2004: 8). A piece of music may remind the listener of warm weather or of feeling good without them being able to formally identify why such is the case. For example, Anderson cites an example of a subject who on hearing the Beatles' song 'In my life' thinks of her dead father even though the father disliked Beatles music (Anderson 2004: 10). Emotions and feelings are invoked by the song rather than the musical identification that the father had with music, unlike Brian's description of his father listening to a Beatles song.

Meaning is also contingently attached to particular songs, timbres or lyrics:

> Certain songs have different meanings for me. If I receive some news, whether it be bad or good, and I'm listening to a piece of music, then whenever I hear that song again it will usually remind of that particular news. Also, if a friend has introduced me to an artist, then whenever I hear that artist it will usually remind my of my friend.
>
> (Paul)

Nevertheless, music acts as a powerful anchor to the subject's sense of their narrative self and their sense of geographical and interpersonal space within which that narrative occurs and is constructed. Not all auditory memories evoke pleasurable responses, especially those in the recent past. Whilst one option is for users to be nostalgic about significant moments in their past, the erasure of shared moments is also easily achieved through the editing of the user's iPod collection:

> I've had a hard time in a relationship over the last few months, and for a while I found it hard to listen to songs which reminded me of the relationship at its best, or other songs which I felt to be my boyfriend's songs – so I edited a playlist with stuff which didn't remind me of him.
> (Emily)

Instant erasure becomes possible at the press of a button, thus empowering the listener who attempts to edit her auditory past. Perhaps in years to come the user will retrieve those auditory markers as the immediate past is bathed in a nostalgic aura.

Nostalgic recall may appear to pose problems for the construction of 'new experiences' as iPod users dream their way through the present. Yet the following young man indicates a more improvisatory and ongoing use of music:

> I like to use it to apply a soundtrack to my life, so I can associate certain events with certain tracks. This can sometimes happen accidentally. For example, I was on a train and my iPod was on a complete random setting. I received a phone call telling me I had been rejected for Oxford University, and 'Everybody hurts' by REM started. Sometimes I choose it, though. When I was walking through London on my way to an interview for UCL I put 'OK Computer' (the album) by Radiohead on, because I wanted to associate the shiny white nature of the album with the feeling of applying to an urban university.
> (Sean)

This user invokes a personalised mimetic on to his surrounding whilst applying the aesthetic principles of his iPod listening on to his surroundings in terms of the 'feel' of being in a specific urban environment. The experiencing of privatised music is translated into the ownership of the space of listening – a joining of mnemonics, music and private space through technologies of sound.

Nostalgia is both individualised and yet commodified in iPod culture. Individualised forms of mediated nostalgia inhabit the same life world as those prefabricated forms of nostalgia provided by the culture industry. These 'sweet ready-mades' reflect the culture industry's attempt to tame the longing for the subject's desire for non-commodified time' (Boym 2001: xvii). Technology acts as both a threat and an enabling medium, offering the iPod user the ability to either embrace or transcend the culture industry's cultural directive to consume in the manner born. The conjuring up of states of nostalgia is located in the historical trajectory of recorded sound.

The mechanical reproduction of nostalgia

Nostalgia and mechanical reproduction go together: experience is reproduced; the dead come back to life; that which is forgotten is bathed in the light of recollection. Mediated nostalgia – nostalgia generated through the record player, the phonograph or the iPod – reverses the irreversibility of time in the mind of the subject. The history of mechanical reproduction is the history of the increased ability of people to create patterns of instant recall. Nostalgia is inscribed into the very technologies of reproduction both visual and auditory. Nostalgia and displacement appear to be integral to the dawn of the mechanical reproduction of sound, creating the ability to conjure up real or imagined memories of home, place and identity. Early research into the use of the gramophone record displays much of the geography of memory, nostalgia and longing that resonates through contemporary iPod use. The Edison survey of US record listeners undertaken in 1921 found that for many, in that country of immigrants, listening to gramophone music transported them back, or linked them to, their absent homes and families, providing them with a 'script of central themes of [their] lives...The process of phonographic remembering included a growing sense of mastery over powerful memories of the past as the listener summoned forth the music that stimulated the emotions linked to memory' (Kenny 1999: 8–10).

The phonograph, placed in the centre of the family home, enabled or sparked these memories through the playing of short two-minute records, of Caruso or of a Central European folk song. Families or parents would listen collectively to the sound of music that reminded them of their old homes far away, or the people they had left behind. In this sense the music may not have had a specific link other than it represented the sounds of Bohemia or Italy, representing a stratified cultural dream pool for these groups of people, even as it was consumed in the domestic spaces of the home. Early descriptions of nostalgia invoke a 'shared' even though often imaginary sensory experience. In contrast to this, nostalgia in iPod culture appears primarily in a privatised state.

Radio continued the collectivised auditory nostalgia of twentieth-century Western society. Douglas noted the shift from the collectivised memories associated with early radio to the more recent post-Fordist segmentalisation of the audience through radio formatting.[2] Yet the collectivised auditory memory evoked by Douglas in describing the ideological nature of early radio listening is superseded by the individualised scheduling of music by iPod users. iPod users wish to control their acoustic experience much more precisely than radio stations are able to provide.

Mobile technologies such as the iPod permit an extension of states of nostalgic recall. A sense of absence is often the lot of the person on the move – nostalgia becomes absence overcome, a mediated presence recalled with the aid of 'solid state' technology. MP3 technologies like the Apple iPod extend the forms of, or rather the retrieval possibilities of, nostalgic recall in everyday life. In the hyper-post-Fordist world of the iPod user their whole musical narrative is at their fingertips, a 'total archive' of their musical past. Consumer culture itself has tapped into and promoted these cybernetic dreams through the development of MP3 technology offering round-the-clock connectivity to the past.

Adorno believed that the commodification of experience created structural social amnesia. As the media stretch out into an ever expanded present – or instant – coupled with information overload so we rarely remember the news programmes of merely two days ago. The rhythm of daily life has become increasingly structured and partitioned by media production and consumption (Lefebvre 2004). Writers have more recently commented that modern culture is awash with the fabricated artefacts of the nostalgia industry itself, in which 'the imagined past is sucked into the timeless present of the all pervasive virtual space of consumer culture' (Huyssen 2003: 10). Yet, in tune with this media overload, which is thought to assault our sensibilities in a welter of social forgetting, come parallel modes of technologically facilitated forms of personal retrieval. Mobile technologies such as iPods not only become digitalised urban Sherpas for many users, they become personalised repositories of the subject's narrative. In the chilly narratives of the anonymous and disenchanted urban spaces moved through comes the urge to centralise oneself – to place oneself. As the iPod user negotiates their way through their auditory mnemonic we need not deny the powerful influence of the media on both the desire for a nostalgic life and the contents contained therein. iPod users personal narrativised nostalgia remains channelled through the commodities of the culture industry. iPod users work, often consciously, within the commodification of experience to eke out the value of their own time and experience.

Nostalgia is invariably a pleasurable experience for users of iPods. The pleasure lies in the very creativity of the exercise, in which nostalgia becomes an urban form of the aesthetic – a successful aestheticisation of experience. Its attraction also resides in the ability of the user to transcend place and time. No matter how transitorily, the user is able to control their nostalgic mnemonic as they manage their journey through urban space. In this scenario the isolated user is isolated only bodily, for in 'reality' they are accompanied through their day by the warm glow of their memories and their associated moods. Daily life becomes infused with the warmth of a narrative presence. iPod users in effect are never alone. The 'imaginary' realm of the user's presence negates the sensory determinacy of the immediate – the tactile and visual world through which they move.

This very negation of the 'present' in its determinacy has been considered to be potentially liberating in the writings of Nietzsche, Lukacs, Bloch, Benjamin and Adorno where they identify the transcending nature of the imaginary – the going beyond that which 'really is' as possessing progressive elements. It is these acts of 'going beyond' which encompass the utopian sensibility of living a life as it should be lived. In a privatised and personalised world of nostalgic reverie, is it the case that these nostalgic desires are structured by a lament 'for a securely circumscribed place…with its regular flow of time and a core of permanent relations? Perhaps such days have always been a dream rather than a reality, a phantasmagoria of loss generated by modernity itself' (Huyssen 2003: 24).

iPod culture, in its privileging of the isolated individual subject, privatises the spaces of urban habitation, furthering the desire to be enveloped in a dream from which they desire not to awaken. This dream world is simultaneously uniquely personal and a structural component of urban culture in the twenty-first century.

11 Sound timings and iPod culture

The cliché about modern technology being the fairy-tale fulfilment of every fantasy ceases to be a cliché only when it is accompanied by the fairy tale's moral: that the fulfilment of the wishes rarely engenders goodness in the one doing the wishing. Wishing for the right thing is the most difficult art of all, and since childhood we are weaned from it. Like the husband who is granted three wishes from the fairy and who proceeds to use two of them by making a sausage appear and then disappear from his wife's nose, so to whomever the genius to dominate nature has granted the ability to see far into the distance sees only what he habitually sees, enriched by the novelty that gives its existence a false inflated significance. His dream of omnipotence comes true in the form of perfected impotence. To this day utopias come true only so as to extirpate the idea of utopia from human beings altogether and make them swear allegiance all the more deeply to the established order in its fatefulness.

(Adorno 1998: 57)

In one day in the modern world, everybody does more or less the same thing at more or less the same time, but each person is really alone in doing it.

(Lefebvre 2004: 75)

iPod culture represents, a distinctive and new 'temporal sensibility' on the part of the subject. This 'temporal sensibility' reflects an attempt to break away and overcome the structured rhythms of contemporary life. Yet, despite the rebellious pronouncements of users, iPod culture remains rooted in the commoditisation of time recognised by both Marx and Weber as central to the workings of industrial nations. Consumers might well go with the flow – embrace the rhythms of culture – or they might resist or fight against the imposed rhythms and timings of the everyday world. Wrestling oneself away from the schedules of the everyday remains problematic, however. The use of technologies like the iPod appears to liberate users from the Fordist and post-Fordist division of time so firmly entrenched within daily urban life. The use of an iPod permits users to transcend the incursive elements of linear time, transforming it into time possessed, partially on their own terms, unlike the use of a mobile phone, which holds a more ambivalent position in the management of users' time. Mobile phones, whilst potentially reclaiming time as the user talks or texts to others whilst on the Tube, in the car or in the office, equally steal time away from users as they feel obliged to answer work calls at home, on their commutes or in their leisure 'time'. The mobile phone potentially makes everything into work, obliterating any distinction between work and leisure, whilst the iPod potentially liberates users from the linear grind of daily life.[1]

iPod users display a heightened sense of incursion by commodity culture, of time managed and time taken away. Everyday life is experienced as increasingly scripted by many iPod users – at work, at home or on their commute – scripted in ways that they become increasingly and painfully aware of: speeded-up work schedules coupled with increased accountability, the rise of the twenty-four-hour economy – the down side of twenty-four-hour consumption – and the need to work ever faster (Gleik 1999). Urban space itself is experienced as increasingly regulated. Representational space becomes saturated with the products of the culture industry, invasively personalised through new technologies such as Bluetooth to the regulated daily movement of people through the city, often predictably gridlocked (Brandon 2002; Kay 1997).

iPod use permits users to wrest back some control from the multiple and invasive rhythms of daily urban life. By focusing in on them, time becomes meaningful precisely through the privatised consumption of sound; their experience is elevated, made 'more real' in its apparent transcendence of linear time. Desire is enabled through technological capability. In doing so iPod users reinscribe mundane linear time with their own very personalised meanings, transforming the intolerable into the tolerable. In a world full of schedules the iPod user claws back time, conceived of as 'free time'. iPod time represents time away from others, schedules and obligations; free time can occur virtually anywhere, any time; it is predicated upon the use of he iPod, and is invariably solitary time. iPod users are sensitive to the management of time yet use the products of commodity culture, like the iPod itself, to fight against the dominant rhythms of daily life. In doing so, societal rhythms remain embodied in and are manifest in users' cognitive orientations to urban experience. Does the iPod user's 'dream of omnipotence' come, as Adorno claims, 'in the form of [a] perfected impotence?' The utopianism of iPod culture is a tentative and potentially self-contradictory one. It is not a Marcusian utopianism whereby consumers become free through the opting out of consumption (Marcuse 1964). Rather, iPod culture represents the immersion of the subject in consumption, with all the ambiguities that this involves, in the belief that control is on their own terms. This chapter investigates the nature and meanings associated with the seeking out of a consumer empowerment that is fully mediated by the products of the culture industry itself.

No dead air: iPods and the micro-management of time

iPod users are planners, spending hours creating playlists for themselves in preparation for a wide variety of listening contexts. Alternatively they sometimes place their trust in the 'shuffle' mode of the iPod, which plays music at random, effectively giving themselves over to their music collection and to the technology of the iPod. Both modes of operation permit users to continually adjust music whilst on the move with a precision that is new, if indeed the desire to do so is not. (Bull 2000)

The carrying of large slices of one's musical library in a small piece of portable technology liberates users from the contingency of mood, place and time, making redundant the contingencies of future moods and circumstances, thus engendering feelings of security in users. Mike, a forty-year-old software consultant form California who spends much of his time travelling on business, plays Bach continually on his travels. Listening to his iPod enables him to 'live where I am. I could be on public transport, in an airport, in a hotel room. The iPod allows me to have my accustomed music environment with me at all times.'

Whilst earlier generations of personal stereo were commonly used as an in-between device – from door to door – the iPod expands the possibilities of use from the playing of music through attaching it to the user's home hi-fi device, plugging it into the automobile radio and by connecting it to the computer at work, thus giving users unprecedented ability to weave the disparate threads of the day into one seamless and continuous sound-track.

Users are able to create a range of strategies enabling them to regain the possession of their time, bringing it into conformity with their desires. What might have previously been understood as 'dead' or 'meaningless' time becomes transformed into the pleasurable time of listening. The mundane commute to work, or the local shopping expedition, becomes imbued with a heightened level of significance for users. Time is increasingly scripted to the beat and rhythm of music. The cyclical and linear components of experience become redrafted in order to transform the monotony of these cycles into something bearable. iPod use extends the field of aspirational reorganisation to include increasing areas of daily life – the dream of living one's life to music becomes for some users a reality. With the increased power of the technology comes the ratcheting up of consumer desire. What was previously acceptable for the personal stereo user is no longer acceptable for the iPod user. The iPod permits users to control time continually. A central tenet of iPod culture is the micro-management of mood, sound and time. Users control their experience by continually adjusting their music to suit their mood, attuning themselves to the micro-management of their auditory experience. With this heightened sensitivity comes the abolition of potentially destructive pregnant pauses or silences that bedevilled previous modes of mobile listening when the tape or CD in the personal stereo ceased playing. These brief silences acquired significance precisely due to their destruction of the continuous flow of experience, returning the user to the contingency of the world which they inhabit.

> I shuffle through songs and allow the iPod to randomly select tracks. I listen to playlists depending on my mood rather than in the past I just played whatever tape I had with me at the time. I also love the on-the-go-playlists and make playlists when travelling. I no longer consider a track list as a static object.
>
> (Frank)

The desire for, and experience of, seamless auditory experience is captured by the phrase 'no dead air' used by Jean, a thirty-five-year-old bank executive describing her morning commute to work in New York. She would scroll though her song titles looking for a particular song to listen to that would suit her mood at that particular moment and whilst listening to the song would scroll through her list for her next choice. Her musical choices would merge seamlessly into one another during her journey time. The ability to adjust one's soundscape to the environment, mood or time in a split second is described by the following user:

> A lot of times I choose a group of random songs in the elevator on the way downstairs – just whatever comes to mind – then, when I get to the subway, while I'm waiting for it I queue up a more extensive, personalised on-the-go playlist. Basically the first time it's just to have something on, and then I make a real playlist for the thirty-or-so-minute subway ride, in which I have nothing else to do but listen.
>
> (Daniel)

Users combine pre-planned playlists with the shuffle function of the iPod – effectively covering every potential possibility of auditory desire:

> I tailor my music and content by activity. Playlists allow me to create sub-sets of music that I can easily call up. It's particularly important for me to have driving, pounding music when I exercise. For commuting it's more quiet and contemplative. I create playlists to tailor my music to my different moods. I often label them as 'Quiet' or 'Exercise tunes' or 'Contemplative' ... essentially just quick clues to content ... Sometimes I'll just blindly spin the scroll wheel and hit 'play'. If the music isn't what I want to hear I'll forward on until I find something that fits.
>
> (Jonathan)

The pliability of MP3 technology empowers users through the speed with which they are able to create and modify sequences of music or talk on the move, enabling them to marry music to fleeting and transitory flows of experience:

> It's a painless process to create a new playlist for every conceivable mood or situation, when, before, burning a CD or MD was a fairly permanent thing and it would have to be a pretty great mix to make it worth while ... there's a significant amount of spontaneity involved with listening on my iPod. I can change to something else whenever I want, I can rearrange playlists as one song gets tiresome or I think another one should be added with a minimum of fuss.
>
> (Kerry)

iPod use represents a rationalisation of time and music enabling users to create flexible playlists or flows of sound that are transformable at speed. Whilst spontaneity may demand planning on the part of the iPod user they frequently resort to playing music at random, thus giving themselves over to the power of the iPod. However, this mode of operation is also subject to intervention as the user moves on to subsequent tracks until finding a suitable sound to match their wishes.

Whilst iPod users spend much time constructing playlists of various descriptions, from genres such as rock, drum and bass, classical to easy listening, happy, sad, morning, afternoon, work, etc – the list is endless – and whilst these often fairly fluid playlists work to calibrate the iPod users experience – to manage or control their sense of time, space and presence – the iPod also permits users to randomly play their music collection – indeed many iPod users also have the smaller iPod Shuffle which plays music randomly or in the same order in a loop. In effect, users appear to give themselves over to their randomly played music collection. The following user explains how he uses playlists and the shuffle:

> I use my iPod in the gym, car, or for a dinner party when I want to dictate my music choices to get it right for the occasion. I use the Shuffle in snatched moments – on the bus, walking to the station – to be reminded about the great music I have tucked away in corners of my iPod. I have written some Applescript, which builds a playlist from the tracks I had heard on the Shuffle when I sync. I use that to go and explore further when I am back at base. I'm happier to switch off the Shuffle than the iPod. I will extend a gym session to finish a track or an album on the iPod. I wouldn't do that with the Shuffle. Not having a screen [on the iPod Shuffle] is amazingly liberating. The Shuffle forces you to listen to the track being played, I don't need to know who it's by, where was I when I bought it, when I heard it first or last. Having a screen to glance at removes this experience.
>
> (Alistair)

Differing modes of control are evident from the above account. Playlists are invoked to control mood or activity, whilst the Shuffle is used to surprise, to enable him explore his music collection in a manner that he wouldn't do by choice – rather as a kind of treasure trove. The taking away of the visual clue to the music provided by the iPod (the Shuffle has no screen) is also described as liberating. Alistair tracks particular songs down when he returns home. Listening thus becomes a mode of exploration:

> I can make playlists for any kind of mood, or just let it play randomly, so that I can rediscover music in my collection that I haven't listened to in a while...I love to just turn the settings to random and then let it jump around my music collection. In this way I can rediscover old favourites, and I get some wonderful juxtapositions that I would have never made on my own.
>
> (Alistair)

The use of the Shuffle enables users to break with their traditional listening habits and preferences, creating new juxtapositions of music for the user to like or dislike, thus extending the user's openness to the variety of music within their own music collection. For some the machine itself is thought to hold the key to the management of desire:

> I like to put my music on random.... I don't like a set playlist in order. There's something about the spontaneity of a random song coming on that I really enjoy ... I don't like it all planned, and I like to be surprised as to what song will come on next. Sometimes it gets weird with the song selection, almost like the damn thing was reading your mood and playing a succession of songs that perpetuate a mood. It makes me wonder if the random function on the machine is just an unbiased algorithm or if my iPod is somehow cosmically connected to me.
>
> (Jason)

In the giving of oneself over to the random play of the iPod users are simul-taneously investing in the value of their own music collection from which the iPod 'magically' selects that which they wish to hear. If it fails, there remains the fast-forward mode. Whatever mode of operation the iPod user chooses, time spent in public, commuting or shopping becomes time repos-sessed through the use of an iPod. Movement and the privatising impulse of cognition become one.

iPod culture and time shifting

In Fordist and post-Fordist consumer cultures leisure is more often than not regulated and prescribed, yet this cultural trajectory has been one of increasing choice in which consumers are increasingly able to choose how they consume 'leisure' time through the plethora of media available to them. Structurally, choice has remained programmed even in a post-Fordist world of niche markets and choice:

> Producers of the commodity information know empirically how to utilise rhythms. They have cut time up; they have broken it up into hourly slices. The output (rhythm) changes according to intention and the hour. Lively, light-hearted, in order to inform you and entertain you when you are preparing yourself for work: the morning, soft and tender for the return from work, times of relaxation, the evening and Sunday. Without affectation, but with a certain force during off-peak times, for those who do not work or those who no longer work. Thus the media day unfolds polyrhythmically.
>
> (Lefebvre 2004: 48)

The polyrhythmic division of the day remains planned and predicted even in the catering for segmental taste markets. Indeed, plenitude of choice does not necessarily correspond to a broadening of taste in a post-Fordist market. Douglas, in her survey of the role and place of the radio in the United States, puts forward a thesis that argues that more choice equates with less diversity of listening:

> Industry spokesmen insist that, especially in large markets, there's more variety than ever, since the listener can choose from a host of carefully crafted and narrowly defined formats. But, within the formats of a particular station, variety is kept outside the door. In promotional ads listeners are assured, for example, that they won't ever have to hear heavy metal, rap, or anything unexpected on their station.
>
> (Douglas 2004: 348)

Post-Fordist modes of consumption, from this point of view, become a form of auditory 'gatekeeping' through which taste is both managed and narrowed. Douglas points to the existence of an industrial dream of auditory control in which the planners of media production orchestrate the multi-rhythms of the consumer's day. Consumer choice becomes embodied and made available in the predetermined structural possibilities of radio channels, itself reflecting the pre-formations of taste embodied in the choices of consumers as they press the radio button down on what is already known and predictable. In Douglas's analysis the post-Fordist economy of plenitude of choice is one of auditory taste ghettoes.

The digitalised economy of the iPod user tells a different story of increased diversity of taste that questions the timings and content of media production. Whilst iPod users might create cognitive ghettoes for themselves as they move through daily life, theirs is interiority rich in media variation. iPod use appears to represent a decentralisation of patterns of consumption, a striving for individualised rhythms and patterns of consumption. Users often have eclectic mixes of music on their iPod, which they arrange in playlists that frequently are categorised not by the genres within which radio channels operate but by mood.

iPod users organise listening schedules to their desires. This often means juxtaposing music from differing genres, which enables them to maintain whatever mood they desire to be in. Digitalisation permits iPod users to rewrite the schedules of daily life – to 'time-shift'. Previous technologies such as VHS players permitted television viewers to reschedule certain programmes by recording them but these activities were very limited in scope. Mainstream providers of the media have desperately embraced the notion of time shifting by placing segments of their programming online ready for consumers to download them and play them back at will. Yet scheduling runs deep in the psyche of iPod users. Wresting themselves away from the preordained scheduling of programmers often results in merely the superimposition of their own schedules, mimicking those of media producers. The rhythm of their day is set to their 'personalised' schedules of listening. iPod culture represents not a rejection of parcelling the day up – for iPod users are indeed constrained by the social division of time which regulates their daily activity: the commute to work, the office day, the industrial schedules that are imposed upon the urban rhythm of daily life – but rather with a reinscribing, a personalisation of those rhythms. The following iPod user articulates the structure of and motivation behind time shifting.

Jim is forty-nine and lives with his wife in a small town in one of the southern states of America and is employed as a software designer and teacher. Often working from home, Jim is partially liberated from the daily routine of commuting. Like many users, he listens to the iPod continually. His is the conscious articulation of an active consumer embracing the virtues of virtuality and its associated possibilities to consume media products where and when he desires. Jim constructs his own media schedule of media programmes and music by daily downloading material on to his iPod. Through time shifting Jim articulates a sense of empowerment deriving from his transcendence of time and place. He is also rebelling against the very commoditisation of media information engendered in contemporary media organisations: the hyper-commodification of both music and speech. Jim expresses an ideology of rugged individualism in his desire to create personalised media schedules for himself. Before the advent of this new technology he described himself as 'a slave to time and location. Now I am almost totally independent of the radio, cassette, CD and electrical outlet.' Empowerment manifests itself in the rescheduling of the auditory day, resulting in the elimination of any unwanted material:

> Elimination of waste: *commercials*. When I listen to music radio there are so many commercials that it becomes pointless. When I listen to television there are so many commercials that it almost becomes pointless.

When I listen to the iPod I can be assured that my thirty minutes of music listening will be thirty minutes of music listening.

Elimination of waste: *drivel*. FM has become AM because the DJs talk over the beginning and end of the songs, and frequently cut off the beginning or end of a song. When I listen to the iPod I can be assured that I will hear the song in its entirety and untainted.

Elimination of waste: *unwanted music*. When I press Play, I can be assured that my iPod will play what I want without filler songs, without commercials, without DJs and without undesired music distractions.

Elimination of waste: *other*. Instead of becoming a mindless receiver of uncontrolled noise, the iPod makes me selective and interactive. I use my iPod to maintain and improve my language skills. I use my iPod to 'read' books I would not normally have the time to read. I use my iPod to listen to time-shifted technical broadcasts and news talk radio.

The above statements appear to represent the distilled image of a heroic hyper-post-Fordist consumer using the products of the culture industry to regain a sense of owned time whilst simultaneously warding off the demons of a culture that destroys the 'authenticity' or usefulness of commodities. In demanding to listen only to what he wants to listen to Jim is eliminating all advertising from programming, the DJs that talk over records, trimming the beginning and end off songs, and eliminating any 'unwanted' music. Jim, in effect, creates his own personalised 'radio station' through his iPod.

Jim articulates use through the active consumption of goods. This hyper-post-Fordist mode of consumption is not an opting out of consumption in the Marcusian mode but rather a reappropriation of his time through the individualising of listening schedules. The content of Jim's radio station is rich indeed:

> Basically, music is nice, but the local FM radio stations are horrid and there are no AM radio stations. Similarly, as I age I care more about news talk radio, books on tape and educational recordings. But my news talk radio programme is on from 11.00 a.m. to 2.00 p.m. and I'd miss most of it. Enter iPod. Now I record streaming webcasts. Then I copy webcasts, books on tape, language tapes and lectures on to the iPod. Then I have a choice of 'my' music, 'my' radio programmes, 'my' books on tape and 'my' educational recordings.

Paradoxically, Jim, like many other iPod users, appears to be fully dependent upon the use of the iPod to structure his day. His independence from the structured regime of the media day is replaced by the imposition of his chosen, individualised regime of listening. His daily schedule of mediated listening is all-encompassing:

> 04.00. Out of bed, iPod on to news talk radio or technical.
> 05.00. iPod on the treadmill playing news talk radio or the occasional 'upbeat' music.

06.15. Off the treadmill and into the shower (no iPod yet).

06.45. iPod on to music for breakfast.

(07.00 to 09.00. Sometimes I listen to a local live newscast.)

07.00. iPod on to news talk radio or technical or language for two hours of housework and/or yard work.

09.00. iPod on to music for an hour of internet news and technical sites.

10.00. iPod on to music for work.

11.30. iPod to yesterday's news talk radio for errands and trip to lunch.

12.00. Since I meet people for lunch, I stow the iPod, but I talk about what I just heard.

13.15. iPod on to books on tape or Euro-pop music after lunch.

17.30. iPod on to news talk radio for afternoon gym.

19.00. iPod off for supper and evening television.

20.30. iPod on for book on tape or Enya music for work and to lead into sleep.

The iPod connects Jim to the 'omniscient microphone' of culture, taking centre stage in the management of daily life. There are very few spaces in the day when Jim doesn't experience the world through the sounds of the iPod. The schedule of daily listening mimics those of the media. Paramount in his account is the need to have daily experience mediated through sounds. Tolerance of experience unadorned, of time unmediated, is low. Many iPod users come to fear unmediated experience – of being left to their own devices:

> I become very bored with exercise. When I go for a walk, or ride my bike, or go to the gym, my mind works constantly and I think of things I need or want to do upon completing my exercise. At the gym it is particularly bad, because the news channels repeat the same stories every thirty minutes and repeat the commercials every ten minutes. Also, at the gym the music is atrocious.

Unpleasant tasks become transformed through iPod use: a half-hour walk may become a one-and-a-half-hour walk if accompanied by the iPod. When out of his routine Jim programmes his iPod to suit:

> If I know I'm going on a trip or doing something out of the ordinary I'll adjust content. For example, I drove from Reno, Nevada, to Ozark, Alabama, in December. For that three-day trip I acquired three new books on CD and uploaded them.

Whilst the rhetoric of individualism is prominent in Jim's description of use, it appears as very much a dependent individualism. Many of his everyday activities are mediated by iPod use. He describes difficulty in sleeping, so takes it to bed. 'If I have insomnia – and I have insomnia a lot – I take the iPod to bed.' Like many iPod users, Jim finds unmediated cognition potentially threatening. Jim is fully dependent upon technology to transcend the traditional technologies of reception – indeed, he has to programme his computer to record his daily input. The history of mobile music technologies is a history of the management of users' experience of time. Paramount in Jim's account is the need to consume the products of the culture industry, to have daily experience mediated through sounds – but within the time schedule and the chosen place of the user.

When users desire to be 'cognitively' free they express this freedom through subordination to technological artefacts like the iPod. Cognitive freedom as defined by many iPod users is practical in so much as it enables them to manage their experience in the desired direction – rather than falling prey to their own volition (unwanted) or the contingencies of the street or, increasingly, the mediated world of the culture industry. iPod users may well be rebelling against a sense of the pre-established harmony supposed to exist between cognition, desire and the commoditised world. Cognitive freedom was central to the Enlightenment project whereby subjects could create sanctuaries for autonomous thought and action away from the encroachments of society – the creation of a private space away from the prying presence of consumer culture. To what extent does the critique of a Fordist culture in which the ideological harmony between subject and object analysed by Marcuse and others in the 1960s appear to be fulfilled or contradicted by iPod culture in its tethering of the subject? Marcuse pessimistically argued that:

> Private space has been invaded and whittled down by technological reality. Mass production and mass distribution claim the entire individual, and industrial psychology has long since ceased to be confined to the factory. The result is, not adjustment, but mimesis: immediate identification of the individual with his society and, through it, with society as a whole.
>
> (Marcuse 1964: 36)

Marcuse thought that subjects had introjected the cultural imperatives of society so fully that they associated themselves increasingly with them. The one-dimensionality thesis has never enjoyed widespread acceptance, as it appears to collapse subjectivity too readily and passively into the structural determinants of society. Yet accounts of 'active audiences', which prioritise cognition over social structure, are equally ideological by voiding the power of structure in its relation to the subject.

The struggle of iPod users to wrest themselves away from the dominance of imposed rhythms whilst remaining locked in the vision of an ordered universe – ordered by them – is the conundrum of iPod culture. The technology of the iPod privileges private life, enhancing the conception of the consumer as an 'isolated subject'. Yet in this privileging of the subject users become dependent, their isolation and control mediated by the hand of commerce and ideology. Just as users wish to liberate themselves from the oppressive rhythms of daily life, so they appear to sink deeper into them.

Weber believed that central to the organisation of an industrialised world was the giving up of control of one's destiny to the bureaucratic workings of culture. To live on someone else's design for your life was at the ideological heart of industrial culture. This was the melancholic certainty attached to the iron cage of capitalism. Security was exchanged for loss of control – to conform in a disenchanted yet secure world. iPod users paradoxically appear to implicitly accept the value of this rationalisation of experience – as Richard Sennett notes: 'Rationalised time [has] cut deep into subjective life' (Sennett 2006: 24) – whilst rebelling against living on the schedules of others. But, of course, iPod users do live on the schedule of others. The world remains the same – despite the therapeutic management of the iPod. Adorno pointed to the conflict inherent in any surpassing the present, arguing that disalienation could take place, in part, only through alienated forms (Adorno 1991). The utopian motivations of many iPod users embody a dystopian reality as they strive to focus in upon the management of their daily lives. For writers like Adorno this is unavoidable – there is no such state as liberation through consumption, only the fetishisation of objects such as the iPod upon which users seek salvation.

12 Endnote

Sound mediations

iPod culture uses communication technology as a support system from dawn till dusk. Yet in the totally mediated world of the iPod user lies the dream of unmediated experience – of direct access to the world and one's emotions.

iPod culture is a culture that dreams of total mediation, yet it is a mediation that paradoxically conceives of experience in its immediacy. Mediated experience – the sounds of the culture industry between the ears fed directly by the headphones placed inside the ears – directly into the experiencing subject – the outside world sinking into silence – or in the bodily movements of the subject as they speak into their mobile phone – as if the other were directly in front of them. Mediated experience appears to be more immediate to the iPod user whilst the technology of the object becomes increasingly invisible, at least whilst it works effectively. Mediated immediacy becomes second nature to the subject as the subject uses their mobile technologies as digital Sherpas to accompany them securely through the spaces and time of everyday life. As one female user commented:

> I found that my most immediate attraction to it was the feel of it in my hand. I wanted to have it with me at all times. In fact in two and a half years I've barely been away from it.
>
> (Virginia)

The dream of unmediated experience has a long intellectual history, from the idealism of a Bishop Berkeley who believed that the world was identical to the image on the retina of the eye – a mimetic fantasy – to that of Husserl, who believed you could bracket out the cultural elements of knowledge to look upon what you experienced untainted by the intellectual and cultural baggage that informed how you actually experienced anything at all. The dream of objectivity – which is, in reality, a dream of unmediated knowledge – thus takes a major place in the pantheon of Western knowledge claims. Mediation – that through which experience occurs – has many disguises, cultural, intellectual, historical and technological. Embodied knowledge is filtered through our very senses – what we hear, see, touch, smell and taste. The practices of 'looking' and 'hearing' are in themselves mediated cultural practices, as are notions of what it is to 'remember' or to 'experience' anything at all. As the anthropologist Kathleen Linn Geurts aptly puts it:

> Sensory orientations, therefore, represent a critical dimension of how 'culture and psyche make each other up' and play a critical role in a person's sensibilities around intersubjective dynamics and the boundaries between self and others. And these sensoriums may affect the very basic features of our ability to judge each other.
>
> (Geurts 2002: 236)

The relationship between the subject – the experiencing sensorium – and the object – that which we experience – is one of mediation. It has a cognitive, a moral, a cultural and a personal dimension attached to it. This point is brought out in a recollection by Theodore Adorno demonstrating that sounds, for example, never come to us raw:

> We can tell whether we are happy by the sound of the wind. It warns the unhappy man of the fragility of his house, hounding him from shallow sleep and violent dreams. To the happy man it is the song of his protectedness. Its furious howling concedes that it has power over him no longer.
>
> (Adorno 1974: 49)

Adorno wrote the above whilst living in exile in Hollywood during the Second World War. Adorno's lament is of one who senses the fragility of home. The wind is a variable upon which cultural specificity is written. One senses that Adorno, for whom Hollywood was a kind of cultural living hell, felt the roof was falling upon him many times. In the years of conflict between the Protestants and Catholics in Northern Ireland, Chinook helicopters regularly hovered over North Belfast – a symbol of UK and Protestant power over the Catholic minority. For many a Catholic the sound engendered feelings of fear, bitterness and oppressiveness. For the Protestants it signified security. For the rest of us it probably signifies *Apocalypse Now*.

The media are deeply implicated in the ideology of unmediated experience. Initially it transformed the relationship of our domestic interiors in relation to what lay beyond. As we sat in the comfort of our armchairs the mediated world flooded in, courtesy of domestic communication technologies like the television set. This world – an audio-visual one-dimensional world, devoid of smell, touch and taste – lured us with the appearance of 'objectivity', of a world which we can experience with our own eyes and ears. As Morley states:

> Television news flatters its 'armchair imperialist viewers' into adopting a subjective position as 'the audio-visual masters of the world', and the

'guarantee' which television offers them is the 'illusory feeling of presentness, this constructed impression of total immediacy...a televisual metaphysics of presence'.

(Morley 2000: 185)

This presentness now moves with us as we move through the spaces of everyday life. It differs from the televisual world described by Morley in so much as the mimetic fantasy is individualised and mobilised – locked into the contents of the user's iPod and placed inside the user's pocket, hermetically sealed from the outside world. Sound in particular is often experienced in its 'immediacy', leaving, as Adorno noted:

> no room for conceptual reflection between itself and the subject, and so it creates an illusion of immediacy in the totally mediated world...Most important among the functions of consumed music – which keeps evoking memories of a language of immediacy – may be that it eases men's suffering under the universal mediations.

(Adorno 1976: 46)

So we have come full circle – back to Bishop Berkeley's notion that the world is no more than the mimetic creation of our own retina, to an auditory resemblance of our cognitive desire. Benjamin noted in relation to film that the subject desired to bring – through technology – 'things' 'closer' 'spatially and humanely' (Benjamin 1973: 217). iPod culture becomes an investigation of how we increasingly bring the auditory world closer to us 'spatially' and, hopefully, humanely.

Notes

1 Sound moves, iPod culture and urban experience: an introduction

1 Over 1,000 iPod users filled in a thirty-four-item questionnaire over the internet. The respondents answered requests posted in the *New York Times*, BBC News Online, *The Guardian* Online, *Wired News* and *Mac World*. These requests were then syndicated and replicated in a wide a variety of newspapers and magazines worldwide. From February 2004 to April 2004 the author received 4,136 requests for the iPod questionnaire. Respondents came mainly from the United States, the United Kingdom, Canada, Australia and Switzerland but also included fewer responses from France, Italy, Spain, Denmark, Finland and Norway. Apple give no regional figures for sales, so it is impossible to tell whether the respondents mirror national use or were a reflection of the use of the specific internet sites on which the requests were posted. Equally, the questionnaire is written in English, thus discounting iPod users with no capacity for written English. The majority of respondents came from social classes 1 and 2, with a distinct bias towards working in new media, advertising and the creative sectors of the economy. Studies of internet research have often found no differences between internet samples and others gained by more traditional methods (Smith and Leigh 1997). The median age of respondents was thirty-four. Fifty-three per cent of respondents were male; age differences between male and female users were insignificant. The questionnaire asked about general iPod use in relation to the use of other communication technologies such as the mobile phone, television, radio and their use of automobiles and public transport. Respondents were asked to describe use over a period of a week and to include data on what was listened to. Twenty per cent of respondents were then asked follow-up questions in response to their initial answers. In addition to the internet sample a small sample of UK users have also been personally interviewed. UK iPod users who were frequent mobile phone users were also accompanied on their daily journeys to work and back. In addition to these data, primary data on automobile and mobile phone which pre-dates iPod use are referred to.

2 Half of Australians possess an MP3 player or its equivalent, whilst the figures in China and South Korea are 70 per cent. Whilst the present study focuses upon iPod users, large numbers of consumers possess alternative-brand MP3 players or mobile phones with music listening ability. Many of the auditory strategies analysed throughout the book are equally applicable to these users. Whilst mobile phones increasingly have MP3 ability, it is not possible to use the phone simultaneously as an MP3 player.

3 Richard Sennett has also used the iPod as a metaphor for the new capitalism. 'In an MP3 player, the laser in the central processing unit is boss. While there

is random access to material, flexible performance is possible only because the central processing unit is in control of the whole' (Sennett 2006: 51). Whilst Sennett mistakenly believes the iPod to be controlled by a laser, the point concerning the power of centralised control masked by the workings of the mechanism itself is well put. Sennett argues that the iPod is symbolic of a consumer culture in which the volume of choice both attracts the consumer and disables them at the same time, 'The iPod . . . disables its user by its very over capacity; the glut of information generated by modern technology threatens to make its receivers passive' (Sennett 2006: 172). Whilst there is some evidence to support this claim – some users find it difficult to listen to one piece of music in its entirety, fast-forwarding because there is so much music on their iPods – in the main users either construct multiple play lists, which structure their listening, or play their machines on 'shuffle' so they need not choose.

4 Lefebvre understood the increasingly influential nature of the media in the constructing of the polyrhythmic nature of daily urban experience: 'Producers of the commodity information know empirically how to utilise rhythms. They have cut up time; they have broken it up into hourly slices. The output (rhythm) changes according to intention and the hour. Lively, light-hearted, in order to inform you and entertain you when you are preparing yourself for work: the morning, soft and tender for the return from work, times of relaxation, the evening and Sunday. Without affectation, but with a certain force during off-peak times, for those who do not work or those who no longer work. Thus the media day unfolds polyrhythmically' (Lefebvre 2004: 48). For Lefebvre this parcelling up of the day was both functional and seductive. Functional, as it was based on prior knowledge of the segmented daily routines of the urban population, seductive in so much as it provided the security and predictability which many consumers found pleasurable. iPod culture represents a new moment in the map of the auditory – the hyper-post-Fordist consumer. iPod culture represents a distinctive and new 'temporal sensibility' on the part of the subject that represents an attempt to break away and overcome the structured rhythms of contemporary urban life. Digital technology has enabled consumers to redefine the nature and meaning of many of their daily schedules, whether it is transforming the experience of their daily commute or the very nature of their media schedules. Consumers may well go with the flow – embrace the structured rhythms of the everyday or fight against these self-same rhythms. Schedules are approached with both trepidation and pleasure.

5 The meaning of urban culture in the present work follows the spirit of Lefebvre's definition in which 'a vacation home, a highway, a supermarket in the countryside are all part of the urban fabric' (Lefebvre 2003: 5). Western culture is primarily an urban culture. This is not to imply that all experience everywhere is identical, that an iPod user walking down a village street is identical to a London commuter. In the village street one is more likely to have meetings with acquaintances than in the city, although more often than not the village dweller is dependent upon the automobile to travel to the local out-of-town supermarket, will possess a mobile phone and be wired up to the worldwide web! The more rural, the more dependent upon the vast array of mobile technologies available to the consumer. We take our urban dispositions with us wherever we travel. Whether one travels to Yellowstone Park in the United States or the Lake District in England, one is likely to hear the dulcet tones of a mobile phone user or the sound system of an automobile as it passes by. (Reed McManus, 'The ring-tone of the wild', *Sierra* 90, January–February 2005.) The author had his own personal experience of the imposition of an urban soundscape on a 'natural' one whilst travelling with a marine biologist in the South Pacific studying the humpback whale, itself a very urban disposition.

On board the ship, which had its engines turned off whilst we were looking at two large humpback whales a mere 50 metres from the ship, the sound of their calls amidst the lapping of the waves and the wind were disturbed by a mobile phone going off. The owner, a Frenchwoman in her thirties, who worked for a fashion magazine in France, answered the phone but had to crouch down with her hand over her other ear in order to be able to hear her call over the sounds of nature. The call was a work call from her office in Paris. Also of interest in this example is the notion of total availability: there was no escape for this user from work, even though she was on vacation on the other side of the globe. Equally iPod users may play music or listen to talking books whilst trekking over mountains, or listen to favourite tracks whilst staring out to sea from a deserted holiday beach.

2 Sound epistemologies: strategies and technologies

1 Schafer, in *The Tuning of the World* (1977), uses the term 'soundscape' to describe the total experienced acoustic environment. This included all noises, musical, natural and technological. Schafer, a composer by trade, was concerned to analyse the changing historical and cultural configuration of soundscapes arguing that it was necessary to understand what effect the configuration of sounds in our environment have in shaping human behaviour. Schafer, however, interpreted all industrial an technological noise as polluting.

2 Connor has pointed to this routinisation of technological innovations: 'Although there were some who were intrigued and amazed by the new invention, in many ways, the contemporary reaction of the coming of the telephone seems to have been "about time too". The telephone had been in use only for months before users began wondering irritatedly why the sound quality was so poor... In periods like the late nineteenth century, and like our own, in which the technological imagination outruns technological development itself, new inventions have a way of seeming out of date, or used up, on their arrival, like a birthday present with which you have been secretly playing in advance' (Connor 2000: 411). However, I wish to point to the attraction that these routinised forms of consumption have in the successful management of experience.

3 A more considered and comprehensive account of the way in which anthropologists used the phonograph to record and study other cultures is to be found in Erica Brady's *A Spiral Way: How the Phonograph changed Ethnography* (1999).

3 Sounding out cosmopolitanism: iPod culture and recognition

1 The sensory specificity of place extends beyond the auditory. Napoleon, who was of Corsican origin, claimed that even blindfolded he would always recognise Corsica because of the pungent aroma of the *maquis* that covered the island.

2 Modern cities have largely undergone an eradication of smell. For a lively discussion of the plenitude of sensory experience in eighteenth-century England see Cockayne (2007).

3 'About one-quarter of the land in London and nearly one-half of that in Los Angeles is said to be devoted to car-only environments' (Urry 2006: 22).

4 No iPod respondent, from the survey of over 1,000 users, stated that they ever initiated interpersonal contact whilst listening to their iPods.

4 The audio-visual iPod: aesthetics and the city

1 'Flanerie is very closely related to other constructions of cultural modernity. Linked to the movements and images that belong to the processes of tourism,

photography, and psychoanalysis, it ultimately charts the aesthetics of modernity that reveals its affinities to the medium of the cinema and its reception of external reality' (Gleber 1999: 6).

5 Interpersonal sound strategies and iPod culture

1 Livingstone has noted, 'Today's media are much more personalised and are increasingly dispersed throughout the home. Children's bedrooms are well equipped with media. Music, books and television are all widely available for personal use, being present in two-thirds of bedrooms' (Livingstone 2002: 39). Hers is not a thesis of social isolation, however, merely an observation that children increasingly choose when and where they choose to interact with others. Bauman more pessimistically notes that 'Homes are no longer warm islands of intimacy among fast cooling seas of privacy. Homes have turned from shared playgrounds of love and friendship into the sites of territorial skirmishes, and from building sites of togetherness into the assemblies of fortified bunkers. We have stepped into our separate houses and closed the door, and then stepped into our separate rooms and closed the door. The home has become a multi-purpose leisure centre where household members can live, as it were, side by side' (Bauman 2003: 102). The sequestering of the home for private consumption existed at the outset of the domestic use of the media. Kracauer noted in the 1930s that physical isolation was not necessarily a prerequisite of cognitive isolation, as radio listeners used headphones to listen to the radio in the 'living' room of the domestic dwelling (Kracauer 1995).

2 McCarthy has noted the way in which 'domestic' forms of media have been increasingly placed in the public areas of cities: 'This proliferation of screens paradoxically makes public spectatorship a particular kind of private experience in which each viewer is provided with a personal sight line distinct from his or her companions, fulfilling a long standing bourgeois ideology of spectatorship as "being alone in a crowd".' (McCarthy 2001: 122).

6 Mobilisation of the social: mobile phones and iPods

1 Two defining consumer technologies of the twenty-first century are mobile phones and Apple iPods. These technologies represent two differing modes of fashion appropriation. The majority of consumers in the industrialised world possess mobile phones, whilst Apple iPods, being a mass produced technology, are endowed with an aura of exclusivity, style and status (Bull 2005; Levy 2006). Central to the marketing strategy of Apple has been to create brand identity through design and advertising that make the use of Apple products 'a way of life'. The products are marketed and interpreted as representing 'imagination, design and innovation'. Klein (2000) argues that Apple no longer sells mere products but the brand itself. In the brand are embodied consumer hopes, dreams and aspirations. Apple consumers often see themselves as distinctive, or individual, through their possession of their iPods, which are visually recognisable to others.

2 Most mobile phone research has concentrated upon the 'young' user – the cash cow of the mobile phone industries which fund much of the research. Mobile phone use is stratified according to the users' place in their life cycle, their occupation and to some extent gender (Castells *et al.* 2007). 'Two in five people (38 per cent) in Britain say they cannot do without their mobile phone. This contrasts with only one in five (19 per cent) who say they cannot do without their desktop computer, internet access (18 per cent), e-mail (17 per cent) or text messaging (15 per cent)' (Harkin 2003: 6).

3 Parents also ask their offspring to call regularly in when out – on the assumption that the checking up on the other is in itself a sign of safety. Parents will often ask their children to call in hourly. This may be construed as a form of parent–child negotiation on the limits to freedom and control but masks a desire for total security on the part of the parent, with parents often allowing more flexibility to children if they carry their phone with them, as if that – the technology – is a security pass to safety (Williams and Williams 2005).

7 Contextualising the senses: the auditory world of automobility

1 Cities vary in their level of automobile dependence, with many North American and Australian cities being virtually totally car-dependent: 'The Automobile City can spread in all directions, offering freedom over space and time. Los Angeles shows how such freedom is soon enslaved to the problems of automobile dependence' (Newman and Kenworthy 1999: 32). Most European cities have a mix of public transport systems and automobility. The model, however, for urban conurbations is increasing car use.

2 Putnam has pointed to the dominance of sole occupancy in automobiles in America: 'One inevitable consequence of how we have come to organise our lives spatially is that we spend measurably more of every day shuttling alone in metal boxes among the vertices of our private triangles. American adults average seventy-two minutes every day behind the wheel...Private cars account for 86 per cent of all trips in America, and two-thirds of all car trips are made alone, a fraction that has been rising steadily.' Equally, Brodsky has commented upon the automobile as 'the most popular and frequently reported location for listening to music' (Brodsky 2002: 219). Comparative analysis discloses that this privatising tendency within automobility is largely a 'Western' phenomenon. For example, Hirschkind (2001) demonstrates that taxis in Cairo are often spaces of contested politicised discourse. In doing so automobiles are profoundly social: they enact the social; both in their denial of other people's private space and in their reconfiguring of urban space generally.

3 'A June 2005 survey of more than 1,200 adults found that 43 per cent of all drivers said they had in the prior six months used a cellphone while driving. A January 2005 survey, also of about 1,200 respondents, found that 40 per cent of drivers said they talked on their cellphones in stop-and-go traffic to pass the time. A still larger study by the US Department of Transportation used direct observation. It found that in 2004 8 per cent of all drivers during daylight hours were using a mobile device and about 5 per cent were using hand-held cellphones...A Harvard University study in 2002 estimated that use of cell phones by US drivers results in 2,600 deaths a year nationwide and 330,000 injuries' (Katz 2006: 3).

8 The auditory privatisation of the workplace

1 In the pre-industrial workplace singing at work was a common activity. Korczynski has pointed to two processes that heralded the decline of singing at work, 'the loss of autonomous pacing of work, and the managerial appropri-ation of the aural space around the labour process' (Korczynski 2003: 13). Power over the auditory space of the workplace meant the power either to pipe music through the workplace for all to hear or to demand total silence. Korczynski points to Taylorist principles being invoked in the workplace whereby the worker was subject to total control, unable to talk, drink or sing (2003: 15). The seductive yet practical role of music in the workplace increas-ingly became recognised. Jones and Schumacher argue that 'management very

often liked to present music as a "gift" ... a signal to their employees that they were trying to create a warm, friendly environment' (2003: 19). The integrationist role of music plays a prominent role in Theodore Adorno's analysis of consumer culture, in which he argues that leisure itself is regimented to the ideologically integrating sounds of music – that the rhythms of the factory increasingly become the rhythms of leisure.

2   This chapter, however, focuses primarily upon the workplace as traditionally conceived. For the most part very few iPod users described habitually using their iPods to work whilst commuting, as distinct from heavy mobile phone users.

10 The nostalgia of iPod culture

1   'The collector is haunted by the knowledge that somewhere on the planet an intact chunk of his past still exists, uncorrupted by time or circumstance' (O'Brien 2003: 16).

2   Douglas noted how music radio has 'so effectively tapp[ed] our emotions... that we develop deep, associative memories between particular songs and our own personal narratives' (Douglas 2004: 12).

11 Sound timings and iPod culture

1   'Time and space, the cyclical and the linear, exert a reciprocal action: they measure themselves against one another; each one makes itself and is made a measuring-measure; everything is cyclical repetition through linear repetitions. A dialectical relation (unity in opposition) thus acquires meaning and import, which is to say generality. One reaches, by this road as by others, the depths of the dialectic' (Lefebvre 2004: 8).

Bibliography

Adorno, T. (1927) 'Curves of the needle', repr. in R. Leppert (ed.) *Essays in Music* (2002). Berkeley CA. University of California Press.

Adorno, T. (1974) *Minima Moralia. Reflections on a Damaged Life*. London. New Left Books.

Adorno, T. (1976) *Introduction to the Sociology of Music*. New York. Continuum.

Adorno, T. (1991) *The Culture Industry. Selected Essays on Mass Culture*. London. Routledge.

Adorno, T. (1998) *Critical Models. Interventions and Catchwords*. New York. Columbia University Press.

Adorno, T. and Eisler, H. (1994) *Composing for the Films*. London. Athlone Press.

Amin, A. and Thrift, N. (2002) *Cities. Re-imagining the Urban*. Cambridge. Polity.

Anderson, B. (2004) 'Recorded music and practices of remembering'. *Social and Cultural Geography* 5 (1): 3–20.

Appiah, K. W. (2006) *Cosmopolitanism. Ethics in a World of Strangers*. London. Allen Lane.

Arato, A. and Gebhardt, E. (eds) (1992) *The Essential Frankfurt School Reader*. New York. Continuum.

Attali, J. (1985) *Noise. The Political Economy of Music*. Minneapolis MN. University of Minnesota Press.

Augé, M. (1995) *Non-places. Introduction to Anthropology of Supermodernity*. London. Verso.

Augé, M. (2004) *Oblivion*. Minneapolis MN. University of Minnesota Press.

Barthes, R. (1985) *The Grain of the Voice*. London. Jonathan Cape.

Barthes, R. (2002) 'The new Citroën', in P. Wollen J. and Kerr (eds) *Autopia. Cars and Culture*. London. Reaktion.

Bassett, C. (2004) 'How many movements?' in M. Bull and L. Back (eds) *The Auditory Culture Reader*. Oxford. Berg.

Baudrillard, J. (1989) *America*. London. Verso.

Baudrillard, J. (1993) *Symbolic Exchange and Death*. London. Sage.

Bauman, Z. (1991) *Modernity and Ambivalence*. Cambridge. Polity.

Bauman, Z. (1993) *Postmodern Ethics*. Oxford. Blackwell.

Bauman, Z. (2000) *Liquid Modernity*. Cambridge. Polity.

Bauman, Z. (2003) *Liquid Love*. Cambridge. Polity.

Bell, C. (1998) *Middle Class Families. Social and Geographical Mobility*. London. Routledge.

Benjamin, W. (1972) *Charles Baudelaire. A Lyric Poet in the Era of High Capitalism*. London. New Left Books.

Benjamin, W. (1973) *Illuminations*. London. Penguin.

Bergson, H. (1998) *Introduction to Metaphysics*. London. Kessinger.

Bijsterveld, K. (2001) 'The diabolical symphony of the Mechanical Age'. *Social Studies of Science* 31 (1): 37–70.

Blesser, B. and Salter, L. (2007) *Spaces speak, are you Listening? Experiencing Aural Architecture*. Cambridge MA. MIT Press.

Bloch, E. (1986) *The Principle of Hope*. Oxford. Blackwells.

Böhm, S., Jones, C., Land, C. and Paterson, M. (2006) 'Introduction. Impossibilities of automobility'. *Sociological Review* 54 (1): 3–16.

Bose, A. (1984) 'Hifi for GM Cars', lecture to EECS seminar, 19 March, MIT Archives MC 261, two audio-cassettes.

Bourdieu, P. (1986) *Distinction. A Social Critique of Taste*. London. Routledge.

Boym, S. (2001) *The Future of Nostalgia*. New York. Basic Books.

Brady, A. (1999) *A Spiral Way. How the Phonograph changed Ethnography*. Jackson MS. Mississippi University Press.

Brandon, R. (2002) *Automobile. How the Car changed Life*. Basingstoke. Macmillan.

Bridge, G. and Watson, S. (eds) (2000) *A Companion to the City*. Oxford. Blackwell.

Brodsky, W. (2002) 'The effects of music tempo on simulated driving performance and vehicular control'. *Transportational Research. Part F* 4, 219–41.

Brown, B. (2002) 'Studying the use of mobile technology in Brown, B. Green, N. and Harper, R. (eds) *Wireless World. Social and interactional aspects of the mobile age*. London. Springer.

Brown, B., Green, H. and Harper, R. (2002) *Wireless World. Social and Interactional Aspects of the Mobile Age*. London. Springer.

Bull, M. (2000) *Sounding out the City. Personal Stereos and the Management of Everyday Life*. Oxford. Berg.

Bull, M. (2001) 'Soundscapes of the car: a critical ethnography of automobile habitation', in Daniel Miller (ed.) *Car Cultures*. Oxford. Berg.

Bull, M. (2004) 'The power of sound and automobility'. *Theory, Culture and Society* 21 (4–5): 243–61.

Bull, M. (2005) 'No Dead Air! The iPod and the culture of mobile listening'. *Leisure Studies* 24 (4): 343–56.

Bull, M. and Back, L. (eds) (2004) *The Auditory Culture Reader*. Oxford. Berg.

Butsch, R. (2000) *The Making of American Audiences. From Stage to Television, 1750–1990*. Cambridge. Cambridge University Press.

Castells, M., Linchuan Qie, J., Fernandez-Ardeval, M. and Sey, A. (2007) *Mobile Communication and Society. A Global Perspective*. Cambridge MA. MIT Press.

Caygill, H. (1998) *Walter Benjamin. The Colour of Experience*. London. Routledge.

Clapson, M. (2003) *Suburban Century. Social Change and Urban Growth in England and the USA*. Oxford. Berg.

Cockayne, E. (2007) *Hubbub. Filth, Noise and Stench in England*. New Haven CT. Yale University Press.

Connor, S. (2000) *Dumbstruck. A Cultural History of Ventriloquism*. Oxford. Oxford University Press.

Corbin, A. (1995) *Time, Desire and Horror. Towards a History of the Senses*. Cambridge. Cambridge University Press.

Corbin, A. (1998) *Village Bells. Sound and Meaning in the Nineteenth Century French Countryside*. New York. Columbia University Press.

Crabtree, J., Nathan, M. and Roberts, S. (2003) *Mobile Phones and Everyday Life*. London. iSociety.

Crissell, A. (1986) *Understanding Radio*. London. Methuen.

Cross, A. (2002) 'Driving the American landscape', in P. Wollen and J. Kerr. (eds) *Autopia. Cars and Culture*. London. Reaktion.

Debord, G. (1977) *Society of the Spectacle*. Detroit MI. Black and Red.

De Certeau, M. (1988) *The Practice of Everyday Life*. Berkeley CA. University of California Press.

De Gournay, C. (2002) 'Pretence of intimacy in France', in J. Katz and M. Aakhus (eds) *Perpetual Contact. Mobile Communication, Private Talk, Public Performance*. Cambridge. Cambridge University Press.

DeNora, Tia (2000) *Music in Everyday Life*. Cambridge. Cambridge University Press.

Denzin, N. K. (1995) *The Cinematic Society*. London. Sage.

Douglas, S. (2004) *Listening in. Radio and the American Imagination*. Minneapolis MN. University of Minnesota Press.

Feld, S. (2000) 'The poetics of Pygmy Pop', in G. Born and D. Hesmondalgh (eds) *Western Music and its Others: Difference, Representation, and Appropriation in Music*. Berkeley CA. University of California Press.

Fischer, C. (1992) *America Calling. A Social History of the Telephone to 1940*, Berkeley CA. University of California Press.

Flichy, P. (1995) *Dynamics of Modern Communication. The Shaping and Impact of New Communication Technologies*. London. Sage.

Foucault, M. (1986) 'Heterotopias'. *Diacritics* 16: 22–27.

Freidberg, A. (1993) *Window Shopping*. Berkeley CA. University of California Press.

Friedland, R. and Boden, D. (eds) (1994) *Now, Here. Space, Time and Modernity*. Berkeley and Los Angeles CA. University of California Press.

Fujimoto, K. (2005) 'The third-stage paradigm: territory machines from the girl's pager revolution to mobile aesthetics', in M. Ito, D. Okabe and M. Matsuda (eds) *Personal, Portable, Pedestrian. Mobile Phones in Japanese Life*. Cambridge MA. MIT Press.

Geurts, K. L. (2002) *Culture and the Senses. Bodily Ways of Knowing in an African Community*. Berkeley CA. University of California Press.

Giddens, A. (1984) *The Constitution of Society*. Berkeley and Los Angeles CA. University of California Press.

Gilroy, P. (2001) 'Driving while black', in D. Miller (ed.) *Car Cultures*. Oxford. Berg.

Gitelman, Lisa (1999) *Scripts, Grooves, and Writing Machines. Representing Technology in the Edison Era*. Stanford CA. Stanford University Press.

Gleber, A. (1999) *The Art of Taking a Walk. Flanerie, Literature and Film in Weimar Culture*. Princeton NJ. Princeton University Press.

Gleick, J. (1999) *Faster. The Acceleration of just about Everything*. London. Little Brown.

Goffman, E. (1969) *The Presentation of Self in Everyday Life*. London. Penguin Books.

Goffman, E. (1971) *Relations in Public. Microstudies of Public Order*. London. Penguin.

Goggin, G. (2006) *Cellphone Culture. Mobile Technology in Everyday Life*. London. Routledge.

Gusfield, J. (1975) *Community. A Critical Response.* Oxford. Blackwell.

Harkiw, J. (2003) *Mobilisation. The Growing Public Interest in Mobile Technology.* London. Demos.

Heidegger, M. (1962) *Being and Time.* New York. Harper & Row.

Henderson, J. (2006) 'Secessionist automobility: racism, anti-urbanism, and the politics of automobility in Atlanta, Georgia'. *International Journal of Urban and Regional Research* 30 (2): 293–307.

Hendy, D. (2000) *Radio in the Global Age.* Cambridge. Polity.

Hirschkind, C. (2001) 'Civic virtue and religious reason: an Islamic counterpublic'. *Cultural Anthropology* 16 (1): 3–34.

Honneth, A. (1993) *The Critique of Power.* Cambridge MA. MIT Press.

Honneth, A. (1995) *The Fragmented World of the Social. Essays in Social and Political Philosophy.* New York. SUNY Press.

Horkheimer, M. and Adorno, T. (1973) *The Dialectic of Enlightenment.* London. Penguin.

Howes, D. (2003) *Sensual Relations. Engaging the Senses in Culture and Social Theory.* Ann Arbor MI. University of Michigan Press.

Huyssen, A. (2003) *Urban Palimpsests and the Politics of Memory.* Stanford CA. Stanford University Press.

Inglis, D. (2004) 'Auto couture: thinking the car in post-war France'. *Theory, Culture and Society* 21 (4–5):197–220.

Ito, M., Okabe, D. and Matsuda, M. (2005) *Personal, Portable, Pedestrian. Mobile Phones in Japanese Life.* Cambridge MA. MIT Press.

Jain, S. S. L. (2002) 'Urban errands: the means of mobility'. *Journal of Consumer Culture* 2 (3), 419–38.

Jenks, C. (ed.) (1995) *Visual Culture.* London. Routledge.

Katz, J. (2006) *Magic in the Air. Mobile Communication and the Transformation of Social Life.* New Brunswick NJ. Transaction.

Katz, J. and Aakhus, M. (eds) (2002) *Perpetual Contact. Mobile Communication, Private Talk, Public Performance.* Cambridge. Cambridge University Press.

Kay, K. (1997) *Asphalt Nation. How the Automobile took over America and how we can Take it Back.* Berkeley CA. University of California Press.

Kenny, W. (1999) *Recorded Music in American Life. The Phonograph and Popular Memory, 1890–1945.* Oxford. Oxford University Press.

Kirby, K. M. (1996) *Indifferent Boundaries. Spatial Conceptions of Human Subjectivity.* New York. Guilford.

Kittler, F. (1999) *Gramophone, Film, Typewriter.* Stanford CA. Stanford University Press.

Klein, N. (2000) *No Logo. Solutions for a Sold Planet.* London. Flamingo Press.

Korczynski, M. (2003) 'Music at work: towards a historical overview'. *Folk Music Journal* 8 (3): 314–34.

Kracauer, S. (1995) *The Mass Ornament. Weimar Essays.* Cambridge MA. Harvard University Press.

Kunster, H. (1998) *Home from Nowhere. Remaking our Everyday World for the Twenty-first Century.* New York. Simon & Schuster.

Lanham, R. (2006) *The Economics of Attention. Style and Substance in the Age of Information.* Chicago. University of Chicago Press.

Laurier, E. (2005) 'Doing work on the motorway', in M. Featherston, N. Thrift and J. Urry (eds) *Automobilities.* London. Sage.

Lefebvre, H. (1991) *The Production of Space*. Oxford. Blackwell.

Lefebvre, H. (1995) *Introduction to Modernity*. London. Verso.

Lefebvre, H. (2003) *The Urban Revolution*. Minneapolis MN. University of Minnesota Press.

Lefebvre, H. (2004) *Rhythmanalysis. Space, Time and Everyday Life*. London. Continuum.

Leppert, R. (2002) *Essays in Music*. Berkeley CA. University of California Press.

Levi, C. (2004) *Fleeting Rome. In Search of la Dolce Vita*. London. Wiley.

Levy, S. (2006) *The Perfect Thing. How the iPod became the Defining Object of the Twenty-first Century*. London. Ebury.

Licoppe, C. (2002) 'France: preserving the image', in J. Katz and M. Aakhus (eds) *Perpetual Contact. Mobile Communication, Private Talk, Public Performance*. Cambridge. Cambridge University Press.

Livingstone, S. (2002) *Young People and the Media*. London. Routledge.

Loktev, J. (1993) 'Static motion, or, The confessions of a compulsive radio driver', *Semiotexte* 6 (1): 14–32.

Marcuse, H. (1964) *One-dimensional Man*. London. Routledge.

Marcuse, H. (1978) *The Aesthetic Dimension*. Boston MA. Beacon.

Massey, D. (2005) *For Space*. London. Sage.

Matsuda, M. (2005) 'Mobile communication and selective sociality', in M. Ito, D. Okabe and M. Matsuda (eds) *Personal, Portable, Pedestrian. Mobile Phones in Japanese Life*. Cambridge MA. MIT Press.

McCarthy, A. (2001) *Ambient Television. Visual Culture and Public Space*. Durham NC. Duke University Press.

McLuhan, M. (1997) 'Acoustic space', in M. A. Moos (ed.) *Media Research. Technology, Art, Communication*. Amsterdam. OPA.

Merck, M. (1998) *After Diana. Irreverent Elegies*. London. Verso.

Miller, D. (ed.) (2001) *Car Cultures*. Oxford. Berg.

Morley, D. (2000) *Home Territories. Media, Mobility and Identity*. London. Routledge.

Morley, D. (2007) *Media, Modernity and Technology. The Geography of the New*. London. Routledge.

Morse, M. (1998) *Virtualities. Television, Media Art, and Cyberculture*. Bloomington IN. Indiana State University Press.

Musil, R. (1995) *The Man without Qualities*. London. Picador.

Negroponte, N. (1997) *Being Digital*. London. Coronet.

Newman, P. and Kenworthy, J. (1999) *Sustainability and Cities. Overcoming Automobile Dependency*. New York. Island Press.

Nussbaum, M. (2003) *Upheavals in Thought. The Intelligence of Emotions*. Cambridge. Cambridge University Press.

O'Brien, J. (2003) *Sonata for Jukebox. Pop Music, Memory and the Imagined Life*. New York. Counterpoint.

O'Hara, K. and Brown, B. (eds) (2006) *Consuming Music Together. Social and Collaborative Aspects of Music Consumption Technologies*. Dordrecht. Springer.

Oldham, G., Cummings, A., Mischel, L., Schmidke, J. and Zhou, J. (1996) 'Can personal stereos improve productivity?' *HR Magazine* 41 (4): 95–9.

Peters, J. (1999) *Speaking into the Air. A History of the Idea of Communication*. Chicago IL. Chicago University Press.

Picker, J. (2003) *Victorian Soundscapes*. Oxford. Oxford University Press.

Puro, J. P. (2002) 'Finland: a mobile culture', in J. Katz and M. Aakhus (eds) *Perpetual Contact. Mobile Communication, Private Talk, Public Performance.* Cambridge. Cambridge University Press.

Putnam, R. (2000) *Bowling Alone. The Collapse and Revival of American Community.* New York. Simon & Schuster.

Ree, J. (1999) *I See a Voice. Language, Deafness and the Senses. A Philosophical History.* London. Harper Collins.

Revill, G. (2000) 'Music and the politics of sound: nationalism, citizenship and auditory space'. *Environment and Planning D. Society and Space* 18: 597–613.

Reyes, A. (2005) *Music in America. Experiencing Music, Expressing Culture.* New York. Oxford University Press.

Rheingold, H. and Kluitenberg, J. (2006) 'Mindful disconnection: counterpowering the panopticon from the inside'. *Open* 11: 29–36.

Robins, K. and Webster, F. (1999) *Times of the Technoculture. From the Information Society to the Virtual Life.* London. Routledge.

Ross, A. (2000) *The Celebration Chronicles. Life, Liberty and the Pursuit of Property Value in Disney's New Town.* London. Verso.

Roth, J. (2004) *The White Cities. Reports from France, 1925–1939.* London. Granta.

Rykwert, J. (2000) *The Seduction of Space. The City in the Twenty-first Century.* London. Weidenfeld & Nicolson.

Sachs, W. (1992) *For Love of the Automobile. Looking back into the History of our Desires.* Berkeley CA. University of California Press.

Schafer, M. (1977) *The Tuning of the World.* New York. Knopf.

Schiffer, M. (1991) *The Portable Radio in American Life.* Tucson AZ. University of Arizona Press.

Schivelbusch, W. (1986) *The Railway Journey. The Industrialisation of Time and Space in the Nineteenth Century.* Berkeley CA. University of California Press.

Schmidt, Leigh (2000) *Hearing Things. Religion, Illusion and the American Enlightenment.* Cambridge MA. Harvard University Press.

Sconce, J. (2000) *Haunted Media. Electronic Presence from Telegraphy to Television.* Durham NC. Duke University Press.

Segrave, K. (2002) *Jukeboxes. An American Social History.* Jefferson NC. McFarland.

Sennett, R. (1977) *The Fall of Public Man.* London. Faber.

Sennett, R. (1990) *The Conscience of the Eye.* London. Faber.

Sennett, R. (1994) *Flesh and Stone.* New York. Norton.

Sennett, R. (2000) *The Corrosion of Character. Personal Consequences of Work in the New Capitalism.* New York. Norton.

Sennett, R. (2006) *The Culture of the New Capitalism.* New Haven CT. Yale University Press.

Seremetakis, C. N. (ed.) (1994) *The Senses Still. Perception and Memory as Material Culture in Modernity.* Chicago. University of Chicago Press.

Shaw, P. (2006) *The Sublime.* London. Routledge.

Shove, E. (2003) *Comfort, Cleanliness and Convenience.* Oxford. Berg.

Silverstone, R. (1994) *Television and Everyday Life.* London. Routledge.

Silverstone, R. (ed.) (1997) *Visions of Suburbia.* London. Routledge.

Silverstone, R. (2006) *Media and Morality. On the Rise of the Mediapolis.* Cambridge. Polity.

Simmel, G. (1997) *Simmel on Culture.* London. Sage.

Sloboda, J. (2005) *Exploring the Musical Mind. Cognition, Emotion, Ability, Function.* Oxford. Oxford University Press.

Smith, M. (2004) *Hearing History. A Reader.* Athens GA. University of Georgia Press.

Smith, M. and Leigh, B. (1997) 'Virtual subjects: using the Internet as an alternative source of subjects and research environment'. *Behaviour, Research Methods, Instruments and Computers* 29 (4): 496–505.

Spigel, L. (2001) *Welcome to the Dreamhouse. Popular Media and Postwar Suburbs.* Durham NC. Duke University Press.

Stallabras, J. (1996) *Gargantua. Manufactured Mass Culture.* London. Verso.

Sterne, J. (2003) *The Audible Past. Cultural Origins of Sound Reproduction.* Durham NC. Duke University Press.

Stockfeld, O. (1994) 'Cars, buildings, soundscapes', in H. Jarviluoma (ed.) *Soundscapes. Essays on Vroom and Moo.* Tampere. Tampere University Press.

Tacchi, J. (2004) 'Nostalgia and radio sound', in M. Bull and L. Back (eds) *The Auditory Culture Reader.* Oxford. Berg.

Taussig, M. (1993) *Mimesis and Alterity. A Particular Study of the Senses.* London. Routledge.

Taylor, C. (1989) *Sources of the Self. The Making of Modern Identity.* Cambridge. Cambridge University Press.

Tester, K. (ed.) (1994) *The Flaneur.* London. Routledge.

Thrift, N. (2004) 'Driving the city'. *Theory, Culture and Society* 21 (4–5): 41–60.

Todorov, T. (1993) *On Human Diversity. Nationalism, Racism, and Exoticism in French Thought.* Cambridge MA. Harvard University Press.

Tonkiss, F. (2005) *Space, the City and Social Theory. Social Relations and Urban Forms.* Cambridge. Polity.

Turkle, S. (2006) 'Tethering', in C. Jones (ed.) *Sensorium. Embodied Experience, Technology, and Contemporary Art.* Cambridge MA. MIT Press.

Urry, J. (1995) *Consuming Places.* London. Routledge.

Urry, J. (1999) 'Automobility, Car Culture and Weightless Travel' (draft). Lancaster University at http://www.lancaster.ac.uk/soc030ju.html.

Urry, J. (2000) *Sociology beyond Societies. Mobilities for the Twenty first Century.* London. Routledge.

Urry, J. (2006) 'Inhabiting the car'. *Sociological Review* 54 (1): 17–30.

Weber, M. (2002) *The Protestant Ethic and the Spirit of Capitalism.* Oxford. Blackwell.

Williams, R. (1977) *Resources of Hope. Culture, Democracy, Socialism.* London. Verso.

Williams, S. and Williams, L. (2005) 'Space invaders: the negotiation of teenage boundaries through the mobile phone'. *Sociological Review* 53 (2): 314–31.

Willmott, Y. and Young, M. (2007) *Family and Kinship in East London.* London. Routledge.

Wolin, R. (1994) *Walter Benjamin. An Easthetic of Redemption.* Berkley. University of California Press.

Wollen, P. and Kerr, J. (eds) (2002) *Autopia. Cars and Culture.* London. Reaktion.

Young, P. (1991) *Person to Person. The International Impact of the Telephone.* Cambridge. Granta.

Index